INDEPENDENCE
CORRUPTED

INDEPENDENCE
CORRUPTED

How America's Judges Make Their Decisions

CHARLES BENJAMIN SCHUDSON

THE UNIVERSITY OF WISCONSIN PRESS

The University of Wisconsin Press
1930 Monroe Street, 3rd Floor
Madison, Wisconsin 53711-2059
uwpress.wisc.edu

3 Henrietta Street, Covent Garden
London WC2E 8LU, United Kingdom
eurospanbookstore.com

Printed in the United States of America

This book may be available in a digital edition.

Library of Congress Cataloging-in-Publication Data

Names: Schudson, Charles B., author.
Title: Independence corrupted : how America's judges make their decisions /
Charles Benjamin Schudson.
Description: Madison, Wisconsin : The University of Wisconsin Press, [2018] |
Includes bibliographical references and index.
Identifiers: LCCN 2018011391 | ISBN 9780299320300 (cloth : alk. paper)
Subjects: LCSH: Judicial process—United States. | Judicial
independence—United States. | Judicial power—United States. | Political
questions and judicial power—United States.
Classification: LCC KF8775 .S383 2018 | DDC 347.73/14—dc23
LC record available at https://lccn.loc.gov/2018011391

supported by a grant of
FIGURE FOUNDATION

To Karen,

my beautiful bride, whom I adore more than words
may express. For fifty years, with courage, loving laughter,
and exquisite spirit, you have been my most challenging teacher
and best friend.

Contents

Preface

Sacred Words

> I don't think writers are sacred, but words are. They deserve respect. If
> you get the right ones in the right order, you can nudge the world a little
> or make a poem which children will speak for you when you're dead.
>
> —Tom Stoppard, *The Real Thing*

I loved playing basketball, and in elementary school I was pretty good. Then
classmates grew taller, and a few years later I was riding the bench for my high
school team. But justice was coming—ten years passed and finally, in the
courthouse gym's lunch-hour games, I was a star . . . well, at least in comparison to thirtysomethings who hadn't stayed in shape.

But all too soon my speed declined, and, approaching forty, I seemed to
have misplaced the skills to "perform" every day. So I cut back, playing every
other day and then even less. I became aware of what, with a wink, I came to
call "crossover time"—those precious few minutes, usually midway through
each game, when I was "on" . . . warmed up and loose but not too tired to hit
the twenty-foot jumper.

Seems that writing this book also may have its crossover time—the precious
few years when I am near enough certain events to remember them and appreciate their significance, yet far enough away to reflect and convey their meaning. Most gently, crossover time takes me close enough to certain people to see
them again, yet distant enough to maintain perspective, free from tears that
otherwise might blur my vision.

How does one know when the time is right to write? I'm not sure, but I
believe that after more than a decade off the bench, my crossover time has
come . . . the time to search for "sacred words" to reach America's judges and
all who care about their independence.

I invite you to accompany my search. Whether my writing will "nudge the
world" by reaching America's judges may be for you and your children to
decide. And whether my words will become a "poem" my own children speak
for me will be for them to judge.

INDEPENDENCE
CORRUPTED

INTRODUCTION
Independence and Corruption

The government may be administered with indiscretion . . . offices may be bestowed exclusively upon those who have no other merit than that of carrying votes at elections; the commerce of our country may be depressed by nonsensical theories . . . but, so long as we may have an independent judiciary, the great interests of the people will be safe.

—Congressman John Rutledge Jr., 1802[1]

[T]he greatest scourge an angry Heaven ever inflicted upon an ungrateful and a sinning people, was an ignorant, a corrupt, or a dependent judiciary.

—Chief Justice John Marshall, 1829[2]

Mugged in Moscow. Sounds like a bad movie, but I wasn't in the cinema. At noon on a sunny spring day, I was in a dim hallway on the wrong floor of an old building two blocks from the Kremlin. A man grabbed my glasses and briefcase and pulled me toward an open apartment door. We scuffled; I regained my property and fled to the street. Down the block, I reentered the building, found the right floor, and hurried to the office of my sponsors, the American Bar Association and the US Department of Justice.[3]

My mugging, I then learned, was unremarkable. "Shouldn't we call the police?" I asked. "What police?" American and Russian officials answered. When I pointed out that the thug, living or lurking just minutes away, posed an ongoing threat, they recounted their own attacks, some similar and others more serious. They explained that mugging had become part of Moscow life . . . that I was lucky not to have been harmed.

I was in Russia teaching prosecutors and judges—first in Tula, the nation's weapons production center; then in Moscow, for a conference of chief judges. I had been directed to address only the subjects the Russian government had specified: organized crime, government corruption, courthouse security, and judges' safety. From that agenda, my mugger, and the weary response, I started to understand Russia's post-Soviet circumstances.

I learned more from the former KGB official who provided my orientation. Formal, fastidious, and vigilant, he always sat nearby at my lectures. Pedagogically rigid, he threatened to cancel my classes when, in answering a question, I strayed from the agenda to talk about battered women. And just before my lecture to the chief judges on organized crime, he warned with words I'll never forget: "Remember, half the judges in your audience take bribes on a regular basis; the other half worry about their lives because they don't."

His words were not hyperbolic. Following the fall of the Soviet Union, when many police went unpaid and quit, criminals helped themselves to law enforcement offices, equipment, and weapons. Some judges, unwilling to obey organized crime's commands, were murdered.

Teaching in Russia following the demise of its police state and, a decade later, in post-Pinochet Chile, I learned of two countries' efforts to re-establish justice systems—to bring transparency to courts that had been secret; to ensure civil liberties for all, including those who still feared becoming "desaparecidos" (the thousands of jailed activists and others who disappeared following Chile's coup d'état). Restoring its strong democratic foundation after "only" seventeen years of dictatorship, Chile succeeded in enacting impressive reforms. But, emerging from centuries of despotism and dominated by organized crime, Russia struggled to do so.

The chief judges I met in Moscow knew they were watched and endangered. Their most urgent concerns went unspoken. Their spoken concerns, however, were ironic. As I described the *secret* legal powers American prosecutors and judges deem essential to fighting organized crime (wiretaps, search warrants, contempt jailings, and others detailed in chapter 2), the Russian judges squirmed. Trying to correct for Soviet abuses, they wanted a new system without such methods. For their new "rule of law," and in their fight against organized crime, they wanted *least* the very powers they needed *most* to protect their nation and themselves.

In Chile, Russia, and many other countries, judges, determined to stock their systems with civil liberties, have turned to America—for statutory examples, and for judicial help in designing their rules of law. The judges I met were not naïve; they knew America's models were imperfect, but they admired our legal ideals and efforts to realize them. Like Congressman Rutledge, they believed that "so long as we may have an independent judiciary, the great interests of the people will be safe." And, particularly given their recent histories, the Chilean and Russian judges were acutely aware of "the greatest scourge" of which Chief Justice John Marshall had warned.

Thus, while focusing on *America*'s judges, we would do well to glance away occasionally, broaden our view, and gain insights from abroad. Doing so, we would, of course, appreciate that America's judges do not "take bribes on a regular basis" or "worry about their lives because they don't." But Congressman Rutledge, as I weigh his words, would not have been satisfied with a *relatively* independent judiciary able to avoid only the most blatant bribes and murderous risks. What was he saying?

Two centuries ago, Congressman Rutledge conceded the possibility—indeed, the inevitability—that from the popularly elected, rough-and-tumble *legislative* and *executive* branches would come some incompetent officials, indiscreet governance, and even "nonsensical" policies. But, he maintained, despite such politically generated problems, "the great interests of the people" still would be safe "*as long as we may have an independent judiciary*."

Why? Why would Congressman Rutledge set "an independent judiciary" as the delicate fulcrum for America's "great interests"? Why did he declare such a standard, separating our two *elected* branches from what, under Article III of our infant Constitution, was our only *appointed* branch?

Congressman Rutledge's words reflect his understanding that legislative and executive decision-making will always be subject to the shifting political pressures of the people. All well and good in many ways, he seemed to say, but only if a politically insulated third branch stands apart to calmly judge, according to fixed standards; to independently determine whether individual liberties were protected, and whether government itself obeyed the law.

But still, why? Why Rutledge's reverence for an independent judiciary? Why Marshall's extreme concern that "the greatest scourge" of "an angry Heaven" would be "an ignorant, a corrupt, or a dependent judiciary"? What do their words recognize?

History answers. America's Constitution—its supreme rule of law—was born in reaction to both unrestrained power and abject impotence. Neither King George nor the Articles of Confederation suffered the inconvenience of an independent judiciary—the king was left unchecked; the Articles, unempowered.[4] History continues to answer. Whether in Chile or Russia or America, Heaven's "greatest scourge" suffocates, enslaves, and slaughters; demagogues reign, mobs rule, judges quiver . . . courts are corrupted, innocent citizens die or barely survive behind barbed wire.

Most Americans seem to understand this, consciously or otherwise. Thus, they almost always seem to accept judicial authority despite the fact (or, depending on their philosophy, *because* of the fact) that the judiciary is, by design, the least democratic branch—appointed judges literally sitting above the people, least responsive to popular whim or will. Indeed, in her stimulating study

Corruption in America: From Benjamin Franklin's Snuff Box to Citizens United, Fordham University law professor Zephyr Teachout identifies not only the "responsiveness to citizens" as "democracy's greatest promise" but also the "barrier of nonresponsiveness that ideally exists between judges and the people" as a vital component of the "American political experiment."[5]

But things change, and America's judiciary changed rapidly. In the Constitution, the founders had established an appointed federal judiciary, insulating it with political protection—life tenure (subject to good behavior), and compensation that legislators and executives could not reduce, regardless of their displeasure with the judges' decisions.[6] But in the Constitution, the founders made *no reference to state judges or elected judges*. The states, however, responded. Often in enacting their own state constitutions (and often drawing on their colonial systems), states soon started establishing their own judiciaries. Thus, America's *judiciary* evolved into a federal/state mix of appointive and elective *judiciaries*, the vast majority consisting of elected state judges.

But would decisions of elected state judges remain untouched by legislative and executive branches? Could such elected judges remain independent while subject to electoral retention reviews or re-elections? Still, without such electoral ligaments to their judges, would Americans respect and defer to judicial authority?

Appointive or elective—the debate has continued throughout our history, judicial shapes shifting over time. For years, the debate pulled me in opposite directions. Witnessing the political posturing of colleagues and sometimes sensing my own, I wondered whether elected judges could ever be independent. At the same time, however, gaining education and sensitization by campaigning, I valued my electoral ties to the people. Moreover, history, with its appointive/elective pendulum swings, cautioned me to resist any simplistic appraisal of the relative merits of these two systems. After all, both historically and experientially, I could point to appointed judges who were unprincipled and elected ones who were fiercely independent. Thus, with judges themselves providing these ironic examples, I concluded that the debate scales balanced.[7]

No longer. Due to four recent Supreme Court decisions, the debate is (or should be) done. These decisions—*Republican Party of Minn. v. White* (2002), *Caperton v. A. T. Massey Coal Co., Inc.* (2009), *Citizens United v. Federal Election Comm'n* (2010), and *Williams-Yulee v. The Florida Bar* (2015)—have transformed America's elected state judges, who account for nearly 90 percent of our nation's judiciary. First, *White* upended constitutional law and judicial ethics codes by allowing judges and judicial candidates to speak out on legal/political issues in the course of campaigning, regardless of whether those issues would be coming before them for decision. Then, taken together, *Caperton*, *Citizens United* (subject to a critical unresolved issue I explore in chapter 14), and *Williams-Yulee* incentivized judges and judicial candidates, as never before, to posture politically in order to secure financing for their campaigns. Chapters 14 and 15 examine these decisions and explain how, even if constitutionally correct, they have generated "a dependent judiciary."

It is that dependency—on preconceived legal/political positions and the campaign contributions that support them—that strips elected state judges of their independence (or, at the very least, of their *appearance* of independence). By contrast, appointed state judges, selected through merit-based processes, are less directly influenced by these Supreme Court decisions. Moreover, such state judges, appointed through various merit-based systems and to various terms, are far less affected than their elected counterparts in other states (though even these appointed state judges may feel political pressure from the elected legislators and governors who appointed them). And although partisan battles and presidential posturing certainly suggest otherwise, *federal* judges, appointed by the president for life and subjected to merit-based review and Senate confirmation hearings, are, in theory, virtually unaffected by these recent Supreme Court decisions. In theory.[8]

Still, as I shall explain, to understand how America's judges really make their decisions, we must focus most sharply on state judges, who make approximately 99 percent of America's judicial decisions, and of whom nearly 90 percent are selected through the same or similar state elective systems as those for the legislative and executive branches. Therefore, increasingly, nearly 90 percent of America's judges now take the bench encumbered by their own campaign rhetoric and beholden to their own donors. At the very least, America's elected judges, even as they may try to maintain their independence, are chilled by the prospect of electoral defeat at the hands of opportunistic opponents who pander politically and, like legislators and governors, raise money from those who support their campaign positions.

Thus, political influence has come to America's judiciary like never before. And, as we will see, while other forms of corruption can compromise judicial independence, only *political* corruption can kill it. With these four Supreme Court decisions, an angry Heaven's "greatest scourge" has arrived; the "great interests of the people" no longer are safe.

But there's much more to the story of America's judicial independence and its corruption. Long before political corruption was propelled by these recent Supreme Court decisions, it was potent. And political corruption does not stand alone. Other corruptions—systemic and individual—corrode; they always have been consequential, remain so today, and will continue to undermine independence regardless of whether judicial selection is reformed. Dissecting independence and its many corruptions will reveal why that is so.

What, exactly, is judicial *independence*? While we may know it when we see it, can we define it? In chapter 3 I shall try. And what is judicial *corruption*? In chapter 3 I shall answer. For now, however, it is enough to have introduced judicial independence historically and systemically, and to understand that, as Teachout explained, a "vast range of inappropriate dependencies and self-serving behavior . . . made up the web of the world of corruption for the founders," and, as Supreme Court Justice John Paul Stevens wrote, corruption "can take many forms. . . . [and] operates along a spectrum" where judges often suffer "threats . . . far more destructive to a democratic society than the odd bribe."[9] The cases we will study highlight that spectrum.

Legislators, lawyers, and judges, of course, may seem the most prominent members of my intended audience, but students, educators, and concerned citizens are just as important. Writing for all, I blend history and contemporary cases, law and memoir. Doing so, I believe, offers a meaningful mixture of messages without which the analysis would be incomplete. And doing so, I hope, will convey the background and nature of our judiciary, the meaning of independence and corruption, the different decision-making dynamics of trial and appellate judges, and the judicial education and political reform needed to revive, strengthen, and preserve judicial independence.

Going behind the bench and into chambers, I shall describe how I, and my colleagues and I, decided actual cases. Therefore, no doubt, while certain chapters, reading as memoir as well as treatise, may seem too "touchy-feely" for some, I believe the human dynamics thus revealed to be among the most consequential components of decision-making. We're going beyond civics lessons and academic commentaries, beyond citizens' assumptions, pundits' positions, and judges' explanations. We're getting inside the judicial skin to feel and understand judging.

As a trial judge for ten years, I presided over tens of thousands of cases[10]—from five-minute hearings to three-week jury trials. As an appellate judge for twelve years, I joined in deciding more than three thousand cases—some clear-cut, resolved with ease; others complex, decided only after months of written and oral arguments, research, and authorship of published decisions. Here we closely examine eight. Why these? They are diverse—civil and criminal, trial and appellate. Each exposes elements of independence and corruption; each illuminates controversies consuming our courts.

- Abortion: *State v. Miller*—the trial and sentencing of a right-to-life leader and her very personal correspondence with the judge who sent her to jail.
- Health insurance: *Peterman v. Midwestern National Insurance*—the appeal of parents and insurers contesting the costly coverage for a premature birth, and the chambered debate over two routes to justice—law and compassion.
- Runaway children: *In the Interest of S.W.*—the sentencing of a teenager, her disappearance, and a judge's decision holding the government in contempt for failing to deliver court-ordered services to her and many other children.
- Sex predators: *State v. Schulpius*—the appeal of a rapist who remained jailed for years despite judicial orders for his release, and America's new "sex predator commitment" laws.
- Murder and the "insanity" defense: *State v. McClain*—the trial and sentencing of a man who murdered his beloved ten-year-old son, and America's "insanity" defense.
- Corporate homicide and punitive damages: *Wischer v. Mitsubishi Heavy Industries*—the appeal of the $100 million jury judgment resulting from the sports stadium construction collapse that killed three ironworkers.
- White supremacists: *State v. Lange and O'Malley*—the criminal trials and sentencings of two "skinheads" and their attempt to disqualify a Jewish judge.
- Electoral conflict of interest: *State v. Clay*—the jury selection, trial, and appeal of a rapist and the politically motivated denial of the new trial that, the judges knew, the law required.

These compelling cases, forming this book's core, present individuals, families, causes, conflicts, and tragedies. They touched me deeply. To do them justice in court, I tried to remember that, under the crushing caseloads and between the lines of every transcript, precious people were coming to our courts—their courts—for help. To do them justice here, I try to help you hear their voices.

Four of these cases I decided as a trial judge, acting alone; four others, as an appellate judge, acting collaboratively with colleagues. Knowledge of the differences between trial and appellate courts should not be presumed.

TRIAL COURTS

Trial courts are the many courts, some federal but mostly state (variously called "county," "circuit," "district," "superior"), that conduct almost all our nation's courtroom business.[11] In both criminal and civil cases, they hold trials (decided by juries or judges) and pre-trial and post-trial proceedings (decided by judges). To reduce confusion, I refer to them all as "trial courts" (or, when necessary to draw the distinction, as "federal trial courts" or "state trial courts").

In trial courts hearing *criminal* cases, one sees pre-trial motions challenging arrests, confessions, or seizures of evidence; jury selection and trials for offenses ranging from disorderly conduct to murder; attorneys arguing to juries and judges; and finally, victims, defendants, defense attorneys, and prosecuting attorneys pleading to judges who pronounce sentences. In trial courts hearing *civil* cases, one may see trials and other hearings involving diverse subjects such as commerce and insurance, divorce and child custody, product safety and medical malpractice, and many others.

Trial courts are action-packed, crowded with witnesses and jurors, spectators and journalists, triumphs and tears. In smaller communities, trial court judges handle a wide variety of cases, criminal and civil. In bigger communities, for administrative ease and subject specialization, trial court judges work in what often are called "divisions"—juvenile, criminal, family, civil, probate, and others.

APPELLATE COURTS

Appellate courts are the relatively few courts, mostly state but some federal, that review appeals—challenges to trial judges' decisions and trial court outcomes.[12] Here, for the most part, we will consider state appellate courts, while keeping in mind that the federal courts provide a similar trial/appellate structure for the litigation of many important issues under federal law.

In most states, we find two levels of appellate courts. While in a few states the nomenclature is reversed, most appellate courts are called the state "court of appeals" (the level above the trial courts), and the state "supreme court" (the level above the court of appeals). Also, in almost all states, the former often is referred to as the "intermediate" appellate court; the latter as the "high" court. Here's the difference.

A state's court of appeals *must* consider any appeal a trial court litigant chooses to pursue. The court of appeals decides the appeal by either affirming the trial judge's decision or reversing the decision, in whole or in part, and returning the case to the trial court for reconsideration or a new trial. Sometimes a losing court of appeals litigant will further appeal to the state's supreme court. But, unlike the court of appeals, which must accept every appealed case, a state's supreme court need review only the few it selects from the many it receives.[13]

Except for days of oral arguments, when attorneys directly address appellate judges in open court, appellate courts are quiet places, with almost all their activity behind closed doors. The judges and their law clerks (recent law school graduates usually serving a year or two in these coveted positions) read trial transcripts containing the verbatim record of trial court proceedings, briefs written by attorneys arguing the issues on appeal, and prior appellate decisions relevant to those issues.

For almost all litigants, a case ends in the trial court; relatively few appeal. For almost all who do, the case then ends in the court of appeals; relatively few appeal to the state's supreme court, and, even if they do, that highest state court usually declines the case. If, however, the state's supreme court accepts an appeal, its decision will conclude the case (except for the rare one that might move into the federal courts or, most exceptionally, to the US Supreme Court).[14]

TRIAL JUDGES AND APPELLATE JUDGES— DIFFERENT DECISION-MAKING DYNAMICS

In a trial court, and particularly in juvenile, criminal, and family courts, emotional subjects and overwhelming caseloads often dissolve in tears. A judge rarely needs reminders of real people and what they suffer; more often, I needed my bicycling commute each evening for comforting separation from court on my way home to my own family. In an appellate court, things are different. The people appear only in print-on-paper profiles traced in the transcripts and briefs bringing their cases. Thus, some suggest, appellate judges may seem more distant and even less "caring," an advantage or disadvantage depending on complex circumstances, some of which we will consider.[15]

Trial judges act alone; their behind-the-scenes decision-making need not be exposed to anyone. And, of course, their processes may be good or bad. Many, often working at home late into the night, study briefs and presentence reports, research law, agonize over issues, and take the bench each day well prepared to consider each case on its merits. I have known many such judges. But I have known others. Unprepared, caring little for the people or their concerns, they may feign impartiality while indulging practices that range from lazy and discourteous to intellectually dishonest, legally unethical, and perhaps even criminal.

But on every case, the trial judge's private decision-making soon yields to public pronouncement in open court—a transparency we may take for granted but one sadly absent from some star-chambered systems abroad. No mere formality, the attorneys' in-court arguments and the judge's public pronouncements help ensure that, almost always, the decision-making has been honest. And a trial judge's decisions are not written in stone; re-argument and reconsideration in open court may occur, and appeal is possible.

Appellate judges, behind closed doors, also read and write alone, but they decide collaboratively. They confer with one another as desired and sometimes convene in open court for oral arguments.[16] Much more writing follows, and later, sometimes months later, appellate judges issue their decisions to the parties, public, and press. Deciding in groups of three or more, appellate judges work under the mutual scrutiny of their colleagues on each case, and, as a result, the "odd bribe" or other overt corruption is less likely than in trial courts. Behind the closed doors of appellate courts I have known excellent and honorable judges, and, again, I also have known others.

Necessarily, this book springs from cases I judged. Inevitably, therefore, it is personal. Thus, even as my experiences guide, they also may lead to tripwires: egotism, dishonesty, and breach of confidentiality.

Egotism

In 1788, during the state debates over ratification of the Constitution, a judge wrote: "The real effect of this system of government, will therefore be brought home to the feelings of the people . . . through the medium of the judicial power. . . . [T]hose who are to be vested with it, are to be placed in a situation altogether unprecedented in a free country. . . . Men placed in this situation will generally soon feel themselves independent of heaven itself."[17]

Independent of heaven itself! Judges, after all, are not known for small egos. By design and of necessity, judges must be strong. At best, they are secure, confident, and *authoritative*, yet gentle and self-discerning. But some may be insecure, arrogant, and *authoritarian*, unkind and, as federal appeals judge Richard A. Posner has written, "often in error, never in doubt."[18]

As a judge, I was exposed to the egotism virus. I tried to stay healthy but was not immune. Now, as an author, unrestrained by attorneys before me and uncorrected by judges above me, might I suffer the sickness? In analyzing America's judiciary but doing so, in part, through cases I judged, might I succumb to self-serving egotism?[19]

Dishonesty

Candid accounts of my colleagues' work and mine will recount not only the public record but private communications. If I fail to honestly reveal my own failings, I will have betrayed my mission. And if, for reasons of delicacy or diplomacy, I fail to accurately describe my colleagues' conduct, commendable and otherwise, I will have become an unfair critic or false apologist. Thus, I ask, how may I honestly disclose problematic elements of actual decision-making while remaining self-discerning and respectful of colleagues, several of whom have died since our years together? And how may I do so while respecting privacy, within the rules of confidentiality?

CONFIDENTIALITY

At first glance, the ethical standards seem clear. The American Bar Association Model Code of Judicial Conduct Rule 3.5 provides, "A judge shall not intentionally disclose or use nonpublic information acquired in a judicial capacity for any purpose unrelated to the judge's judicial duties."[20] Such a standard, I believe, is sound for several reasons, not the least of which is that, without it, the candor of appellate judges' case consultations would constrict. Still, "unrelated to the judge's judicial duties" may be in the eye of the beholder. Moreover, such standards must be reconciled with others that encourage judges to write and teach to increase understanding of the judiciary.[21]

Confidentiality has costs. Unless judges speak out, how will we learn how they really make their decisions? In this least transparent branch of government, how could we see? Critics comment on how judges *should* make decisions, and cynics speculate that "they all do it" otherwise. But no one—concerned citizen, activist whistleblower, investigative journalist, regulatory official—really knows.[22] And, apart from theoretical treatises, no judge has revealed how judges really decide real cases.[23] Why? Why must policy makers and the public continue to wonder, with only criticism, cynicism, and speculation to guide them? Why? Because, pun intended, judges *can't tell* how judges really decide.

Figuratively, many judges *can't tell*; they do not discern their own decision-making processes. Judge Posner has asserted that they "are not fully conscious of the beliefs that determine their judicial votes."[24] Consumed by caseloads, they have no time to reflect on (or write about) their own reflective processes. Blinded by their biases, many do not know what may be blocking their view. Sitting so close, many lack the perspective to identify and differentiate the factors, correct or corrupting, that form their decisions. Paraphrasing criticism of King Lear by one of the king's daughters, Judge Posner observes that "most judges have ever but slenderly known themselves."[25]

And literally, many judges believe, they *can't tell*—they're not allowed. As noted, however, the Model Code's preclusion—"unrelated to judicial duties"—may allow for more openness than judges assume, and standards vary from state to state. Further, apart from such uncertainties, Judge Posner saw something a bit more suspicious: "[M]ost judges are cagey, even coy, in discussing what they do. They tend to parrot an official line about the judicial process (how rule-bound it is), and often to believe it, though it does not describe their actual practices. . . . Judges have convinced many people—including themselves—that they use esoteric materials and techniques to build selflessly an edifice of doctrines unmarred by willfulness, politics, or ignorance."[26]

This judicial reluctance to discuss decision-making, Judge Posner argues, "makes the scholarly study of judicial behavior at once challenging and indispensable."[27] Instead of biographies or quantitative analyses, "we need *critical* studies of judges."[28] And, I would add, we need critical studies of judges *by judges*. As federal chief judge Irving R. Kaufman declared: "Judges have the duty to speak on matters that affect the judicial system because the public interest cannot be served by silence. Silence is not always golden."[29]

Thus, depending on one's viewpoint, judges either properly protect or all too conveniently conceal their decision-making processes. At what point does proper privacy end and counterproductive concealment begin? The answer may vary from case to case. The answer also may vary over time. Unquestionably, whatever one's admiration for transparency, one should recognize the value of confidentiality in judicial decision-making in practice.[30] And yet there is a big difference between cases pending and cases completed, later considered in a reflective light.

What is appropriate here? To truly understand how America's judges make their decisions, I believe it necessary to touch untouched topics and examine honorable and dishonorable judicial conduct. To honor and protect judicial independence, without which the "great interests of the people" will be lost forever, I believe we must push and probe where others have not, exposing chambered decision-making that has always been concealed.

The cause is compelling; the time is now. Respectfully, therefore, I ask you to come with me into our courts and carefully open our chamber doors.[31]

Part One

JUDGES

I

WHO'S THE JUDGE?

If changing judges changes law, it is not even clear what law is.

—Judge Richard A. Posner[1]

Today, thousands of men, women, and children, many with lawyers, will walk into America's courtrooms hoping judges will be . . .

Will be what? As I was about to write, "fair," I saw the "dishonesty" tripwire just inches away and jumped into the arms of a joking friend. His quip was simple, answering what often is the first question clients ask their lawyers: "Who's the judge?" The circuitous route to his punch line is essential to our analysis.

For the first ten years of my judicial career, I heard juvenile and criminal cases, presiding over hundreds of jury trials and, daily, deciding dozens of motions and sentences. Early on, I encountered a peculiar problem: "substitution." Here's how it works.

Court clerks randomly assign each new case to one of the county's judges. Then, depending on each state's laws, any party in a civil case, and any *defendant* in a juvenile or criminal case, may be able to "file a substitution" in order to avoid the assigned judge and require random reassignment to another.[2] Typically, that party or defendant can do so administratively—not in the courtroom before the judge but in the clerk's office, hidden from judicial view. In this manner, the party may jettison the originally assigned judge *without giving any reason.*

"Substitution" differs from the better-known but far less frequent "disqualification" or "recusal" (two terms describing the same thing), available in every state, which allows any party in any case to appear in court and ask the assigned judge to step aside "for cause" or due to "prejudice." This can be confusing, but, thanks to the 2016 controversy surrounding Donald Trump's assertion that a federal judge of Mexican heritage should have disqualified himself from a case,[3] this area of law—and what does *not* constitute judicial prejudice requiring recusal—has come to be better understood.

Unlike "filing a substitution," which is common in those states that provide
such a statutory right, requesting recusal is rare and risky; most often, it requires an attorney to appear in court and, in person, tell the judge why he or
she should not hear the case. Therefore, except when merely alerting the judge
to an obvious reason for recusal (for example, "Your honor, your wife will be
a witness in this trial"), the attorney is, in effect, asserting, "Your honor, my
client fears [or, less euphemistically, "I believe"] you won't be fair." If the judge
denies the request, that party then is stuck with that judge *and* any antago-
nism that may have arisen from the request itself.[4]

Filing a substitution also may run other risks, particularly in smaller counties with one or only a few judges. There, a substitution request may be awkward (anonymity would be unlikely), inconvenient (travel to another venue
for trial might be needed), and detrimental to the professional rapport the
attorney hopes to have with that judge in other cases. But in a large county
where many judges may be assigned to a specialty (felonies, for example,
where I served in a division with six other judges), substitution is no-risk and
may be sound strategy.[5]

"Substitution" is not our first encounter with "federalism," our constitutional system's allowance for significant legal differences among the states.[6]
Recall that in my introductory chapter I could not even comment on judicial
confidentiality or appellate structures without accounting for different ethical standards and different names for courts in different states. Now, even to
the fundamental question "Who's the judge?" America answers in many ways,
through a multitude of *systems*—federal, state, territorial, tribal, military, and
others. While similar in many respects, these systems have important differences. Therefore, throughout this book, my words may meet your "Wait . . .
that's not the law here." Maybe so. My analysis, however, will apply to most
states or, at least, be instructive, notwithstanding system distinctions.

To summarize:

- "Recusal" (or "disqualification")—available in all states to all parties in all
  cases. It is requested in court, on the basis of a stated allegation of prejudice or
  the appearance of prejudice. It is granted or denied at the judge's discretion, as
  often as necessary to avoid conflicts of interest or other appearances of potential impropriety.
- "Substitution"—available in some states to all parties in civil cases, to all
  defendants in juvenile and criminal cases, and to prosecutors in some states. It
  is requested in the clerk's office, on the basis of nothing stated. It is granted
  once, administratively and automatically.

Thus, for my ten years as a trial judge, substitution allowed defendants and their attorneys, without appearing before me or revealing any reason for their request, to compel random reassignment of their case to another judge. In both my juvenile and my criminal court assignments, many did so—so many, in fact, that had I wanted to check in the clerk's office to learn which attorneys were substituting, it would have been impractical to do so. With virtual anonymity, attorneys were telling me, "Your honor, we want *anyone* but you."[7]

I was puzzled . . . and embarrassed. Doing my best, attempting to conduct court with care and courtesy, I could not understand why so many defense attorneys were advising their clients to avoid me. Enter my friend, Charles F. "Chuck" Kahn Jr., a fine attorney with extensive experience in criminal defense who, a few years later, would become a judge.[8] Earnest, soft-spoken, and dry-humored, he delivered the reassuring punch line: "Remember, defense attorneys have two possible reasons to substitute—they believe their clients *will not* get a fair hearing from you or, more likely, they know their clients *will*."

More seriously, Chuck explained that, for defense attorneys, I presented a dilemma. Many, he said, wanted clients before me in cases where they could legitimately challenge police conduct. They respected what they considered my careful review of motions to invalidate arrests or suppress evidence. They believed I would be willing to grant their motions on the basis of constitutional principles even though, in their view, other judges might gloss over such "technicalities."

So why substitute against me? Chuck went on. As much as these attorneys wanted me to review their challenges to police conduct, they wanted no part of me on the day of sentencing. Apparently, I had come to be known not only for faithfulness to constitutional principles but also for "tough" sentencing and, just as problematically, for unpredictability.[9] In short, defense attorneys could not count on me to accept the guilty plea/sentencing agreements—"plea bargains"—they had negotiated with prosecutors.

Thus, the dilemma: defense attorneys must decide whether to substitute when the case begins; a defendant is not allowed to litigate pre-trial motions before one judge and then take an off-ramp to another for trial or sentencing. And since relatively few defendants claim police misconduct but almost all plead guilty, a sentencing (though not the sentence) is virtually certain.

Chuck was right, and the defense attorneys were right, too. They had perceived that, in criminal cases, I had a judicial "philosophy." I believed that it never should be easy for government to take away freedom—arrests and other police conduct require serious judicial review—but when government does so lawfully, criminal conduct should meet appropriate consequences. Therefore, while carefully considering attorneys' sentencing arguments—whether in support of their competing recommendations or their plea agreements—I, unlike many judges, felt free to chart a different course, even if that meant much more (or much less) incarceration than recommended. Thus, to be sure, and often to the consternation of the attorneys before me, I exercised *independent* discretion in sentencing.

So what's the point? Substitution . . . an interesting anecdote, perhaps, but why detail its intricacies here?

First, substitution exposes a legal procedure that poses the primary question from all who enter our courts: "Who's the judge?"

Second, substitution spotlights "federalism." It reveals that, even in answering such a seemingly simple question of judicial assignment, our legal systems have devised many answers. Barely opening America's courtroom doors, we bump into big differences, making our justice systems all the more interesting and our analyses all the more difficult.

Third, substitution goes a long way toward proving the public's opinion that judges matter. Yes, of course, judges matter in the systemic sense of sixth-grade civics, but as we ask how judges really make their decisions, substitution suggests that *each judge* matters in the personal sense. Thus, litigants ask, "Who's the judge?"—male or female, young or old, liberal or conservative, married or single, Republican or Democrat . . . "Mexican" or otherwise? Looking into courtrooms up and down the courthouse corridors, what are the odds through each door?[10]

Finally, in substitution—in what otherwise might seem the most mundane of procedures—we can't help but acknowledge our own selfish interests in *the* judge. Thus, challenging the presumption with which I almost began—that litigants walk into courtrooms hoping judges will "be fair"—we might feel our own hearts pounding if we imagine ourselves in court. Do we want the judge to be fair? Might we prefer that the judge be biased . . . biased in our favor?

Thus, litigants learn what cynics sense and scholars confirm—*the* judge matters. Even though the laws are set, each case starts with judicial roulette. In every civil and criminal trial court, despite the "rule of law," one judge, deciding alone, matters. In every appellate court, despite the "rule of law," groups of judges, deciding together, matter. And in appellate courts, that may seem all the more remarkable given that the trial is over, the transcript typed, the briefs written, the oral arguments done, and given that the judges, reading the same record and researching the same law, often disagree. As Judge Posner observed, "Nothing is more common than for different people of equal competence in reasoning to form different beliefs from the same information."[11]

Whether in trial or appellate courts, judges matter; their differences make a difference. But can that be fair? If we as a nation subscribe to the "rule of law," should the ruling of law differ depending on the courtroom door? How can justice jump, strut, stumble, and fall from one courtroom to another? The answers are behind the scenes. From shadowed robing rooms to spotlighted courtrooms, judicial dramas emerge—scripts written, parts cast, judges interpreting roles and delivering lines. But where are the producers, and who are the directors?

2

THE PROSECUTOR'S PERSPECTIVE

Meek young men grow up in libraries, believing it their duty to accept
the view which Cicero, which Locke, which Bacon, have given;
forgetful that Cicero, Locke, and Bacon were only young men in
libraries when they wrote these books.

—Ralph Waldo Emerson, *The American Scholar*

In a book about how judges really make their decisions, why present the prosecutor's perspective? Because it is the perspective that reflects the experience of
much of America's judiciary. While earlier in our nation's history judges could
have come from various careers, legal and nonlegal, now and for many years,
in almost every state, judges have been required to be attorneys.[1] And while
some judges have come from private practice or other fields of public service,
many more have launched their judicial careers from prosecutorial ones.

More exactly, many state judges once were *state* prosecutors.[2] Often referred
to as "assistant district attorneys" or "assistant state's attorneys," they practiced
in state courts, prosecuting state criminal cases. While terminologies and procedural details differ in more than fifty ways, prosecutors' standards and duties
are similar in all states. And, depending on what each state counts as a "case"
(a murder charge; a speeding ticket), it is in the state courts that juries and
judges handle well over 90 percent of America's legal business.[3]

This may seem surprising. What about all the other cases, big and small?
After all, we've heard the expression that some squabble doesn't amount to a
"federal case." And most Americans, if they encounter courts at all, do so at
local levels where "Judge Judy" presides, where small claims are settled, where
traffic tickets are bargained and paid. What about them?

These courts, federal and local, are important. But they do not handle the
cavalcade of cases that consume America's state courts every day—burglary,
child abuse, delinquency, drunk driving, murder, sexual assault, and other criminal charges; family, divorce, insurance, probate, real estate, commercial cases,
and a host of other civil matters. All these cases come to state court judges,

many of whom spent their "formative" years as state prosecutors. And that is where I began.

In 1975, after graduating from the University of Wisconsin Law School, I accepted a position as an assistant district attorney—one of fifty-five appointees of Milwaukee County District Attorney E. Michael McCann, the elected official responsible for prosecution of state crimes in the courts of Wisconsin's biggest county.

I was fortunate. District Attorney McCann was an exemplary public servant. A gifted trial attorney, he was honest, hard-working, politically astute yet faithful to his legal duty apart from politics. Modest in manner and lifestyle, he conveyed compassion. At staff meetings, he urged his assistants to bring what he termed "the milk of human kindness" to their pursuit of justice. He reminded us that so many of those we served—victims, witnesses, and, yes, defendants—had been touched by tragedies. Thus, he preached, while we could promise little, we must always offer courtesy and the kindness that may well have been absent from their lives. And, he implored, we must always be true to our ethical duty—not to win or count convictions but to "do justice."[4]

Unavoidably, and often at an all too early age, prosecuting attorneys hold life-changing authority and discretion. Fulfilling what the law terms their "quasi-judicial" function, they evaluate evidence, police conduct, and the merits of a case before charging (or not charging) a person with a crime.[5] They must vigorously prosecute criminals in courtroom battles but also maintain balance—disclosing evidence favorable to the defense, moving to reduce or dismiss charges in light of new evidence or circumstances, recommending probation or softer sentences when incarceration would be unfair. In short, before cases come to court, and then throughout litigation, prosecutors must make discretionary decisions similar to those made by judges.

That's the legal model throughout America. And while some states, county by county, may suffer unfairness from unwise or politically motivated prosecutors, many others are well served by those who remain true to their mission—"do justice."

In 1975, when I entered the prosecutor's office, I was dripping with idealism. Just fourteen years earlier, as a fifth-grader ten days shy of my eleventh birthday, I had watched John F. Kennedy's inauguration on the tiny TV a teacher had brought from home. I remember feeling personally challenged by "Ask not what your country can do for you. . . ." Now I wanted to answer with "what I could do for my country." And in dream-come-true fashion, I soon received special assignments that allowed for the pursuit of my ideals. What I did not realize was that three of these eventually would be woven into the fabric of my judicial robe.

FAILING TWO WOMEN

In my first week, I was assigned to help design a program for battered women. Part of "Project Turnaround," I was among the new federally funded state prosecutors in the US Justice Department's initiative to "turn around" the system's focus from defendant rights to victim and witness needs. The program we developed—America's first for battered women in a prosecutor's office— became a national model, leading to my interview on the PBS *MacNeil/Lehrer Report* and to my presentation of a paper to the US Commission on Civil Rights.[6]

Heady stuff for an idealist just out of law school. Far less ego-stroking were the endless hours with women, battered by boyfriends or husbands, ignored or ill-served by police, torn between fear and family, finally desperate enough to come, almost always alone, to our office.

Our "breakthrough" (after all, this was 1975, just as America was waking to the reality of such violence) was to respect each woman and to recognize the seriousness of what she and, often, her children were suffering. We—three prosecutors and one social worker—cared about them. We tried to empower the women as "experts" in their own cases, enlisting them to help evaluate their options. We drew on legal and community resources, following through with supportive services as they braved the legal system.

One afternoon, in addition to the many young women seeking our services, an older woman, Ada Shellough, came to the cubicle that had become my office. In a calm, quiet voice, she told me of her fear—not for her own safety but, rather, for that of her daughter and grandchild. She explained that her son-in-law, Leonard Collins, a Vietnam veteran, was unstable and violent. She said he recently had become more explosive because of his belief that she was asking county social services to remove the grandchild from his home.

Ms. Shellough seemed sincere. I believed her. While with other complainants I might have issued an "order-in" letter allowing an alleged abuser to come in for further review, I was concerned that such a letter in this case could detonate the dangers Ms. Shellough feared. I wanted to investigate further, but only after Mr. Collins was in custody. Therefore, that very afternoon, before giving him the chance to tell me his side of the story, I took the unusual step of charging Mr. Collins and ordering a warrant for his arrest.

The next day, Leonard Collins found Ada Shellough before the warrant found him. Probably before the warrant was even processed, he bayoneted her to death. (I never learned whether social services actually intended to remove the child from his home or whether Mr. Collins knew of Ms. Shellough's visit to my office.)

I attended Ada Shellough's autopsy. In a dim and dreary examination room, deep inside an old edifice of courtrooms and law enforcement offices, I watched the coroner cut her open. Standing a few feet away, I looked into her body. Feeling faint, I sat and continued to watch her torso probed—for evidence, for prosecutorial purposes. I listened to the coroner narrate, tape-recording the anatomical details of her death, soon to be recited in court.[7]

This was not the first time I watched medical professionals crowding over a corpse (nor would it be the last). When I was seventeen, my brother and I came home one afternoon to find our mother on the floor, stricken by a pulmonary embolism. I tried to revive her; I watched paramedics try to save her. Eight years later, for reasons I did not discern but accepted as a matter of undefined faith, I felt I owed Ada Shellough my presence. I also told myself that, as a matter of professional principle, I should see the potentiality with which I would be dealing every day. To cast away whatever callousness could come from caseloads, I should see the flesh-and-blood humanity of each person who would depend on me for justice.

CONFRONTING DECEIT

After one year working with battered women, I was assigned to investigate what, according to a newspaper exposé, appeared to be fraud in Medicaid-financed social work agencies. Again, I was swimming in unknown waters. Until 1975, battered women had not gained attention from prosecutors in any programmatic way, and until 1976, while Medicaid recipients were regularly prosecuted for fraud, Medicaid providers—doctors, nursing home owners, and others—had avoided audits and investigations.[8]

Why me? To understand a typically underfunded big city DA's Office and to sense the work of overworked prosecutors, then and now, it is important to recognize that I received these unusual assignments not because I was good but because I was new—new as in expendable, new as in available but "not ready for prime time" prosecuting felonies before juries.[9] Thus, suddenly (and, I would say, prematurely), I found myself directing major white-collar crime investigations in which I was dealing with defendants who employed seasoned attorneys, some of whom had landed positions in prestigious firms precisely because of their previous employment *as prosecutors*.

While I probably would not have been assigned to the Medicaid fraud cases had I not gained District Attorney McCann's confidence working with battered women, I still was inexperienced. Whether assisting women or pursuing white-collar crooks, I was working investigatively, outside the courtrooms where my colleagues were facing judges and juries every day. Thus, I was not getting a feel for how the evidence I was discovering would play out in a trial. As a result, while sometimes moving smoothly, I also stumbled, as we shall see.

The fraud was brazen, doctors and agency owners guzzling at an unguarded fountain of federal funds. For example, Dr. Alice Dean, a child psychiatrist, "examined" hundreds of children for minutes but, for each one, billed Medicaid for two hours of "individual psychotherapy." Then, prescribing psychotherapeutic treatment for every child, she referred them to Family Outreach Social Service Agency, the other half of the "Medicaid mill," which, in turn, defrauded Medicaid by billing for psychotherapeutic services in excess of those actually provided by its social workers. Another agency, Crossroads Academy, operating alternative schools, obtained psychotherapy prescriptions from another psychiatrist. Crossroads then billed Medicaid for individual psychotherapy— some nonexistent, some consisting of group field trips to Milwaukee baseball games during a season when, I must concede, my beloved Brewers' efforts were rarely therapeutic.[10]

But here, my purpose is less to describe Medicaid fraud and more to relate a lesson learned while investigating Crossroads. So now, let us better understand white-collar crime investigation (and the methods spurned by the Russian judges at my lecture) and then see the courtroom scene of the next prosecutorial experience that proved so important in my judicial preparation.

In cases of sophisticated white-collar crime or organized crime, special investigative methods often are needed. Why? Consider the contrast. Whereas most street crime is known—suffered by victims, observed by witnesses, reported to police—many organized crimes remain hidden. Moreover, whether drug kingpins or corporate executives, the leaders conceal their roles, insulating themselves by rewarding, coercing, threatening, and harming their lackeys. Thus, moving up the pyramids of such organizations, we find that the most important witnesses are the ones least likely to cooperate with law enforcement.

Therefore, to investigate such crime, prosecutors rely on more than the usual policing. First, prosecutors need *secrecy*—to secure witnesses and their cooperation without exposing them to retaliation or revealing the investigation. Next, prosecutors need five legal powers, over and above the usual: (1) subpoena—to require reluctant witnesses to appear for interviews; (2) immunity—to assure co-conspirators that, in exchange for truthful testimony, they will not be prosecuted; (3) contempt—to incarcerate co-conspirators who refuse to cooperate even after having been granted immunity; (4) subpoena duces tecum—to "follow the money" by compelling disclosure of business and banking records; and (5) search warrant or, in rare cases, wiretap or other electronic surveillance to obtain eavesdropped evidence.

With the exception of search warrants, these special powers are neither necessary nor available to police pursuing street crime. In the federal and most state systems, these powers are authorized through secret grand juries, under the supervision of a judge. And in some states these same powers are provided through procedurally different but functionally equivalent proceedings: the "one-man grand jury" or "John Doe."

Mere announcement of a grand jury or John Doe often is enough to motivate cooperation. Knowing that a subpoena can compel their appearances, witnesses and even co-conspirators, often with their attorneys, meet with prosecutors; they work out agreements exchanging information and the promise of truthful testimony for immunity or favorable sentencing recommendations. They usually do so discreetly, outside the grand juries and John Does where, usually, only the most resistant witnesses and targeted conspirators appear, under subpoena.

Whether in grand juries or John Does, one encounters a judicial role largely unknown to the public—judges as investigators, working in concert with prosecutors. Drawn from the regular judicial ranks and assigned by chief judges or court administrators, such judges never preside over cases ultimately coming from charges filed as a result of such investigations. Rather, while still maintaining the neutrality necessary to judge a prosecutor's requests for subpoenas, searches and wiretaps, immunity and contempt, such judges join the investigative effort. Depending on personality, experience, and interest, they may do so in a relatively detached or a deeply involved manner.

The investigation of Crossroads Academy took place through a John Doe. For our purposes here, three procedural differences distinguish the John Doe from a grand jury. While both are secret, taking place in closed courtrooms or other courthouse facilities, only in the John Doe (1) is an attorney allowed to accompany a witness for questioning; (2) is a judge present during questioning; and (3) does the judge, not grand jurors, formally decide whether criminal charges will be issued.[11]

So it was in a beautiful old courtroom, in a secret John Doe proceeding, that I questioned Carol Cook, vice president of Crossroads Academy, Inc., accompanied by Crossroads' attorney. I did so before Judge George A. Burns Jr., an experienced, charming, and savvy gentleman who, silver-haired and black-robed over his golf shirt, looked exactly as central casting would have wished.

Mrs. Cook, who, coincidentally, lived in a majestic Milwaukee home just two blocks from my more modest one, owned Crossroads with her husband, the corporate president. As she took the stand, she seemed calm and composed, an executive doing her duty. But what she did not know was that, weeks earlier, Judge Burns had granted my motion to immunize her administrator, who had told us how she and Mrs. Cook sat at the Cooks' dining room table and prepared bogus bills.

With that information, cooperation from other witnesses, and documentary evidence, I had carefully prepared my questions so as not to reveal too much too soon. Not knowing what we knew, not suspecting that we held smoking-gun evidence from her own home, and apparently not having confided in her attorney, who otherwise would have advised her to remain silent or cut a deal, Mrs. Cook testified. For almost an hour, all proceeded as planned. I gently questioned Mrs. Cook, feigning interest in the operation of Crossroads. Then, cautiously, my questions escorted Mrs. Cook to her dining room and the details of her billing.

Question by question, I coaxed Mrs. Cook into a corner from which she could not escape. With details that could have come only from her administrator, I artfully crafted the ultimate, incriminating questions—questions that should have drawn Judge Burns's applause, and Mrs. Cook's confession.

Instead, she lied. In response to my first logically ironclad question, she lied. I tried again, rephrasing my exquisite inquiry. She lied again. No applause. No confession. And I became flustered. "But . . . then . . . how . . . ," I stammered. Mrs. Cook was cool; I was sweating.

Judge Burns called a recess and invited me into chambers. Placing a fatherly hand on my shoulder, he asked, "Charlie, hasn't anyone ever lied to you before?" His words seemed facetious; his tone was not. Judge Burns, watching my reaction to Mrs. Cook's lies, seemed to understand something about me, about my background, about my naïveté. He continued: "Charlie, did you really expect her to confess and hand you the keys to her prison cell? Go back out there, ask your questions, let her lie, and then charge her with *perjury*, in addition to Medicaid fraud." And that's what we did. Eventually, Mrs. Cook pled guilty, taking the fall for her husband and allowing him to remain free to care for their infant, born during the first months of her imprisonment.

But what about me? I brooded; I pondered Judge Burns's question; I wondered why, at age twenty-six, I had to think about whether anyone ever had lied to me before. And, although I imagined that, at one time or another, perhaps in summer camp or playground encounters, some kids must have lied to me, I otherwise came up empty. As best as I could recall, I had, at least in this regard, led a charmed life, surrounded by family and friends who, whatever their limitations, were honest. How fortunate—and how unfortunate for one working in the criminal justice system.

I had little instinct for deception, no radar for deceit. I had no understanding of the self-destructive illogic that had led so many I would encounter to harm themselves and others; to lie, cheat, and steal as a way of life. I had no experience with dishonesty except my own, consisting of childhood thefts—most memorably (I finally confess), of a one-dollar Duncan Imperial yoyo from Bear's Reliable Pharmacy—which I had rationalized as rare and inconsequential.

Blessed by good guidance from my wonderful family, my "default" was to believe and trust, leaving me, as a prosecutor, particularly unprepared. So, at twenty-six, I was stumped by "Hasn't anyone ever lied to you before?" As a judge, I would need to correct for my own innocence as I judged others' guilt.

Nailing an Omelet to the Wall

Minutes after midnight on February 7, 1976, Bruno Dreyer, a seventy-eight-year-old cognitively disabled patient, walked out of the Glendale Convalescent Center into near-zero air.[12] He trudged through deep snow to the chain-link fence bordering the nursing home grounds, collapsed, and froze to death. Mr. Dreyer was found later that morning still clutching the fence, but his chart's last entry for that same day read: "12–7 a.m. Side rails up. Checked every two hours. No problems. Slept well."

The coroner convened an inquest into the cause of death.[13] In two days of testimony, state inspectors and nursing home staff members described the deplorable conditions and understaffing that, they believed, allowed Mr. Dreyer to "elope." Days later, the news broke—the coroner recommended criminal charges.

Time passed; headlines faded. I was vaguely aware of the nursing home news, but uninvolved. Just completing my first year in the DA's Office, transitioning from the battered women's program to the Medicaid fraud investigations, I still lacked courtroom experience; I still was expendable. But now working white-collar crime cases, I was one of only a few in our office familiar with John Doe investigations. So it should have come as no surprise when District Attorney McCann handed me the inquest transcript to review. He also cautioned that investigating a patient death might seem like trying to "nail an omelet to the wall."

Little did I know what was coming. Little did I suspect that I was about to begin a six-year effort that would take my work to the courtrooms of Chicago and Milwaukee, the governors' offices of Illinois and Wisconsin, a five-week jury trial, national notoriety, and appointment as a judge.

After reading the inquest transcript, I advised District Attorney McCann that, like the coroner, I suspected the three Chicago owners of maximizing profits by filling their nursing home with patients while emptying it of staff. Could we prove it? Could we discover any evidence connecting their conduct to Bruno Dreyer's death? Could we prove that these men, owners of dozens of nursing homes in four Midwestern states, who, for all I knew, might never have even set foot in Milwaukee, had, in a criminally liable sense, pushed Mr. Dreyer out into the freezing air? Could we prove their knowledge and actions, beyond a reasonable doubt, to twelve jurors?

I had no idea. But I knew the inquest evidence fell short of proving much at all. Therefore, I advised, in order to discover more evidence, a John Doe would be necessary and a year of investigation might be needed. I was right about the John Doe but overly optimistic about the timeline. For the next two years, District Attorney McCann resisted pressure to pull me from the privacy of my office and assign me to courtroom duties. For two years, complying with the judicial order of John Doe secrecy, he deflected accusations that Bruno Dreyer's death had been swept under the rug.

Meanwhile, assisted by a registered nurse interning with our office and by special agents of the Wisconsin Justice Department, I pored over business records and patient charts, interviewed more than one hundred witnesses— staff members, patients' relatives, and professors of gerontological nursing— and questioned suspected co-conspirators. Finally, finding no single smoking gun but many wounding weapons, we charged six defendants—the three own-ers, their corporate partnership,[14] their assistant who traveled between Chi-cago and their many nursing homes, and the Glendale administrator—with reckless homicide for Mr. Dreyer's death, and fifty-eight counts of patient abuse for the life-endangering skin deterioration and weight loss suffered by fifty-eight neglected patients.

The investigation had been difficult for many reasons, not the least of which was that the fifty-nine patients featured in our charges were dead, cognitively disabled, or so infirm that they could not testify. And almost all were alone; only two were visited by relatives able to describe their loved ones' suffering. Thus, most of the trial evidence would be circumstantial.

The prosecution theory, however, was simple: greed. Our investigation had uncovered conduct more despicable than I could have imagined—conduct that would stand as a warning to policy makers prone to "privatizing" and, in so doing, mixing profit motives with human services. To understand, a bit more background. . . .

For many years, the Glendale Convalescent Center had been a big nursing home, caring for hundreds of elderly patients. But, despite its size, Glendale had maintained a "Ma and Pa" atmosphere through the dedicated efforts of its husband/wife owners. On site daily, they knew their staff, helped their patients, cared about care, and treated both patients and staff with affection and respect. In the 1970s, however, converging circumstances led to the sale of Glendale and many other independent facilities to nursing home conglom-erates. For Bruno Dreyer, two of those circumstances proved fatal.

First, across the country, many states were trying to reduce institutionali-
zation—of prisoners, and of the physically disabled and mentally ill living in
state facilities. (Motivating this movement were two theories: that reducing
the reach of government would reduce taxes; and that de-institutionalizing
prisoners and patients would give them the chance to fare better at home or
in smaller community-based facilities.) Second, financing the health services,
Medicaid now would provide the coverage, pegging payments to the level of
care—the more disabled the patient, the greater the care and, therefore, the
higher the government's payment to the caregivers.

Legislators, eager to cut budgets, closed old "asylums" and other state health-
care facilities. But in all too many instances, and perhaps foreshadowing the
"repeal/replace" subterfuge used to attack Obamacare years later,[15] they failed
to fund the in-home and community-based care that was to have replaced
them. The abhorred vacuum formed, and profiteering filled it. Where public
officials may have seen potential for cost-effective conversion from institution-
alization to more humane personal care, others saw nursing home empires.
Perfect crimes were coming.

The new Glendale owners bought dozens of nursing homes in Illinois,
Indiana, Missouri, and Wisconsin. They courted big new customers—state
governments needing alternatives to old institutions—contracting to house
the countless patients leaving the abandoned state hospitals. And they found
perfect victims—helpless patients who, in most cases, could not cry out; isolated patients who had no visiting relatives to complain or advocate on their
behalf; developmentally disabled patients for whom Medicaid would pay the
most. The Glendale owners recruited such patients and, almost every day, from
their Chicago office, called their on-site administrators and asked: "What's the
count?"

One year before Bruno Dreyer's death, state nursing home inspectors issued
an "Order to Correct Deficiency," requiring Glendale to remedy a staffing short-
age so severe "as to jeopardize the health, safety and welfare of the patients."
Instead, Glendale continued to increase the patient population and cut supplies and staff. The remaining nursing aides were unable to bathe, toilet, dress,
and ambulate patients; unable to reposition bedridden patients every two hours,
as required by code, to prevent bed sores; unable to assist "feeders" who needed
spoon-by-spoon help to prevent life-threatening weight loss.

A year later, just before Mr. Dreyer's death, state inspectors again cited
Glendale for insufficient staff and again ordered correction. Glendale again
ignored the order. Then, five days later, Bruno Dreyer eloped and froze. He
had been living on Glendale's most secure ward because of his history of wandering within and away from the nursing home. But on the night he died, the

entire staff responsible for more than two hundred patients on his and two other wards consisted of one nurse and two nurses' aides.

At the five-week trial of the Glendale administrator, jurors heard from fifty-one witnesses for the prosecution and a few for the defense. They heard from Glendale's nursing director and other staff members who had complained to state inspectors, petitioned the owners and administrators for help, and, in countless charts, recorded that they had failed to feed or reposition bed-ridden patients "due to lack of staff." They heard of the owners' daily phone call, "What's the count?" And the jurors learned of the last words in Mr. Dreyer's chart: "12–7 a.m. Side rails up. Checked every two hours. No problems. Slept well." The authoring aide tearfully testified that, instead of actually checking patients, she had followed orders to sit at her nursing station and, chart by chart, write such false entries.

After three days of deliberation, the jury found the administrator guilty of reckless homicide and patient abuse.[16] Years of litigation and appeals involving the other defendants followed. Ultimately, all were convicted, two were incarcerated, and the corporate partnership paid maximum fines.

As a result of the Glendale cases, the Chicago owners lost all their nursing homes, at least in Wisconsin and Illinois. Wisconsin and other states rewrote their laws regulating nursing homes, thus improving oversight and strengthening enforcement.[17] All too immodestly, I felt my idealism validated. True to my Wisconsin roots, I recalled the camper's quip: "Anyone who thinks the little guy can't make a difference never spent a night in a tent with a mosquito."[18]

The Glendale prosecution brought much notoriety and, in doing so, helped build my bridge to the judiciary.[19] How? While the legal details may merit a law school lecture, here we'll simply trace the topic of "extradition" and how its legal turns led to my judicial appointment.

Historically, extradition is a polite bow to federalism—an expression of respect for the independent status and legal system of each state. Designed as an expeditious process through which one governor calls to another, "Send that crook back here," extradition is administered through brief hearings in state courts.

Usually, a defendant is arrested, jailed, and then "rendered" to the extraditing state in little more than the few days needed for preparation and transmittal of the "governor's warrant" from one capitol to another, and then to court. There, typically, defense attorneys object to extradition, but only to adjourn the proceeding the few days they need to examine the paperwork, confirm the existence of the underlying charge, and advise defendants to "waive extradition" and surrender to the extraditing state. Although a particularly resistant defendant or litigious lawyer can prolong the process a month or two, they have little reason to do so. Why? Because in the state where a fugitive is found, the court does not address the merits of any charge; it only reviews the formal legality of the governor's warrant. Therefore, languishing in a local jail, a dilatory defendant would only postpone surrender to the state where the underlying charge could be contested.

Thus, extradition hearings usually are fast formalities. Rarely do judicial reviews reveal any basis for delay, usually involving nothing more than a technical defect in the paperwork, quickly corrected. But for the Glendale owners, extradition litigation lasted ten years!

How could they delay for a decade, making this extradition battle the longest in American history? Why would they do so? They devised an unusual strategy based on a unique legal theory tenuously tied to a corporation's legal status. And, already elderly at the time of their arrests, they did so to delay the day they might be convicted and sentenced to prison.

Upon their arrests in Illinois, the three owners appeared in a Chicago courtroom before the Cook County chief judge. Their attorneys challenged the extradition warrants in what, at first, seemed the usual formal fashion. Then, because the defendants had surrendered to the Illinois authorities and were not "flight risks," they were released pending resolution of their extradition. The owners then directed their attorneys to go to Wisconsin, plead guilty to all charges on behalf of one of the other defendants—their company—and pay the maximum civil and criminal fines, totaling $135,500. Their attorneys did so; their company promptly paid. Then, tapping into extradition's governor-to-governor historical foundation, they availed themselves of a little-known procedure—an "extraordinary hearing" in each state—before legal counsel for Illinois governor James Thompson and Wisconsin governor Lee Sherman Dreyfus.

Confused? Here's the key. Once the Glendale owners' company, the NR-1 Trust, had pled guilty and paid the fines, they were able to assert a novel defense, both in court and at the gubernatorial hearings. They argued that their company, while registered as a corporation in Wisconsin, really was not a corporation at all, not a separate "party" or "person" that could stand as a defendant in a criminal case. Instead, they contended, because the NR-1 Trust, under Illinois law, was a "partnership," it was their alter ego, an entity legally indivisible from themselves, the partners. Thus, they maintained, although in Wisconsin the NR-1 Trust was registered as a corporation, it remained a partnership—a partnership that had pled guilty and completed its sentence by paying the fines. Thus, they, the partners (alter egos of their partnership), could not be prosecuted again. Double jeopardy!

Their argument failed, but it consumed years of litigation and appeals. Eventually, the Glendale owners were extradited and convicted. They paid additional penalties but were not imprisoned. But, before concluding that these delays were advantageous only to the defendants, consider my calculation. Because of the owners' ages and health, I believed it unlikely that they ever would be imprisoned. Thus, I thought, the next best deterrence could come through long litigation and prolonged publicity. And indeed, that occurred. Once or twice each year, newspapers told of our success fighting for extradition and, eventually, gaining convictions of all six defendants.[20]

Thus, for thirteen years, from the night of Mr. Dreyer's death to the day of the owners' sentencings, this single case publicized the prosecution's perseverance and success, thus deterring others who otherwise might have contemplated such crimes. Along the way, this case carried me into the "extraordinary hearings" before the governors' legal counsel. What I did not learn until later was that Governor Dreyfus held special concern for nursing home patients and, as a result, had shown keen interest in the case. When he denied the defendants' request to block extradition, he called me. With the governor on hold, my secretary tried to find me, but, because I was in court, I was unavailable. Later, returning to my office, I was greeted by a "While You Were Out" slip on which was written the governor's message: "Go get 'em, tiger."

Thus, Governor Dreyfus—a man I had never met and with whom I shared no political affiliation—took an interest in me. Not long thereafter, through an aide's phone call, he encouraged me to apply to fill a judicial vacancy. I was intrigued. But I was too young and, besides, the governor was a Republican. So, in that first call, mentioning that I had volunteered for two years in the 1972 presidential campaign of George McGovern, the Democratic candidate, I conceded that my prospects seemed slim. The aide replied, "Well, the governor's quite an independent guy himself."[21]

So I became a judge, then Wisconsin's youngest. My rapid rise left me targeted for both understandable envy and perfectly fair skepticism. I joined the skeptics in wondering whether, at age thirty-two, one could possibly possess the wisdom worthy of judicial authority.[22] And I became a judge with a prosecutor's perspective. My seven years in the DA's Office had prepared me for the judiciary in important ways, though certainly not all. Difficult decision-making and deep involvement with people, rich and poor, police, good and bad, and judges, honorable and otherwise, had given me invaluable background. Ironically, however, service in an excellent, ethically anchored prosecutor's office also had left me unprepared for the judicial pettiness and political infighting I soon would see.

I became a judge both propelled and impeded by biases and inclinations, at least some of which grew from my prosecutorial experiences. From battered women and tragic deaths, I carried *compassion*, even when such sensitivity could consume me or conflict with law. From white-collar criminals, I learned of my lingering *naïveté* and the vigilance I would need to prevent it from inuring me to the deceits of those coming before me. And from my mosquito-in-the-tent success, I deepened my "ask not" *idealism*, even as such success might inflate my estimation of my own judgment.

Nothing is novel in the notion that experience shapes one's character and career. But in America's judiciary, where independence is the ideal and corruptions are so influential, the nature of prosecutorial shaping is of particular importance. It may prove problematic if unacknowledged; constructive, but only if understood. Either way, as we will see, the prosecutorial shaping of America's judiciary is critically consequential.

3

THE
DECISION-MAKING IDEAL

"To decide impartially," according to Socrates, is the essence of judicial virtue.[1] So package "impartiality." Deliver it with gavels and robes to all judges on their very first day. That was easy. But on their second day, what happens? Case by case, impartiality, unguarded, seems to have been misplaced or surrendered, stolen or sold. By their second day on the job, judges without independence have found themselves unable to protect impartiality from forces tipping their scales.

What is judicial independence, and from what (and from whom) must it be protected? In America, whether in the founding fathers' earliest writings or Google's latest search, we can find countless reflections on judicial independence and its role in our society.[2] And, apparently, there's no end in sight. In their meta-analysis, *An Evaluation of Cross-National Measures of Judicial Independence*, professors Julio Ríos-Figueroa and Jeffrey K. Staton wrote, "The increasing number of scholarly attempts to define and measure judicial independence speaks to how crucial [it] has become in several theories of economic development, rights protection, and the rule of law."[3]

Still, no definition has commanded consensus, and while the "increasing number of scholarly attempts" may continue to refine "judicial independence," almost every judge I know would simply say, "I know it when I see it." I offer this intending no disrespect for either scholarly efforts or judicial instincts but, rather, with fascination for both. Indeed, it may be that, collectively, scholars and judges themselves are onto something. It may be that "judicial independence," unlocked from any single semantic cell, regains the freedom essential to its meaning.

If so, this could help explain why scholars, increasingly, and judges, as always, seem to define judicial independence by isolating it less and *feeling* for its contextual meanings more. Judicial independence is "complex and nuanced," wrote law professor Laurie Levenson, and is "an elusive and multi-layered concept that is difficult to define," concluded federal judge Paul L. Friedman.[4] And Ríos-Figueroa and Staton seem to be suggesting acceptance of more nuanced research reflecting "concepts that are not directly observable." These concepts, they say, are "latent, and for this reason[, their] measurement requires inference."[5]

To accept such inferential research (and, I would maintain, experiential insight) is not to ignore the very valuable analytical dissections scholars have performed. Notwithstanding the lack of definitional consensus, certain definitional concepts are helpful, including at least three we will explore in the actual cases we consider: (1) *systemic* and *individual* judicial independence; (2) systemically *external* and individually *internal* sources of corruption; and (3) *de facto* and *de jure* systems to protect independence.[6]

Whatever their definitional disagreements, scholars and judges agree: *independence protects impartiality*. Canon 1 of the ABA Model Code of Judicial Conduct opens, "A judge shall uphold and promote the independence of the judiciary."[7] Why? Why does "independence" form the foundation for the first canon of judicial conduct? Charles Gardner Geyh answered: independence protects decision-making from corruption; only independence, he explained, "makes impartial decision-making under the rule of law possible."[8]

What might I add to the definitional discussion? With admittedly less scholarship on my vitae than we might want but with a wealth of experience under my belt—twelve years litigating before dozens of judges, twenty-two years judging thousands of cases at trial and on appeal, and forty years teaching law students and judges from every state and many other countries—I should be embarrassed if, in a book about judicial independence, I failed to offer at least a small contribution. Thus, to the "elusive and multi-layered concept" I now propose this addition to the analysis: *judicial independence is decision-making embodied by (1) genuine and full inquiry, (2) intellectually honest reasoning, and (3) humility.*

Genuine and Full Inquiry

When Socrates counseled that "[f]our things belong to a judge" and first posited "to hear courteously,"[9] he was, I suspect, recommending more than manners. I believe he understood that "to hear" is hard. To truly hear is to listen carefully and sincerely, initiate inquiry, cultivate communication, gather and clarify information, and understand emotions as well as words. To hear "courteously" also is to inquire sensitively, bringing patience and persistence to fully expose the facts and motivations carrying human conflict to court.

INTELLECTUALLY HONEST REASONING

When, in 1838, a young man spoke to the Young Men's Lyceum of Springfield, Illinois, he discussed "the perpetuation of our political institutions," warned of mob violence threatening the rule of law, and declared: "Passion has helped us; but can do so no more. It will in [the] future be our enemy. Reason, cold, calculating, unimpassioned reason, must furnish all the materials for our future support and defence [*sic*]."[10]

Still shy of thirty, Abraham Lincoln was a lawyer and a legislator. He "expressed a concern that would haunt him and shape his political personality: what would become of America when its founding fathers were gone, their disciples were gone, and the new generation had no great leaders to inspire it with the original ideals of the republic?"[11] Thus, a young man, whose countenance would come to convey agony and compassion, preached reason, "cold, calculating, unimpassioned reason," as the quality that "must furnish all the materials for our future." Why? Why would Lincoln relegate revolutionary passion, which he revered, and elevate "unimpassioned reason" to guide the founders' grandchildren?

Lincoln was not denigrating passion—revolutionary passion creating a nation, intellectual passion creating a constitution, or sexual passion creating life. Indeed, "clearly Lincoln, this acolyte of pure reason and remorseless logic, was also a romantic."[12] But Lincoln was a man of law. He recognized that reason, most of all, would offer Americans an irreplaceable opportunity: the opportunity of time—time, without violence, to develop law that, in turn, would stabilize our society's foundation. He understood that our Constitution had not yet formed the perfect union but, rather, had offered Americans a chance—a chance for continuity from which we could "form a more perfect union" and, possibly, "establish justice."[13]

That opportunity would depend on all three branches of government but, ultimately and most of all, on the judiciary. The chance for time and continuity would depend on Americans' confidence that, in going to court, they could fairly and nonviolently resolve their differences. And their confidence in the never-ending effort to "establish justice" would depend on judges and their *independence*.

Remarkably, all that was well understood as revolution loomed and, two centuries later, as constitutional crisis consumed Congress. "In 1774, our first patriots considered an independent judiciary as the most precious of our rights," wrote Congressman Fisher Ames in 1806.[14] And in the midst of Watergate, as President Richard Nixon challenged judicial authority, he was rebuffed by Senator Sam Ervin, who reminded America that "an independent judiciary

is perhaps the most essential characteristic of a free society."[15] Yet, just as remarkably, perhaps, the constitutional framers, while extolling an independent
judiciary (indeed, the lack of judicial independence in the king's courts was
among the reasons for declaring independence),[16] detailed the structure and
functions of the executive and legislative branches but said almost nothing
about the judiciary. "Details to follow," they seemed to say—a matter for Congress and state legislatures to sort out later.

One may move through history, from Lincoln to Ames to Ervin, to elaborate this aspect of judicial "independence"—intellectually honest reasoning—
and clarify its importance. But its essential value is easy to see. Two simple
scenarios should suffice. (1) The teenager asks, "May I use the car tonight?" The
responsible parent responds with *genuine and full inquiry*, asking why, when,
where, with whom, and whether homework is done. *Honest reasoning* then
applies the family rules; the engine revs or remains garaged. (2) The witness
swears to tell "the whole truth" and, after the attorneys' *genuine and full inquiry*,
the judge instructs the jurors to apply *honest reasoning*—to evaluate witness
credibility and all the evidence, unswayed by "sympathy, prejudice or passion"
and, on the basis of "reason and common sense," render their verdict.[17]

HUMILITY

Without this third leg to stabilize the judicial stool, independence wobbles.
Why? Consider the ideological consciousness of many judges, in light of Nobel
laureate Paul Krugman's advice: "Everyone has an ideology, a view about how
the world does and should work. Indeed, the most reckless and dangerous
ideologues are often those who imagine themselves ideology-free . . . unaware
of their own biases. What you should seek, in yourself and others, is not an
absence of ideology but an open mind, *willing to consider the possibility that
parts of the ideology may be wrong.*"[18]

But to punctuate the point, we can do even better than a Nobel Prize winner. In Philadelphia, "[t]here was an unspoken consensus" that Benjamin
Franklin "was the wisest man in the room." On the last day of the convention he said: "I confess that I do not entirely approve this Constitution at present, but Sir, I am not sure I shall never approve it: For having lived long, I
have experienced many Instances of being oblig'd, by better Information or
fuller Consideration, to change opinions on important Subjects, which I once
thought Right, but found to be otherwise. It is therefore that *the older I grow
the more apt I am to doubt my own Judgment, and to pay more respect to the Judgment of others.*"[19]

And about Benjamin Franklin and the other founding fathers, Joseph Ellis,
a Pulitzer Prize–winning historian, concluded: "Not their hubris but their

humility has made the lasting difference. They knew they did not have all the answers."[20]

While Krugman, Franklin, and Ellis were reflecting on the political realm, their reverence for humility applies all the more poignantly to the judicial. After all, while political ideologues compete openly with one another and, therefore, often are "humbled" by foes, judges, to a great extent, operate covertly. And while one politician's ideology alone rarely is decisive, judges, often sitting alone or nearly so, have the last word, their robes concealing preconceived ideologies, their power unchecked.

Thus, as Krugman suggests, while the politician would be well advised to hone humility and allow for "the possibility that parts of the ideology may be wrong," I suggest that judges *must*, like Franklin, "doubt [their] own Judgment" to reach the independence ideal. And, for the judge, such humility, in Franklin's words, must "pay more respect to the Judgment of others"—even those of different or disagreeable ideologies.

So very humble is such phrasing, and so very sweet. And so simplistic such homilies may seem in the judicial realm. Let's get real. After all, we're preparing to examine how judges *really* make their decisions and to consider, among many factors, how different personalities may account for strikingly divergent decisions. And we're also preparing to examine the very different decision-making dynamics of trial judges, acting alone, and appellate judges, conferring and deciding together. So set aside humility for the moment and consider, let's say . . . arrogance. Arrogance—exactly what we wouldn't want in a judge? Not so fast. As Harvard law professor Noah Feldman pointed out, "Many of the greatest [US Supreme Court] justices have been irascible, socially distant, personally isolated, arrogant or even downright mean." Indeed, on the Supreme Court, "personal friction can fuel constitutional importance . . . greatness may be found in difficult personalities." Thus, he concluded, while "great justices need independence and a fierce commitment to constitutional principle, [they] don't need a judicial temperament."[21]

So, to say the least, it's complicated, and humility (or arrogance, for that matter) often plays out quite differently in the trial court and appellate court settings. Still, in my view, true humility, even if masked by arrogance or other offensive personality traits, is an essential element of judicial independence. It opens the mind, creating the opportunity for wise judgment.

With humility comes a judge's tender touch, even for those whose manner may seem strange. With humility comes a judge's courtesy, even for those whose philosophies may offend. With humility comes a judge's courage to decide in ways that to some may seem soft, to others too tough. With humility comes a judge's wisdom in welcoming an attorney's challenge and honoring a higher court's reversal.

With humility comes a judge's proud adherence to precedent, in spite of personal disagreement. With humility comes a judge's deference to legislative enactments, in spite of political displeasure. And, though it happens rarely, with humility may come a judge's principled and painstaking decision to break from the past and chart a meticulously well-reasoned new course.

CORRUPTION

Independence, protecting impartiality, can be threatened and corrupted. But how and why—and by what or whom? What is corruption?

Corruption, of course, can be bribery. Deuteronomy 16:19 warns, "You shall not judge unfairly; you shall show no partiality; neither shall you take a bribe; for a bribe blinds the eyes of the wise, and perverts the words of the righteous." Some judges, as we will see, cross the biblical line and jettison independence altogether by selling their decisions.[22] But corruption encompasses much more. As Justice John Paul Stevens recognized, "There are threats of corruption that are far more destructive to a democratic society than the odd bribe."[23] Such threats may be ever-present because, as the attorney and journalist Patrick Radden Keefe wrote, corruption is a "regrettable feature of our natural condition."[24]

The term "derives from the Latin *corrumpere*, which can mean to bribe, but also to mar or destroy."[25] It may entail the "[i]mpairment of integrity, virtue, or moral principle" or "a departure from what is pure and correct."[26] Two constructions may be particularly helpful in considering corruptions of judicial independence. Economist Robert Klitgaard offered a formula: corruption = monopoly power plus discretion minus accountability.[27] And Keefe, identifying common themes among several definitions of corruption, distilled them to "the conflict of interest that arises when *private imperatives* intrude upon the public sphere."[28]

Such constructions broaden our understanding of judicial corruption. They reach many if not all the "private imperatives" we will consider—from alcohol addiction to religious belief to electoral ambition—that vitiate the virtues constituting independence. Thus, moving far beyond the "odd bribe" in order to encompass forms of corruption "far more destructive to a democratic society," we would do well to think of "corruption" as *any bias or private imperative that intrudes upon genuine and full inquiry, distorts intellectually honest reasoning, or undermines the humility essential to independent judicial decision-making.*

Further, for the judiciary, we must extend this to include the *appearance* of such bias or private imperative that seems "to exert outsized control,"[29] potentially leading the public to doubt the impartiality of judicial decisions. This distinction is important. Codes of judicial ethics require judges to ensure not only "fairness" but also the "appearance of fairness." Therefore, judges must be alert to ways in which their conduct and statements, their friendships and affiliations and those of family members, may be viewed in relation to cases coming before them.[30]

One should not enter any discussion of corruption without considering Zephyr Teachout's insightful work, *Corruption in America: From Benjamin Franklin's Snuff Box to Citizens United*.[31] Most sharply, she focused on the evolving historical concepts and legal configurations of corruption *as bribery* and, in fascinating detail, framed the Supreme Court's decision in *Citizens United*, which we will consider in chapter 14. In doing so, Teachout also located bribery in relation to other forms of corruption. Thus, she not only broadened our understanding of bribery but also showed (1) that "corruption" includes not only the quid pro quo exchanges of money and political favor but also the less brazen acts resulting from attitudes and even some unavoidable circumstances; and (2) that "corruption," from the founders' debates to academics' recent writings, has commanded the attention of activists and scholars, and, if our liberties are to survive the mounting threats to judicial independence, must continue to do so.[32]

Teachout joined others I've just mentioned in reminding us that "[c]orruption, in the American tradition . . . encompasses many situations where politicians and public institutions serve private interests at the public expense"—that, in the founders' view, corruption "cover[ed] innocent activity as well as insidious transactions," and that not only money but "other reasons—narcissism, ambition, or luxury—could lead people to place private gain before public good in their public actions."[33] For the founders, corruption was (and, for Teachout, corruption remains) "the core reason for political decline."[34] It "defeats liberty."[35] And yet, she maintained, "corruption's worst dangers may be overcome by structure and culture."[36] No surprise, therefore, that "the Constitution was designed in significant part as protection against corruption."[37] Indeed, Teachout declared, "In the construction of the Constitution [the founders] were trying . . . to create structures such that private and public interest would be aligned as frequently as possible."[38] As Justice Stevens explained, the founders "discussed corruption 'more often in the Constitutional Convention than factions, violence, or instability,'" and added, "It is fair to say that '[t]he Framers were obsessed with corruption,' which they understood to encompass the dependency of public officeholders on private interests."[39]

Notwithstanding corruption's paramount importance, defining it, whether in the days of the founders or today, has remained difficult. Teachout conceded that "corruption is an important concept with unclear boundaries," and that "corruption" is a particularly "tricky word for lawyers because it has different kinds of meanings."[40] Rather than precisely defining it, she elaborated that "[c]orruption describes a range of self-serving behaviors . . . when private interest *excessively* overrides public or group interest in a significant or meaningful exercise of political power."[41] That, I think, is important. By qualifying "private interest" in this way, she acknowledged the normalcy of unavoidable private interests; she focused on the importance and historical difficulty in defining and measuring what might be *excessive*. Moreover, while not insisting on exact moral measurement or legal definition, she declared that "[t]he concept of corruption requires one to consider motivations," and to "use definitions" that embrace "the 'emotionalism' usually associated with corruption."[42]

I agree. As we explore judicial independence and corruption, we will be challenged—to think *and* feel; to analyze America's values in legally specific terms, but also to feel decision-making with holistic sensitivity. Emotions and motivations—of judges, of those depending on them for justice, and of ourselves in learning about them all—are essential to our understanding.

So now, moving from past to present, from definitional to decisional, we return to real courtrooms; to real cases before trial judges and appellate judges. We're ready to appraise both exemplary examples of impartiality and unconscionable betrayals of independence.

Part Two

IN CHAMBERS

4

THE TRIAL JUDGE

Birth, Aborted

State v. Monica Migliorino Miller

Methinks we have hugely mistaken this matter of Life and Death.
—Ishmael in *Moby-Dick* by Herman Melville

On September 25, 2012, twenty-two years after last seeing Monica Migliorino Miller and sentencing her to jail, I received a package containing an autographed copy of her book, *Abandoned: The Untold Story of the Abortion Wars,*[1] accompanied by this letter:

It has been many years since you and I last saw and spoke to one another. Of the people I am sending this book to, you are one of those for whom it is more difficult for me to say what I wish to say. Perhaps it is because I always felt that you, somewhere in the pit of your soul actually understood why people like me would break the law to defend the unborn. But, yeah—I have to say, in the end you disappointed me—and of course sent me to jail for 9 months. Perhaps you have changed—or perhaps you still consider yourself to be both pro-choice and pro-life—as I think in your 21 page sentencing statement you were describing yourself—and perhaps considered this to be the American ideal.

I am sending my book to you—just newly published . . . because you are featured in this work. I hope I have been fair. I have tried to tell the truth. I hope, if nothing else, this book will help you see the struggle for the right to life from those who have lived that struggle. It is a record of how pro-lifers endured, entered into that struggle and the story of the victims we tried to save. It is our story and theirs—a story in which you play a part in that by the "luck of the draw" I wound up in your courtroom.

Abandoned is at once a history—an effort to preserve an important moment in time that would otherwise be lost if people who lived this battle didn't record it. But, yes, I wrote this work to reveal the tragedy of abortion—to help people see the injustice of depriving the innocent of their right to exist.

I welcome your feedback—and I truly wish you well and ask God to bless you.

I replied, in part:

Thank you for taking the time to author such an important book. Your inteligence and sincerity were always evident and now your personal account can contribute to the understanding of a critically important issue. We need not agree on every point for me to admire your passion, your compassion, and your dedication to the principles you hold dear. And we need not be politically aligned for me to be grateful that a person as good as you (rather than those of less integrity) . . . succeeded in publishing an earnest account of a difficult time.

I sincerely hope you are well and that your growing (I'm pleased to read) family is thriving. I shall forever be grateful that "by luck of the draw" you came into the courtroom where I presided. I considered it a privilege to try to do justice in your case, and as was true in all cases—and particularly in yours—I will forever agonize over my uncertainty as to whether I succeeded.

This drama's opening acts were performed many years earlier. In 1990, Ms. Miller, then a Marquette University lecturer and doctoral candidate in theology, walked into the courtroom where I was presiding. Once again, she had been arrested for militant antiabortion actions and, this time, charged with three misdemeanors: disorderly conduct, unlawful assembly, and obstructing an officer.

Miller's conduct went well beyond that of most abortion protesters but was not unusual among those who escalate their actions from placard-carrying demonstrations to physical obstruction of patients and staff. On this morning, Miller and others entered a building in which a clinic was located. They occupied the stairwell and entryway, securing themselves to railings with chains, locks, and pipes loaded with hot tar to prevent police and firefighters from cutting or blow-torching them free. When an officer attempted to extricate one of her colleagues, Miller resisted. In her book, she recounted the confrontation:

When it became apparent that those closest to the door would soon be arrested, Wendy Fulcher and I took hold of each other's arms and hung on to one another. . . . [Milwaukee Police] Sergeant [Robert] Moe . . . placed his hands on Wendy's arm and began to pull.

"Monica, let go of her arm," Moe ordered.

"I can't let go, Sergeant. Babies are scheduled to die here."

"I am ordering you to let go," Moe commanded, his voice rising in frustration and anger.

"I'm sorry, I can't. I'm here to defend the unborn and I cannot let go."

"If you don't let go now, you're going to be charged with obstructing an officer."

. . . I remained silent and did not let go. It took Moe [and his partner] only a few additional seconds of tugging to pry Wendy loose from my grasp. A moment later, two other officers came up and pulled me out of [another protester's] grasp. I let my body go limp in passive resistance. . . . The officers dragged me several feet down the hallway and left me there. I got up and began to race back to the door but, before I could get far, I was tackled and handcuffed.[2]

Many law enforcement officers and several hours were needed to clear the protesters.

As director of Citizens for Life, Monica Migliorino Miller had become a leader of antiabortion demonstrations and an often-arrested clinic protester. This was, however, her first appearance before me, and it was not entirely by "luck of the draw." At random, Miller's case first went elsewhere, where a judge recused. Her case then was reassigned, again at random, to another judge, who also recused. These two judges had concluded that their beliefs about abortion were so strong that they might not be fair or at least might not be able to ensure the appearance of fairness.

Then, at random, Miller's case came to me. I could have recused and sent her back to the clerk for yet another reassignment. Instead, at her first hearing, in open court, I discussed my possible recusal with both Miller's attorney and the prosecuting attorney. I thought I could be fair and said so. I explained that I had thought about abortion issues and, truly, was torn. I said that, although I admired the principled determination of clinic demonstrators, I also respected each woman's right to choose. I disclosed that my wife was pro-choice and, on at least one occasion, had joined a counterprotest for clinic protection. I added, however, that Karen and I sometimes differed politically, and that her pro-choice advocacy would not affect my decisions.

But what did I fail to say?

First, I did not disclose that I wanted the case. I was drawn to legally challenging and controversial issues. Politically ambitious, I welcomed a front-pager.[3] Moreover, I wanted Miller's case all the more because other judges had recused. I would be pleased to have court watchers surmise that the prosecuting and defense attorneys would hand their "hot potato" only to a principled, independent judge.

Second, I did not disclose that, while truthfully declaring that Karen would not influence my decisions, I also could not help but wonder how she and her friends would feel if I made any decision at odds with their pro-choice position. Miller might have assumed as much, but still, I did not reveal my thoughts.

Third, I did not disclose that, in reading accounts of comparable cases, I had come to disagree with judicial denials of defendants' requests to testify about their motivations and their justifications for breaking the law to protect the unborn. The prosecutor probably would have been concerned about my leanings on this important evidentiary issue. Both parties probably would have been interested in learning that, with Holocaust heritage in my heart, I was sympathetic to the "righteous" who risk their lives to rescue the innocent.

Fourth, I did not disclose that, although I respected principled civil disobedience, I also believed that righteous leaders, from Thoreau to Gandhi to King, accept incarceration as a critical element of their commitment. What importance might that have held for Miller? What impact might that have had on her evaluation of whether to substitute against me?

And, finally, I did not disclose that, in these years when abortion demonstrations were tearing at the American fabric (fifty thousand arrests nationally in two years, as documented in my sentencing decision), I had become increasingly concerned. Thus, I wanted a case that would give me the chance to address these issues and perhaps even offer fresh insight that might help reconcile the apparently irreconcilable.[4]

Thus, the moment Miller walked in, my independence was "corrupted," as broadly defined. I wanted the case. I was concerned about consequences with Karen and her friends. I was likely to provide the key evidentiary ruling Miller desired but, should she be convicted, was also likely to send her to jail. And, in addition to judging *her* case, my ambition, albeit altruistic, would motivate me to aim her sentencing at a nation of cases.

I offer this now as neither apologist nor confessor. And I offer this without the naïve notion that other judges would have been any less encumbered by their own concerns. My purpose is not to second-guess recusals, or recusals refused but, rather, to tease out the tension—the tension between *independence* and *corruption*. And if in this book I am to presume to judge other judges' struggles, should I not begin by exposing my own? So, in Miller's case, we confront factors that may have compromised my independence:

1. Ambition, and desire for notoriety, perhaps leading me to gently guide the in-court recusal conversation in ways that would encourage the attorneys to ask that I stay on the case (and, indeed, they did so);

2. Holocaust heritage, perhaps leading me to admire Miller and grant her evidentiary request to present "justification" testimony, which other judges had excluded from other trials;

3. Spousal influence, however subtle, perhaps leading me away from other anti-choice rulings;

4. Personal philosophy, perhaps leading me to sentence Miller to substantial incarceration, consistent with my sense of righteous civil disobedience; and

5. Egotistical altruism, perhaps driving my desire to judge more than Miller's case in order to save a small part of the world.

Thus, by the day of sentencing, I was where I wanted to be—sitting with the chance to succeed where others had failed, to author the *definitive* decision, compassionate and strong, that, in historically honed terms, would show the way for judges throughout America. Did I succeed? No, but in an unusual, written sentencing decision, drawing from history and literature as well as from the law, I tried.

I sentenced Monica Migliorino Miller to jail. She left me little choice, declaring that she would not pay a fine, do community service, or comply with conditions of probation prohibiting unlawful acts. Even had she said otherwise, however, I would have ordered incarceration because of her prior offenses and apparent incorrigibility. Her conduct, still "nonviolent" as she and some others termed it, now included not only the unlawful blocking of clinic doors but also physical resistance to police efforts to remove them and, as detailed in chapter 6, she had declared that even shooting a police officer would be warranted to protect the unborn.[5] I ordered the maximum sentence on each count but, because the three offenses were inextricably connected, treated them as one; the sentences would be served concurrently, totaling nine months.

Predictably, my decision was both praised and condemned.[6] An appeal brought legal affirmation.[7] In Milwaukee, clinic confrontations dropped dramatically.[8] Miller, however, was only temporarily deterred. She resumed her protests. Less than two years after her sentencing, she was arrested again and, once again, her case came before me. But because Karen had increased her clinic protection efforts in the weeks preceding Miller's most recent arrest, I reached a different recusal conclusion. To preserve the appearance of fairness, I disqualified myself.[9] Never again would I see her in court or preside over any clinic protest cases.[10]

In 2013, after reading her book, I emailed Miller:

By most any measure, *Abandoned* is superb. Your writing is beautiful—
passionate yet restrained and, I think, excruciatingly fair. I cannot imagine a
better book that tells the story of a pro-life activist. Most remarkably, however, is that, somehow, in telling your story you are always telling the story
of the children—with your calm yet thunderous voice, you give them voice.
You elevate the unborn, honoring their lives from the moment of conception,
cherishing their memories long after death. . . .

I am pro-life. I have always believed that life begins at conception. I do not
need science to support that proposition. How can it be otherwise? How can
any expectant parent ever have the slightest doubt—Mom feeling the changes
within; Dad, with trembling delight, putting ear to belly.

How can I reconcile these beliefs with my role in your life? That's not easy
(and, perhaps someday, that's another conversation). Can I answer that question? Yes. Am I at ease with my answer? No. And might part of the answer be
that, perhaps, I simply did not have your courage? Yes.

Two days later, she replied:

I have been pondering [your email]. You are a remarkable person for having
written it—most remarkable is the depth of your humility. Also remarkable is
the depth of your ability to understand the essence of what abortion repre-
sents. I believe that you do, on a very real level—get it! You understand—no
one could say the things that you did in your letter to me and not understand.
And I believed that on a real level you understood 23 years ago . . . your letter
meant more to me than perhaps you'll ever know. I cried.

You should know, and I hope that my book reflected this—going to jail was
a blessing to me—God brought a great deal of good out of it—He made it a
good thing. Indeed, I would consider it a blessing if it were His will I wind up
there again before this battle for life is over . . . and God be with you.

This, from the woman I sent to jail. This, years after she served the sentence I
ordered—a sentence condemned by her friends, praised by pro-choice advocates—a sentence I probably would order again today, despite my misgivings.

In 2014, the US Supreme Court, in a unanimous decision, struck down a
state law confining protests (including antiabortion "counseling") to areas at
certain distances from clinics, behind "buffer zones." Reducing such restrictions, the Court underscored the First Amendment's constitutional line to protect demonstrators' free speech.[11] The Court said nothing, however, that could

countenance the kind of conduct that brought Monica Migliorino Miller to a jury trial and sentencing before me many years ago.

I shall always wonder whether I was fair. Now appreciating personal correspondence with a woman I admire, I also reconsider whether I may have strayed—from the case I was judging to other missions I was seeking. And here, together, we will consider how ambitions may eclipse humility, how corruptions can compromise judicial independence.[12]

5

THE APPELLATE JUDGE

Birth, Premature

Peterman v. Midwestern National Insurance
Company, Special Products, Inc., Frank A. Busalacchi,
and Visuals Plus, Inc.

In 1992, birth again commanded my attention. But this was different—a premature birth, not an aborted one; a civil case, not a criminal one; an appeal, not a trial; a case decided with two colleagues, not alone; and a case that released a judicial tantrum—an emotional explosion from a volatile colleague who, in the years to come, would teach me so much, both good and bad.

As tantrums go, this one was instructive. It offered the chance to understand two decision-making philosophies, one of which would make no room for the other and either of which, in the absolute, could be corrupting.

A few months into my first year on the Wisconsin Court of Appeals, I received the briefs. While merely one among the many new appeals my colleagues and I reviewed each month, this case was much more complicated and compelling than most. Like a Russian novel, its issues would need untangling; its characters, a roster.

John and Kathy Peterman—a young couple
Visuals Plus, Inc.—their employer
Unnamed—Visuals' insurance administrator
Frank Busalacchi—Visuals' insurance agent
Special Products, Inc.—Mr. Busalacchi's insurance agency
Midwestern National Insurance Co.—Visuals' new group health insurance
    provider

The facts, however, were clear and undisputed.[1] In 1983, John and Kathy Peterman started working for Visuals Plus, Inc., a company that provided group health insurance to its employees and employed an insurance administrator to advise them. Although John and Kathy were *individual* employees, their insurance initially was structured as *family* coverage—for John, as an employee, and for Kathy, as his dependent.

In 1988, Visuals Plus changed insurers, having accepted a proposal from insurance agent Frank Busalacchi and his agency, Special Products, Inc. The new group plan would be through Midwestern National Insurance Company. Making their transition to the new policy, John and Kathy filled out the required forms and learned of one structural change: Midwestern, instead of providing one policy for John with *family* coverage for dependents, would provide two *individual* policies for John and Kathy. Prudently, therefore, Kathy asked Visuals' insurance administrator about coverage for pregnancies and children. The administrator told Kathy that, when needed, she could convert to family coverage.

About a year later, Kathy, a few months pregnant, advised Visuals' administrator of her due date, July 25, 1989, and requested family coverage. The administrator advised Special Products and Midwestern to make the change. Special Products and Midwestern advised Visuals, and Visuals, in turn, advised Kathy, that she could convert to family coverage in June, the month before the expected birth.

But no one advised the baby.

More than three months early, the Petermans' baby girl arrived. Visuals' administrator then instructed John and Kathy to complete forms for conversion from individual to family coverage. They did so. Midwestern, however, maintaining that the Petermans had no family coverage at the time of birth, denied insurance for the costs of delivery and "premie" care.

Thus, stage left, enter the lawyers.

The Petermans sued Midwestern, Special Products, Mr. Busalacchi, and Visuals, claiming breach of contract, bad faith, and negligence. Midwestern, Special Products, and Visuals, denying liability and pointing fingers in all directions, sued one another. And covering this state court spaghetti was a sprinkling of parmesan ERISA (Employee Retirement Income Security Act), the federal law that regulates group health insurance.

In the trial court, Judge Francis T. Wasielewski attempted the untangling. He did so without a trial, or at least without the type of trial most might imagine—with testimony and with a jury evaluating evidence. Instead, on motions from the parties for "summary judgment," he reviewed the *undisputed* facts, together with the strenuously disputed legal arguments, to reach his conclusions.

This is not uncommon. Here, as in so many cases in which insurance companies dispute coverage, their lawyers fight their own clients, competing companies, or both. And here, as so often is the case, the facts were known, the chronology was clear, the insurance terms were written, and the law was certain. All that remained was legal research, argument, analysis, and decision— not much room for heart. That does not mean, however, that Judge Wasielewski's task was easy. The interplay of many parties, levels of liability, and intersecting laws presented quite a puzzle. Fortunately, he was an intelligent and conscientious judge.

Ultimately, my two colleagues and I affirmed some and reversed other parts of his decision. In our decision, almost as if no baby were involved in what, to me at least, seemed a heart-throbbing drama, we declared: "The precise question we must address in this case is whether ERISA, under its federal common law, recognizes claims supported by the doctrine of estoppel."[2]

I felt differently. Thus, although I joined in my colleagues' decision and reached the same conclusion, I also drafted a short "concurring" opinion offering my rationale. I thought the "precise question" actually was whether common sense and compassion would play any part. If so, John and Kathy and their baby would win (and, for all I cared, Midwestern, Special Products, and Visuals would go to a padded cell where their lawyers would duke it out until they could agree on who would pay what). And if not . . . well, add one more family's voice to the call for national health insurance. What was the basis for our decision? Even now, re-reading it, I'm not sure. The verbiage is convoluted, the reasoning difficult to discern. No guiding precedent emerges. And I still wish we had resolved the appeal as I suggested in my concurring opinion:

Wandering through the maze of America's competitive insurance industry, parents often change health care coverage. Sometimes they do so because they become unemployed; sometimes because they change employment; sometimes because they or their employers locate more attractive or affordable insurance programs.

Sometimes, to their amazement, they later learn that their change caused their loss of crucial coverage. Sometimes, based on persuasive promotions from insurance companies and explanations from employers, they could neither anticipate nor reasonably expect that their children would lose coverage too.

Sometimes, as a result, children suffer. That children suffer is tragic at any time, under any circumstances. That children suffer due to loss of insurance, resulting from adult decisions beyond their control and beyond their parents' control, is tragic and unjust.

. . . I add only a few words to assure that, within the maze of legal analysis, we not lose sight of a child—one very little girl who, along with her family, would have suffered had we not found our way to this fundamentally humane and just application of law.

With special pleasure, therefore, I concur and emphasize the message of Justice Harry Blackmun who, in another legal maze, also searched for the health and safety of a child:

> [T]he question presented by this case is an open one, and our . . . precedents may be read more broadly or narrowly depending upon how one chooses to read them. Faced with the choice, I would adopt a "sympathetic" reading, one which comports with dictates of fundamental justice and recognizes that compassion need not be exiled from the province of judging.[3]

For the Petermans, particularly in the absence of clear and certain precedent, why did we not echo Justice Blackmun's call, in a close call, for compassion?

Judge James Smith, one of my two colleagues on the case, answered. Indeed, my concurring opinion, a draft of which he had just received, brought a livid Judge Smith banging on my chambers door and bursting in even before I could say, "Come in." He threw down the draft and threatened that, unless I withdrew it, he would write his own concurring opinion, which, he said, would be brutal. Blasting Justice Blackmun's words, Judge Smith asserted that "compassion" was exactly what we *must* "exile from the province of judging."[4]

A minute later, Judge Smith calmed. Once he realized I was salvageable, or at least genuinely interested in understanding his concerns, he assumed the mentoring role—a role he had played so well on earlier occasions, patiently guiding me along my appellate court learning curve.[5]

For almost an hour, in one of the most meaningful conversations of my career, we discussed our approaches. And I really was listening. After all, Judge Smith was an experienced trial and appellate judge, a prominent author, and a member of the faculty of the George Washington University National Law Center. He was, in my opinion, the most well-read and intellectually strong member of our appeals court.

Judge Smith explained that our job was to reach correct *legal* conclusions, nothing more and nothing less. Our decisions must be logical, uncompromised by compassion or sentiment. Further, he maintained, we always must take a "linear" approach, logically arranging the issues and resolving them in order, as the answer to each question triggered analysis of the next. Moreover, he explained, while any given issue might seem to be a close call, once resolved, it might just as well have been a "slam dunk." The closeness of a close call was of no consequence—on to the next issue, unencumbered by any lingering doubt.

I expressed my respect for his approach. I added, however, that in my experience, some cases resist linear logic; some situations seem more spherical, some issues more holistic. I did my best, but Judge Smith wasn't buying. Calm and conciliatory, however, we agreed to continue thinking and writing to see whether we might agree, at least on some principles. The result, which we drafted together, was a footnote stating, in part: "Our conclusion [in favor of the Petermans] . . . is arrived at through the process of deductive legal reasoning. Although Justice Blackmun's dissent, as quoted by [Judge Schudson's] concurring opinion, can be read as suggesting that courts should color their legal analysis with 'sympathetic reading[s]' in order to reach a specific result, all of us, including the author of the concurring opinion, agree that result-oriented judging is improper."[6]

"Result-oriented judging"—what's wrong with that? Is not *fairness* the standard? Is not *justice* the goal? And if so, should not a just *result* always be the tail wagging the judicial dog?

To answer, and to understand how judges make their decisions, we need to set one last heavy stone in our foundation—an unwieldy one, difficult to place. And, indeed, our next chapter, also unwieldy and difficult to place in this book, requires our return to theory just as we were grasping practical tools from our case studies. But bear with me. The next chapter's theoretical focus is essential to seeing how judges really make their decisions, and its perspective would not be possible without the positioning provided by our first two studies—one from a trial court, the other from an appellate court. Now, with Ms. Miller and the Petermans as our guides, we consider what, for judges true to the independence ideal, often becomes the decisional pivot point: the standard of review.

6

STANDARD OF REVIEW

Casting the Legal Drama

Two cases, both about birth—one criminal, at trial and sentencing; the other civil, on appeal. Did my decisions reflect "result-oriented" judging? Did they deviate from the independence ideal? And if so, might it have been independence itself and the corresponding absence of accountability that fostered them?

Pondering such a paradox, Charles Gardner Geyh wrote, "Independence in appropriate measure can shield judges from external threats that undermine their capacity to uphold the law, but independence in excess can enable judges to act on their internal biases or predilections and disregard the law."[1] To further consider that possibility and prepare for the six cases to come, we turn to "standard of review," *the* legal concept that often determines a judicial decision.

"Standard of review" is powerful. Often controlling case outcomes, it can cause trial judges to accept verdicts with which they disagree; it may require appellate judges to reach conclusions they dislike. Principled, independent judges always abide by standards of review; others sometimes comply but may manipulate or disregard them.

But if "standard of review" is such a big deal, why is it almost unknown outside legal circles and almost never mentioned in the press? Well, as we're about to see, it's no fun. Legalistic, it can be complicated. Dry and resistant to easy analysis, it repels polemics. However misleading, "Court Approves Gay Marriage" is an easier headline than "Court Concludes, under Its Standard of Review, That Statutes Restricting Marriage to a Man and a Woman Violate Rights Guaranteed by the Constitution."

While many people may disagree about whether journalists are pandering or efficiently informing, pushing sales or conserving ink, most would acknowledge that "Court Approves Gay Marriage" misrepresents the ninety-two pages of opinions in the Supreme Court's 2015 decision *Obergefell v. Hodges*.[2] Moreover, contrary to what most would assume from press reports, the dissenters' primary point was *not* that the majority *approved* something bad but, rather, that the majority's decision deviated from the proper *standard of review* or, more precisely, from a proper determination of *who decides.*

Chief Justice John Roberts, writing the primary dissenting opinion, conceded that he might be bucking "strong arguments rooted in social policy and considerations of fairness."[3] He maintained, however: "The majority expressly disclaims judicial 'caution' and omits even a pretense of humility, openly relying on its desire to remake society according to its own 'new insight' into the 'nature of injustice.' As a result, the [majority] invalidates the marriage laws of more than half the States and orders the transformation of a social institution that has formed the basis of human society for millennia. . . . Just who do we think we are?"[4]

Did the Supreme Court majority justices *favor* gay marriage? Their decision does not say. Does Justice Anthony Kennedy, author of the majority opinion, *like* gay marriage? His words do not tell. As legislators, would the justices, majority or minority, have voted for or against state laws allowing gay marriage? Who knows? The opinions neither support nor oppose the policies at issue in the challenged state statutes. Thus, Chief Justice Roberts declared:

> [T]his Court is not a legislature. Whether same-sex marriage is a good idea should be of no concern to us. . . .
>
> Understand well what this dissent is about: it is not about whether, in my judgment, the institution of marriage should be changed to include same-sex couples. It is instead about whether, in our democratic republic, that decision should rest with the people acting through their elected representatives, or with five lawyers who happen to hold commissions authorizing them to resolve legal disputes according to law. The Constitution leaves no doubt about the answer. . . .
>
> The real question in these cases is . . . *who decides* what constitutes "marriage"?[5]

All right, interesting enough, but confusing. Where does "standard of review" worm its way into the analysis? How could it be so powerful as to push aside the juicy dispute—the goodness or badness of gay marriage—and substitute such a dull debate?

To answer, we'll spotlight several sections of America's legal stage. There, we'll find the cast—legislators, jurors, trial judges, and appellate judges—working from the same script but entering different scenes and playing very different roles. Our program notes explain.

LEGISLATORS

They're center-stage, Act One, debating policy and enacting law in the form of statutes, which, they say, reflect the people's will. Governing everything from taxes to traffic to treason, these statues may be warranted or unwise, but unless someone challenges them and proves they violate the Constitution, judges leave them alone.

JURORS

In the audience, indistinguishable from all other ticketholders, they come on stage only when cast. They then listen to witnesses and figure out who's lying and who's telling the truth; they weigh the evidence and, finally, deliberate. Before doing so, however, they listen to the judge's instructions defining the legal terms—"burglary," for example, or "negligence," or "punitive damages," or "reasonable doubt," and many others—to guide their deliberations. And while, case to case, instructions will vary according to the subject at trial, the judge in *every* case will direct the jury with words like these:

> It is the duty of the jury to scrutinize and to weigh the testimony of witnesses and to determine the effect of the evidence as a whole. You are the sole judges of the credibility, that is, the believability, of the witnesses and of the weight to be given to their testimony. I am the judge of the law, only.
>
> There is no magic way for you to evaluate the testimony; instead, you should use your common sense and experience. In everyday life, you determine for yourselves the reliability of things people say to you. You should do the same thing here.[6]

The jurors then leave the stage for the privacy of the jury room, where, in confidential discussion, they reach their verdict.

TRIAL JUDGES

As the drama develops, they assume prominent parts. Some of their lines are short, rigidly written; others, long and variable. They resolve the lawyers' disputes before, during, and after a trial, without any involvement of a jury. Judges do *not*, however, evaluate witnesses—that's the jury's job. They do *not* figure out what happened—that's the jury's job. They do *not* render a verdict—that's the jury's job (though when, as often occurs, the parties "waive" their right to a jury trial, the judge, performing the jury's role, does all these things). And while, in *civil* cases, they might modify or overturn a jury's verdict, that is the exception. And in a *criminal* case, a judge never overturns a jury's verdict.[7]

When the jury's jobs are done, trial judges make a variety of decisions—resolving postverdict motions, primarily in civil cases, and sentencing defendants in criminal cases. In all postverdict motions and sentencings, judges are guided by law but exercise *discretion*, the most critical concept in judicial decision-making. Indeed, to understand how standards of review can control judicial decision-making, we need to consider the *degree* of discretion; that is, the latitude the law allows a trial judge. Let's take a look.

Post-verdict Motions

Following the verdict in a *civil* case, a party that deems the verdict unfair may ask the judge to change it. If the judge also believes the verdict is unfair, will the judge do so? That all depends—on whether the unfairness flows from a *legal* error a judge can correct or from credibility calls the jury could make. A judge's disagreement with a jury's conclusions about witnesses and evidence is not enough; under the standard of review defining whether and to what extent trial judges may modify verdicts, judges are to restrain themselves from substituting their opinions for jurors' conclusions about subjects in the jury's realm—witness credibility and evidence.

That is one of two reasons why, in *criminal* cases, jury verdicts almost always stand. While in civil cases legalistic issues may complicate a jury's work and require the judge's intervention, criminal cases most often turn on witness credibility, and credibility is the jury's call. In short, America's justice system came to say that, when sizing up witnesses, twelve jurors are wiser than one judge.

The other reason is constitutional. In a criminal case, if a jury says, "Guilty," a judge still can order an acquittal for some legal reason, though that happens rarely; I *never* did so. But if a jury says, "Not guilty," a judge must never change the verdict to "Guilty." "Not guilty" was the jury's call, not the judge's; to change that verdict or allow a new trial would be to deny the defendant's Sixth Amendment rights—to a jury trial (just had one) and against double jeopardy (after acquittal, not another one).

Complicated? Yes, but actually these standards conform to common sense. And here our purpose is less to digest the details and more to taste trial practices enough to understand the reasoning underlying legal standards that control how judges review decisions of other decision-makers—that is, how "standards of review" demarcate the range of a judge's discretion. Further, as we will see, the range of discretion varies according to whether we're watching a trial judge or an appellate judge. For now, still watching the trial judge, we continue.

Sentencing

With death penalty cases as the only exception, sentencing is exclusively the trial judge's decision.[8] In fact, in criminal cases, jurors deliberate, return their verdict, hear the judge's words of thanks, and leave—or leave only to return minutes later to watch the sentencing from the public gallery. Then, as spectators, these ex-jurors might learn things they were not allowed to know at the trial—most significant, the defendant's criminal record. Why?

With few exceptions, American law holds that the "unfair prejudice" of a defendant's criminal history outweighs its "probative value"—that is, that a jury's knowledge of the criminal history would likely lead to an unfair assumption (bad record, must be guilty) unrelated to the evidence.[9] Thus, our courts strictly separate the trial and the sentencing. At trial, the jury focuses on evidence of the alleged crime, undistracted by the defendant's past. At sentencing, the judge focuses on the crime *and* the criminal. Needing to know the defendant's history to sentence fairly, the judge widens the lens to see factors shielded from the jury's view.

Sentencing is the most discretionary of all judicial decisions. The restrictions on trial judges are few: legislators set their limits—the maximum possible penalty and, sometimes, the minimum; appellate judges set their sentencing criteria—the seriousness of the crime, the circumstances of the defendant, and the protection of the community. (And appellate judges, setting their own standards for reviewing trial judges' sentences, mostly demurred, leaving trial judges' sentencing discretion almost unlimited.) Thus, as citizens sometimes lament, two defendants in virtually identical circumstances may receive drastically different sentences from different judges, the outcomes determined by "luck of the draw." (We'll consider much more about sentencing in chapter 9.)

APPELLATE JUDGES

Most often, their roles are silent. But in the last act, they may come on stage, and, when they do, all others listen. They do not preside over trials, see witnesses, or hear testimony; they do not decide post-verdict motions or sentence anyone. Instead, reading trial transcripts, they remain distant from what jurors and trial judges experienced—expressions and body language, tone and tears. Thus, appellate judges are poorly positioned to make credibility calls and, accordingly, do not do so. In effect, the standards of review tell them, "Don't even try; defer to the jurors and trial judges; they were in the courtroom."

Appellate judges are, however, better positioned to decide the trial's legal issues. After all, while trial judges, sitting alone, must make quick calls ("objection" / "overruled . . . sustained") and, with only a little more time, decide post-verdict motions, usually without research or consultation, appellate judges take time, read briefs, do research, and confer with clerks and colleagues. Thus, on strictly legal issues needing no credibility call, the standards of review tell appellate judges, "Your turn; do not defer to trial judges; you're better able to decide."

These many actors may make our legal drama difficult to follow. For the public, this multilayered decision-making, complete with different standards of review and degrees of discretion, may seem unnecessarily complicated. In my view, however, it is sublime—an Oscar-worthy casting of the correct decision makers who, playing the right roles, convey accountability and humility, the third irreplaceable virtue of judicial independence.

So, in summary, consider the following.

The Question: "Who's Telling the Truth?"

- *The decision maker*: *jurors*, in position to listen to every word and watch every expression.
- *The humility*—overheard in the jury room: "While tentatively, I feel this way, the judge just told me that, before reaching a verdict, I must carefully consider each of your eleven perspectives."

The Question: "Did the Jury Err?"

- *The decision maker*: *the trial judge*, in a position to evaluate the whole trial and, in post-verdict motions, the attorneys' legal arguments about the jurors' judgments.
- *The humility*—overheard in the trial court: "Counsel, your *legal* point is well taken, and I may conclude that the verdict must be modified. But your other arguments address issues that could have turned on witness credibility. I might have made that call differently, but it was the jury's to make. Even if I disagree, I must not substitute my judgment for the jury's."

The Question: "Did the Trial Judge Err?"

- *The decision maker*: *appellate judges*, poorly positioned to review any decision that depended on up-close-and-personal views at the trial, but perfectly positioned to review anything evident in a transcript, particularly when enhanced by briefs, research, and collaborative decision-making.
- *The humility*—eavesdropped behind closed doors and read in written decisions: "Reviewing strictly *legal* issues, we are ready, willing, and able to substitute our judgment for that of the trial judge. But in many areas—evidentiary rulings that could have gone either way, and sentencings—we might not agree with the trial judge's discretionary decision, but we defer."

Thus, early in every properly written appellate decision, readers should see (but often may skim over) what often proves pivotal: the standard of review. So, for example, in her appeal, Monica Miller presented four issues, the last of which was "whether the trial court misused its discretion" in sentencing. The court of appeals responded, first stating its standard of review.

> Sentencing is addressed to the sound discretion of the trial court and our review is limited to whether that discretion was misused. Furthermore, "our review is conducted in light of a strong public policy against interference with the trial court's sentencing decision."

The court of appeals then continued, invoking precedent and explaining its decision in light of its limited discretion in reviewing a sentencing.

> The primary factors, to be considered in sentencing, *and weighed as the trial court chooses*, are: "the gravity of the offense, the character of the offender and the need to protect the public." Other relevant factors include the defendant's past record and history, personality, remorse, repentance and cooperativeness, the defendant's need for rehabilitative control, and the rights of the public.

Finally, the court of appeals concentrated on the merits of my decision.

> The trial court's sentence in this case, supported in a twenty-one page written decision, painstakingly considered these factors as they apply to Miller. The trial court concluded:
>
>> The maximum sentence is just in consideration of (1) the seriousness of the crimes, (2) the several substantial layers of victimization, (3) the dangerousness of the defendant, (4) the defendant's criminal record, (5) the defendant's refusal of any alternative to incarceration, . . . (6) the importance of deterring others, (7) the need to protect other citizens, including children, and (8) the importance of protecting the Constitutional rights the defendant would deny to others.
>
> The trial court's consideration of the facts of record in the context of these relevant factors reflects a proper exercise of discretion.
>
> Miller contends that her sentence is illegal because the trial court also relied upon impermissible factors. [At the sentencing hearing], [p]rior to [pronouncement of the sentence], Miller and the trial court discussed the morality of her action. In the . . . discussion, Miller was emphatic:

I refuse to pay the fine . . . if one is imposed. I cannot accept probation. . . .
I will not do community service as a sentence. . . . [I]f a police officer is
escorting a woman into an abortion clinic and somebody were to shoot the
police officer . . . I could not say that that pro-lifer did something immoral.

The trial court relied on this statement, in part, in its sentencing. Miller
argues that this reliance impermissibly punished her for expression in contra-
vention of the First Amendment. It did not. "The expression of the belief
bears directly on the possibility of rehabilitation and is evidence of the danger
[Miller] will pose to the public if she believes she can violate its laws with
impunity." Thus, the statement was a proper consideration at sentencing.[10]

Accordingly, the court of appeals concluded that "Miller's sentence was
proper."[11] But note, it never said the sentence was wise or just. The court never
said that, had it sentenced her, it would have reached the same result. Instead,
staying within its appellate range of discretion, the court of appeals recited
the standards for its review and measured whether my decision was a legally
proper, reasonable exercise of discretion.

Similarly, though under different standards of review, the court of appeals,
in the Petermans' case, reviewed the challenges of several parties to the trial
judge's decisions on their motions for summary judgment. After summarizing
the facts and before presenting our decision, my colleagues and I recited the
standard of review, writing:

Summary judgment is appropriate when there is no dispute of material fact
and the moving party is entitled to judgment as a matter of law. On review,
appellate courts apply the summary judgment standards in the same fashion
as trial courts. In summary judgment cases we review the matter de novo.[12]

"De novo" is the standard directing appellate judges not to defer but, instead,
to take a fresh look. After all, in a case like Peterman, where the attorneys agree
to submit undisputed information to a trial judge, appellate judges, like the
trial judge, are not watching witnesses or considering credibility. Instead, like
the trial judge in such a case, they are looking at exactly the same materials the
attorneys had submitted for the trial judge's decision on strictly legal issues.

In both Miller and Peterman, as in almost every case on appeal, the appellate judges' written decisions declare the standards of review. Front and center,
before the analysis and conclusion, these standards deliver two reminders:

1. Listen, folks—lawyers, litigants, citizens, press—we're not necessarily saying
   what we want, what we believe, what we would have done had we been writing

the rules or rendering the verdicts. Instead, we're reiterating the range of our reach, the degree of our discretion, the limits of our power. Within these parameters, we're offering our conclusions about the *lawfulness* of the jury's and the trial judge's decisions.

2. And listen, we're not trial judges, and we're not acting alone. On strictly legal questions, we will take a fresh look and, sometimes, substitute our decision for that of the trial judge. On discretionary matters, however, we will defer to the trial judge's closer view unless we encounter that rare instance when the judge failed to consider what must be considered or reached a conclusion clearly beyond the bounds of reasonable discretion.

I believe that with such standards of review—whether *de novo* for fresh consideration of strictly legal issues or *deferential* for much more limited consideration of evidentiary questions (sometimes further divided between "due deference" and "substantial deference," depending on yet another subclassification of subjects)—*humility* weaves within the fabric of judicial robes. No small achievement.

While standard of review once seemed hopelessly elusive to those outside our courtrooms, it now is familiar to millions of Americans. How? Professional sports—to be exact, managers' and coaches' challenges. The parallels are perfect. As we TV viewers await the review of video replays enabling officials to scrutinize an umpire's or referee's split-second decision, commentators remind us that, in doing so, the officials' final decision will not turn on whether they agree with the on-field call but, instead, on whether the on-field call was "clearly wrong." That's the standard of review. Accordingly, close calls are upheld; only blatant errors are overturned.

Granted, standards of review still may sound like the sort of verbiage for which attorneys are infamous and judges disdained. But now, sports fans have a feel for them and appreciate their logic. And I, without reservation, defend them. Standards of review *logically* delegate legal responsibilities and, in doing so, help maintain judicial humility. Without knowing their pivotal importance, we would not understand how America's judges really make their decisions.

Finally, as we conclude our consideration of this difficult subject, let us consider how standards of review *prescribe process*, and let us ponder the importance of process in how America's judges really make their decisions.

I recall words I first heard as a young prosecutor. Commenting on a frustrating but legally correct judicial decision, District Attorney McCann counseled: "In a good court, you get *law*; if you also get *justice*, that's a bonus." I thought I understood what he meant, but now I ask: If indeed you get law, do you not also, *necessarily*, get justice?

The question takes us back to the Petermans and my chambered debate with Judge Smith: decision-making—linear or spherical, legalistic or compassionate? Should compassion be included in decision-making, or, as Justice Blackmun feared, must it be exiled from the province of judging? And do our answers change as we walk from the trial court to the appellate court?

I do not have *the* answer, and I doubt a single answer could be correct. I believe, however, that for almost all cases *on appeal*, Judge Smith offered the better argument. For all his seemingly arrogant my-way-or-the-highway manner, his premise actually may have been the more humble. After all, Judge Smith's decision-making process revered . . . process. Given his premise—that strictly legalistic, issue-by-issue analysis would lead to the legally correct answer—he did not ask about "justice" but, instead, *presumed* true justice as the inevitable byproduct of precedent, time-honored by deferential process. And while my less linear, more holistic approach may have seemed sweeter, it was, stripped to the bone, more *self*-righteous—less deferential to all those judges who had come before, it was less humble.

Thus, in *Obergefell*, I was all the more impressed by Chief Justice Roberts's dissent, homing in on humility: "The majority expressly disclaims judicial 'caution' and omits even a pretense of humility. . . . Just who do we think we are?" He continued:

> The majority today neglects that restrained conception of the judicial role. It seizes for itself a question the Constitution leaves to the people, at a time when the people are engaged in a vibrant debate on that question. And it answers that question based not on neutral principles of constitutional law, but on its own "understanding of what freedom is and must become."
>
> The legitimacy of this Court ultimately rests "upon the respect accorded to its judgments." That respect flows from the perception—and reality—that we exercise humility and restraint in deciding cases according to the Constitution and law. The role of the Court envisioned by the majority today, however, is anything but humble or restrained.[13]

Without explicit references to standards of review, Chief Justice Roberts offered standards supporting the fairness of *placing the right questions before the right decision-makers*, whether they be legislators, jurors, trial judges or appellate judges.

Still, Judge Smith's unqualified faith in legal process may have been flawed. Judge Posner, throughout *How Judges Think*, provides the rebuttal. He notes that even doctrinaire "legalists" must "acknowledge that their methods cannot close the deal every time" and that "legalism so often fails to yield a determinate result."[14] And, to be sure, Chief Justice Roberts's patience with democratic process must somehow have its limits. Otherwise, such judicial faith and patience, in the extreme, renders acquiescence to even the most extreme injustices—internment, enslavement, and extermination. Sometimes, long before enough people scream and legislatures respond, courageous judges must set aside precedent, break with tradition, and shake society awake.

Was 2015 such a time? Was same-sex marriage such a cause? Did *Obergefell*, for reasons of conscience, compassion, and Constitution, compel slower-moving democracy to yield to jarring judicial insight? Five justices thought so; four did not.

I have an opinion, both heartfelt and legal, but here I am not taking sides. And, unfairly perhaps, I have quoted Chief Justice Roberts's dissent at length without giving equal time to Justice Kennedy's majority opinion. But I do so not to argue the merits of same-sex marriage. I do so to punctuate the point—the importance of humility and its essential position in judicial independence. On that, I suspect, all nine justices would have agreed.[15]

Judges, if true to America's evolved, precedent-based, logically linear process, usually will come close to independence—to decisions anchored in neither yesterday's sentimentality nor today's fleeting sense of "justice." And although I still believe compassion, in the hands of a thoughtful trial judge, comfortably shares space with law and logic, I also have come to conclude that, with only rare exceptions, compassion finds only an uncomfortable fit in an appellate decision.

We need not resolve the legalistic/compassionate debate for all, or for all judges, or for all time, to better understand that *both* strictly linear logic and uncapped compassion can influence judicial decision-making. We can consider both. As we reflect on our two cases about birth and as we go on to study six cases about life and death, religion and politics, we can watch for judges avoiding or applying legal standards, ignoring or respecting their proper discretionary range, losing or finding their humility, skewing corrupted decisions or maintaining independence.

7

THE TRIAL JUDGE

Life, and a Lost Teenager

In the Interest of S.W., a child under eighteen years of age

> Careful the things you say
> Children will listen
> Careful the things you do
> Children will see . . . and learn
>
> —Stephen Sondheim, "Children Will Listen"[1]

On an autumn morning in 1983, my second year as a judge, I arrived early at the Juvenile Court Center, a complex of facilities including a jail for teenagers; offices for prosecutors, probation officers, and social workers; and several courts. Walking into chambers a half hour before cases were scheduled, I was surprised to be greeted by John Johnson, the county's chief judge. Something was up. This was an unexpected visit for which he would have had to have driven some distance, from either home or the main courthouse. And he looked troubled.

"Jack," as he liked being called, was a man I had known eight years. Appearing before him as a prosecutor, I had come to admire him. A former police officer and prosecutor, he was quiet, twinkle-in-the-eye kind, and thoughtful. As chief judge, he had been supportive and complimentary of my efforts. Thus, I was astounded when, after a brief greeting, he said, "I'm reassigning you . . . I'm just getting too much heat."

Jack explained that since I had issued a decision two days earlier, he had been besieged by county social workers and their union leader demanding my ouster. I tried to stay steady as I imagined my career careening, my reputation ruined. I asked Jack if he had read the thirty-six-page decision prompting the uproar; he had not. I implored him to do so before making such a move. And, in an awkward role reversal, I cautioned our chief judge, a much older and wiser man, that if, as judges, we knew nothing else, it was to pause when others would push us into a quick decision.[2] He agreed, and I gained a twenty-four-hour reprieve.

What was going on? What decision had provoked such pressure? Well, it's a long story, but an important one that reveals much about America's justice system and about judicial independence and corruption. Here's the background.

Like many others just beginning their judicial careers, I had been assigned to juvenile cases—custody and protection of abused and neglected children; "termination" of parental rights; trials of juveniles charged with crimes; "waiver" of juveniles to adult courts for violent felonies. Such has been the custom in many large jurisdictions—assignment of new judges to juvenile courts for a few years of experience to prepare them for graduation to adult courts.

How misguided. Juvenile courts, many justice system officials agree, are the most important and challenging, the most legally complex, and the most emotionally draining. Nowhere else, except in small jurisdictions where one or a few judges handle everything, does a judge see such variety—the criminal law mix of misdemeanors and felonies; the civil law mix of custody, placement, and specialized juvenile law subjects of termination and waiver. Nowhere else does a judge struggle to manage the emotions flowing from nonstop cases of neglected infants, abused toddlers, and violent teenagers.

And nowhere else are hopes so high, and so unrealistic. I often felt like the Wizard of Oz, crouched behind the curtain. But, instead of hiding, I wanted to jump out and scream at the parents: "Don't look at me like that . . . what did you expect? I don't know you . . . I had nothing to do with what brought you here . . . I have no magic . . . and now, after messing up this kid for years, you're asking me, in minutes, to take you all back to Kansas."

Each day was a heartbreaking endurance test—overwhelming caseloads, lunch minutes not lunch hours, bathroom breaks just long enough for the midday rotation of stenographers whose wrists, at our pace, could sustain only a half day.

Tremendous fulfillment found its way as well—making the right call that saves a child or restores a family; years later, meeting young men and women sporting smiles and surprising me with, "Remember me? You were *my* judge," and telling me of their careers and families and the difference I had made in their lives. But those moments were rare.

Even *before* my first day, I felt the futility. How well I remember coming to the clerk's office, a few days before my first day on the bench, and asking for files of the cases I would be hearing the first week. Blank stares; then, "You want what?" The staff explained that while they might be able to gather some for me in advance, their procedure was to deliver each day's files just before court convened. But, I asked, how could I prepare for the hearings? More puzzled looks . . .

Soon, I understood. Each day, I was assigned an average of thirty scheduled cases, plus emergencies and various unscheduled hearings. And the files held so many case histories, presentence reports, and psychological evaluations essential to the decisions I was to make that it was impossible to read them all in advance or keep them straight. At most, as each case was called, I might take a minute or two to skim the reports and read the psychologist's concluding paragraph. I then would hear arguments from the attorneys, pleas from the children and family, and, often most influential, recommendations from social workers and probation officers from the Department of Social Services.

In short, in heavy-caseloaded juvenile courts throughout America, judges cannot prepare as they should, cannot evaluate as they desire, and cannot independently determine what the law requires: decisions in the "best interests of the child." And it only gets worse . . . much worse than in adult courts. Allow me to explain.

Every day, many of these juvenile court decisions are "dispositions"— sentencings or "placement" orders governing the next year of a child's life: who will have custody—where, with what supervision, treatment, or incarceration? Make the right call, save a child; make a mistake, await tragedy. Find the files . . . read the reports . . . search for crystal balls.

For an adult court judge, only criminal sentencing is comparable, but it's so much easier. The options are few and familiar: prison, jail, probation, fines, and community service. But a juvenile court judge chooses from among many more alternatives: maximum-security reform schools; semisecure residential treatment centers; group homes; homes of parents, foster parents, adoptive parents, relatives, and friends. And the many residential treatment centers are spread throughout the state and beyond, offering very different urban and rural environments, specializing in diverse services such as drug treatment or family therapy.

How does a judge decide? Bad enough that the judge has not reviewed the files and read the reports, but now the judge must make the call without knowing much, if anything, about the possible placements. How in good conscience could I order children into programs about which I knew nothing, in facilities I never had seen?

Well, I was assured, the solution was readily at hand. County and state social service departments employ social workers as liaisons to treatment centers, near and far. They know the facilities and their programs and, at "staffings," learn about the children. Thus, they are able to consider the options and find the best fit for each child, the fit they then recommend to the judge. And the judge, of course, with no time to probe, has no choice but to defer.

My trust, however, was tempered by sad stories about treatment in such residential centers nationwide. And I could find neither theoretical nor statutory justification for blind judicial acceptance of social workers' recommendations. Thus, within my first weeks on the bench, I called the state court administrator and, diplomatically, insisted that he locate a retired judge to take my place on the bench for one week while I traveled the state to visit these facilities, *unannounced.*

I was in for a pleasant surprise. Scraping away my skepticism, the staff at many treatment centers welcomed me enthusiastically. Dedicated and, I thought, justifiably proud of their programs, they seemed pleased that a judge would visit and watch them work. (In fact, of the many I visited, only one was deficient, thus foreclosing further placements.)

These reform schools, treatment centers, and group homes were very different from one another in locations, sizes, age groups accommodated, and programs. The right facility for one child might be dead wrong for another. Most ominous, staff members explained that many court-ordered placements were bad fits, leaving them wondering why judges were spending all that money only to send children to centers where they would be inadequately served.

Still no expert, I now had at least some sense of these centers. I was better able to understand and question the recommendations in court. Suddenly, words that had seemed innocuous gained importance. "The Department recommends . . . ," social workers advised. Now this stilted bureaucratese caught my attention. Suspecting a bad match, I asked, "But what do *you* recommend?" Again, the answer: "The Department recommends . . ."

I pushed, questioning placements that seemed senseless. Social workers squirmed. Some refused to answer. Some said they had been warned to never deviate from "staffing" determinations. Some called supervisors, who quickly came to court. But a few expressed relief when ordered to offer their own professional opinions. And then, social workers conceded, some staffing recommendations had been based not on the "best interests of the child" but, rather, on the best *fiscal* interests of the Department.

My schooling continued. I learned that the county held different contracts with different treatment centers, similar in some respects but varying in placement numbers and payment rates. The Department, operating within budget constraints and under cost-cutting pressures, harbored financial incentives hidden from the law and often inconsistent with children's needs.

So, for example, the Department, choosing from among many residential treatment centers for placement of a teenage burglar whose break-ins resulted, in part, from drunkenness, might recommend a center despite knowing that it had no program for alcohol abuse. Many judges, however, particularly in jurisdictions where judges do not specialize in juvenile cases but instead "rotate" from one assignment to the next, do not know one center from another. They have little choice but to acquiesce. Over time, in juvenile courts with heavy caseloads, entrenched social workers, including many excellent ones demoralized by the directives they felt forced to obey, usurped judicial discretion. To this day, judicial rubber-stamping permeates many of America's juvenile courts.

During periods of tax-cutting pressure, it's even easier to find fiscal factors leading to concealment or misrepresentation. Thus, social workers then may misinform judges of the appropriate placement options. But that's far from the whole story, and, historically, the story becomes much more interesting. It helps explain why, despite (and, ironically, because of) good intentions, social service bureaucracies breached the boundary separating them from the judiciary, thus compromising judicial independence in America's juvenile courts.[3]

In 1899, America's first juvenile court was established in Chicago, and, by 1917, juvenile justice systems had formed in all but three states. "Regarded as 'one of the greatest advances in child welfare that has ever occurred,' the juvenile court . . . system was part of a general movement directed toward removing adolescents from the criminal law process and creating special programs for delinquent, dependent, and neglected children."[4]

This was the Progressive Era. Social theorists and legal historians came to view these new juvenile justice systems as stunning accomplishments, providing children and families with previously unavailable protection and services. The rationale was clear:

> Reformers believed that separation from the adult justice system was critical for three reasons: (1) Children committed crimes not from a sense of evil or malice, but rather from a sense of need. A child's crime was an expression of pain, a signal that something was not right with the individual or family. The child needed help, not criminal court punishment. (2) Children suffering abuse or neglect might have to be removed from the family, an action that required special procedures to [confidentially] evaluate the circumstances of the family and the needs of the child in order to balance their respective rights. (3) *Those responsible for decisions about delinquent, abused, or neglected children should have the special inclination and expertise needed to understand the young.*[5]

Who had such "special inclination and expertise"? Certainly not judges, particularly those just testing their training wheels before cycling on to the adult courts; not judges, unschooled in pediatrics, psychology, and other disciplines critical to the consideration of these cases. But social workers—a new set of professionals born from progressivism—were ready. They soon came to play the leading role in the new juvenile courts.

The leading role? Indeed. I arrived at a scene populated by career juvenile court social workers, many of whom were highly skilled and selflessly dedicated to the children and community. But many also were dominating in ways that reflected little regard for their lawful place in the juvenile justice system. Some, when they disagreed with judicial placement decisions, ignored them or even rewrote the dispositive words on court orders above judges' signatures.[6]

It was that leading role that I, not knowing so at first, was confronting with my question, "But what do *you* recommend?" It was that role I was challenging by insisting on an honest answer. And, most of all, it was the role I was recasting *merely* by introducing what I believed to be traditional, *independent* judicial authority.

My two colleagues at the Juvenile Court Center, two very able senior judges nearing retirement, helped me reach out. Forming committees and meeting with social workers to share concerns, we listened, explained law, clarified respective lines of authority, and reached agreement with the Department of Social Services on key issues. When, nevertheless, violations of our court orders continued, we warned that judges have "contempt" authority to enforce their orders.

Still, social workers ignored orders; flagrant violations continued. Finally, a sixteen-year-old girl offered the opportunity—indeed, the obligation—to do what only judges can do: not cajole in committee meetings but apply law with precision and power in open court. In the lengthy decision that brought the chief judge to chambers that morning, I had done so.

I found a social worker, her supervisor, and the Department of Social Services in contempt *and placed the Department under my supervision*. The decision, *In the Interest of S. W.*, tells the story.[7] I offer it here, abbreviated but still lengthy, not only to relate details essential to understanding the law and high stakes in this case but also, and particularly for the benefit of lay readers, to present an example of judicial methodology—the facts/law/conclusion progression of decision-making that is fundamental to judicial independence.

This decision addresses whether the County Department of Social Services and two of its social workers are in contempt of court for violation of a court order.

I. FACTS OF THE CASE

SW is a teenage girl who, at age sixteen, was adjudicated as a "child in need of protection or services" on the request of her parents who sought this court's jurisdiction as a result of their inability to care for, control, or provide for her care or treatment. This court's dispositional order placed SW in her parents' home, under the supervision of the Department. Consistent with the conclusion of SW's psychological evaluation, the agreement of the parties, and the recommendation of the Department, this court ordered that SW and her parents participate and cooperate in counseling supervised by the Department.

Three months later, SW was arrested and charged with four crimes. She was held in the juvenile jail until an opening became available in the semi-secure Children's Home [a short-term group home, one mile from the Children's Court Center, where children may live while their cases are pending]. Then, two weeks later, when SW failed to appear for her pre-trial conference, the court was informed that she had run away from the Children's Home. A warrant was issued for her arrest. The next day, SW appeared in court and was released to her probation officer for a pre-placement visit to Newberry House, a [long-term] group home.

Five weeks later, SW was found guilty of forgery. At her dispositional hearing, everyone recommended probation with placement at Newberry House. The key question was whether probation should include an initial period of inpatient drug and alcohol treatment, or whether outpatient counseling while living at Newberry House would meet SW's needs.

This court ordered one year probation with placement at Newberry House under the Department's supervision. The court also ordered SW to participate in outpatient drug and alcohol counseling, and scheduled the case for a review of SW's cooperation and progress. Adjourning the case two months for that hearing, I spoke directly to SW.

THE COURT: You will participate one hundred percent in the programs set up for you in drug and alcohol treatment. One beer is one too many. One missed appointment is one too many. You say you don't need the thirty-day inpatient program, [but] just break these rules and that's where you will go—not as a punishment, but because it then will be clear that that's the alternative we will have to follow. You see, the law requires that I do what I can to make sure you don't destroy your life with drugs and alcohol. From what I am reading here and . . . been told, that's what you have been doing. You're not a bad person at all. You're a good person with all kinds of ability. I understand you're even an excellent athlete, is that right?

SW: Yeah.

THE COURT: Well, you won't be for long with drugs and alcohol. So it's not that I'm trying to be hard on you. It's just very clear that drugs and alcohol and your future do not mix. They've really made a mess of your life in many ways. So it's going to be important that I have a report on the next date that tells me just what your cooperation has been over these next sixty days. *Let it be clear with the Department, though, that if there is a violation, you don't have to wait sixty days to come back. If there is a violation of any of these rules and conditions, return the case here immediately so we can get started on this inpatient program right away.*

Hearing those words at that hearing were not only SW and her parents, but also her lawyer, probation officer, Department supervisor, and the prosecutor. The written order prepared by the court clerk and provided to all parties specified "that a report be made as to child's cooperation and if conditions are not as ordered, the matter is to be brought back before the Court IMMEDIATELY."

At the scheduled review hearing two months later, a Newberry House social worker, a Department supervisor, and the Department's lawyer were among those who appeared in court. SW did not. She had absconded from Newberry House just nine days after the previous hearing and had not returned in the following seven weeks. SW's parents advised the court that they had not been told of their daughter's departure; that they had assumed she was complying with the order; that they even had received a bill from the Department for the Newberry House placement, and had paid the bill.[8] SW's probation officer acknowledged that she remembered the court's order to return the case immediately in the event of SW's violation, but that she had waited until the review date, nonetheless. Thus, this court issued a warrant for SW's arrest, seven weeks after it would have done so had the Department complied with the order.

All the parties and all those working with SW acknowledge that this court's Dispositional Order was valid. All agree that SW's circumstances were extremely serious, and that her best interests required a carefully monitored program of drug/alcohol counseling. All agree that the runaway from Newberry House and the resulting failure to obtain such counseling were serious violations, posing severe risks to SW's health and safety. Moreover, no one disputes that in failing to return the case to court immediately, as ordered, the Department and its employees increased the potential risks to SW by depriving this court of the opportunity to issue a warrant and return her to court for implementation of the order.

What, then, should be the judicial response to the violation of the order by the Department and its employees? Is a contempt finding appropriate? Or should this court view the violation as an unfortunate but inevitable occurrence when government attempts to serve human needs, through a Department operating with inadequate resources?[9] To appreciate the appropriateness

of a contempt finding, and the need for a strong judicial response to this violation of the court order, it will be helpful to understand that the violation in
SW's case is neither isolated nor unusual.

II. ADDITIONAL BACKGROUND

SW's case is but one of many this court has seen during the last sixteen months
where the Department fails to implement court orders, violates court orders,
and/or fails to advise the court when a child's violation of an order includes
the most crucial conditions of treatment and placement. [Six cases then were
detailed.]

The three juvenile court judges found such violations to be so serious and
frequent that they met with Department personnel several times to emphasize
the need for the Department to develop procedures to (1) guarantee efforts to
implement court orders and, at the very least, (2) assure the return of cases
to court when children ran from placement. Pursuant to what this court is
advised is a Department rule [stopping the Department's payment for the
placement, opening the resulting vacancy for another child, and thus adding a
financial disincentive to seek a runaway's return] cases are "closed" when an
"AWOL" lasts fourteen days. (In such AWOL circumstances, the Department
advises police and a "missing" report is filed. But, as the judges emphasized to
the Department, a "missing" report does not order police to look for a child.
Such a report merely establishes the child's status when found as a victim or
perpetrator of crime. On the other hand, the judges emphasized, returning the
case to court allows a judge to order a warrant, which does bring about police
effort to find the child.)

In addition, based on research and recommendations of the Children's Court
Citizen's Advisory Board, the judges announced a policy mandating return to
the court of any child who failed to comply with a court-ordered condition
of drug/alcohol counseling or treatment. The judges had been advised that,
of all children placed under such orders, 40% to 50% were noncompliant.
Moreover, the judges were advised that in almost all such cases, probation
officers and social workers were not returning the children to court. The policy
included: "When a child fails or refuses to comply with a court order for evaluation or treatment, the Department will return the child to court for judicial
action. The judge will take whatever steps are necessary, including possible
commitment to a custodial setting for treatment, to guarantee enforcement of
the court order."

Thus, the seriousness of the Department's noncompliance can be considered in a number of ways: (1) The Department's violation occurred even though
the court's order followed the Department's recommendation. (2) The violation

occurred even though the court admonished both SW and the Department that any noncompliance would require SW's immediate return to court. (3) The violation occurred despite efforts of the juvenile court judges to gain the Department's compliance with court orders, and even after enactment of the new, more explicit judicial policy requiring prompt notification of a child's noncompliance or elopement from placement.

The Department leadership consistently has expressed its agreement with the judicial policy. In fact, Department staff members were on both the Citizen's Advisory Board and the subcommittee that reviewed the problems and developed the policy. The Department has had a change in leadership in the last year, and the new director and his senior staff give every indication they will bring about improved performance. Still, as can be seen with SW and other recent cases recounted here, the violations of court orders continue unchecked, and the dangers to children and the community persist.

III. Juvenile Court Statutes and the Law of Contempt

What is the appropriate judicial response? What authority does the juvenile court have in relation to the Department? Although the statutes do not specify the manner in which a court is to enforce compliance with orders, they do clarify that courts must not ignore violations.

The statutes explicitly direct that courts not only make orders to serve children and the public, but also that courts make sure orders are carried out. [The decision then quotes five statutes that do so.] Thus, the court is not merely to advise, recommend, or suggest. The juvenile court fulfills its statutory responsibility by "providing judicial procedures" that "assure," and "enforce," and "effect" the statutory objectives. The statutes require implementation of a dispositional order, and require the court to exercise authority to guarantee implementation:

> In any dispositional order . . . *the judge shall decide on a placement and treatment . . .* [and] *shall employ those means necessary to maintain and protect the child's well-being . . .* and which *assure the care, treatment or rehabilitation of the child. . . . Any party, person or agency who provides services for the child shall be bound by the court order.*

Further, it is clear that the Department is not free to revise a dispositional order without judicial approval [statute cited]. Most clearly, the statutes specify that "powers and duties" of the Department derive from court orders [statutes quoted]. Moreover, a court's authority to direct a Department employee to do precisely what was ordered in SW's case also is explicit: "It is the duty of each person appointed to furnish services to the court to make such investigations and exercise such discretionary powers *as the judge may direct*. Such person *shall keep informed concerning the conduct and condition of the child* and *shall report thereon as the judge directs* [statutes cited]."

My decision then offered an extended analysis of contempt law, *describing the danger if only willful and maliciously motivated violations could be deemed contemptuous*:

> A court could be impotent to respond to violations of court orders, no matter how serious, when the violations seemed to result from the inherent problems of a large bureaucracy. Malice would be absent; responsibility would be diffused; intent would be invisible; and judicial orders could be ignored or changed by those ordered to implement them. Despite the specificity of an order, those responsible for implementation could assert "misunderstanding," or "lack of communication."[10]

Finding both statutory and "inherent" authority to invoke contempt authority, I held SW's social worker and her supervisor in contempt and ordered them to pay fines. Most significantly, I held the Department in contempt and required reform, ordering that it:

> develop policy and train staff to assure: a) reasonable understanding of the statutes governing the juvenile courts; b) implementation of court orders; and c) consideration of appropriate alternatives and legal actions when a child under Department supervision violates a court ordered condition for placement and/or drug/alcohol treatment; and that the Department submit to this court within sixty days a written report of the actions taken to develop and implement such policy and training.[11]

The decision was front-page news, but not all good. The morning paper headlined, "Two Social Workers Found in Contempt."[12] The afternoon paper, in a story headlined "Judge Raps Fines for Caseworkers," reported criticism from a surprising source—the new presiding juvenile court judge (not Chief Judge Johnson or the two senior colleagues who had helped forge our agreements with the Department): "'I am extremely concerned about the potential impact upon the entire staff of Children's Court,' said [the presiding judge] in an interview. Asked for his opinion, [he] said: 'These are professional people. They make mistakes like everyone else. But these mistakes and other matters must be placed in perspective. A mistake is one thing, a contempt is another.'"[13]

And the next morning's press helped explain why Chief Judge Johnson was waiting for me. The headline: "Union Set to Petition for Transfer of Judge Schudson." The story:

> A petition seeking the transfer of a Children's Court Judge who fined two county social workers $100 on contempt charges will be circulated Thursday by the workers' union, a union official said Wednesday.
>
> The petition will contend that Circuit Judge Charles B. Schudson acted unreasonably and harassed the workers, said Dan O'Donnell, president of Local 594 of District Council 48 of the American Federation of State, County and Municipal Employees.
>
> O'Donnell also indicated that he believed the Department of Social Services and its social workers are being made scapegoats for society's ills.
>
> Schudson declined to comment, saying a county lawyer already has said the case will be appealed.
>
> "Needless to say," Schudson added, "doing the right thing is not always popular." . . .
>
> O'Donnell said the union's petition will be addressed to [the] Chief Circuit Court Judge. . . .
>
> "He (Schudson) was elected to be a judge. He's trying to be judge, parent and social worker," O'Donnell said. . . .
>
> "We all are understaffed and the workers are doing the best job they can under the circumstances. Schudson is holding them liable for the imperfect world in which we live," O'Donnell said.
>
> O'Donnell said the union had made a mistake when it endorsed Schudson's election. He said it was also a mistake not to have pushed for Schudson's [transfer from] the Children's Court center sooner.
>
> O'Donnell said he was approached by "a number of concerned employees regarding the public ridicule and harassment" in Schudson's court.[14]

Fortunately, during the twenty-four-hour pause Chief Judge Johnson had permitted, the winds shifted. He read the decision and agreed with it. We both were buried by calls and letters supporting it, and an organization of foster parents countered the union's petition with one of its own calling for me to stay in juvenile court. I provided copies of the decision to key media figures, and asked them to read it and comment as they saw fit.[15] They did so.

The *Milwaukee Journal* focused on judicial independence. Its lead editorial declared that social workers changing court orders "to fit the convenience or

opinions of the staff . . . would pose an intolerable condition for any judge"
and that my transfer "would deal a severe blow to the concept of an independent judiciary." The editorial concluded: "To transfer Schudson under such
circumstances would be to yield to the dictates of a politically powerful union.
That would be totally improper, and dangerous to the best interests of the
judiciary."[16]

Perhaps most influential, the communications director of the CBS TV
affiliate recorded an "auditorial," which aired repeatedly for two days:

> There's a very serious unfairness occurring here at the Children's Court Cen-
> ter. One of the most dedicated judges the center has ever had on the bench
> is being maliciously maligned. Judge Charles Schudson fined and held in con-
> tempt of court two social workers. He did this because they ignored his court
> orders . . . orders that directly affected the welfare and security of a teenager.
> The judge's decision angered the union to which the social workers belong and
> the union is now demanding he be transferred. . . .
>
> The social workers might tell us they're overworked . . . and we would
> agree . . . yet that is no reason to disobey a court order. We've read the judge's
> decision and we've read the [statutes]. It's obvious he not only had the legal
> authority for his decision, but had an obligation to do what he did. Judge
> Schudson's future now lies in the hands of [the] Chief Judge. . . . We're con-
> fident [he] will render a fair decision. However, we feel to transfer Judge
> Schudson would be a terrible loss to the juvenile justice system. . . . Actually,
> Schudson should be commended for bringing public attention to the serious
> problems . . . that have been frustrating judges and justice for many years.

So I survived. I stayed in juvenile court—but not necessarily due to good
judgments or wise decisions, either Chief Judge Johnson's or my own. Shifting
political winds seemed to have blown him off but then back on course. Press
efforts to prevent "a severe blow to the concept of an independent judiciary"
proved pivotal. Ideals of independence do not always steady America's judges
as they sail heaving seas.

Yes, I survived, but more important, the contempt decision survived. The
union and social workers protested, and the Department asked me to stay the
order pending appeal. But when I said no, and when the Court of Appeals
upheld that decision,[17] the Department complied. Having never submitted
its petitions, the union withdrew its request for my transfer; the union president, in the privacy of Chief Judge Johnson's chambers, voiced his agreement
with my decision and apologized for whatever "embarrassment" he might have
caused. The staff members found in contempt resigned or were reassigned.

For the next year, Henry Plum, an attorney and national educator on juvenile law, joined me in preparing training videos and presenting seminars to the Department's more than three hundred probation officers and social workers. Not surprisingly, on anonymous evaluations of their court-ordered classes, some offered caustic comments. But with time, favorable feedback grew and, eventually, our educational efforts gained grudging respect.

After one year, I issued a second decision acknowledging the Department's cooperation and declaring that the Department's continuing compliance would "purge" the contempt and relieve the Department of court monitoring. The decision concluded: "Almost one year passed before SW was found. Her silent consolation, and that of her family, will be that her disappearance brought about judicial action and Department[al] response[,] which will assure services to children and protection to the community for the future."[18]

Reading these concluding words now, I worry that SW's story may sound like a boastful tale of judicial triumph. In fact, the case was among the most painful experiences of my career. More important, the case serves as a revealing account of both an institutional failure and a teenager's tragedy. It describes juvenile justice in America, which still suffers restricted resources, bureaucratic abuse, and judicial ignorance, apathy, and cowardice.

I hasten to add, however, that while many juvenile court judges, crushed by caseloads and controlled by fiscally driven bureaucracies, fail to maintain independence, many others are among the most idealistic and dedicated public servants I have known. Through an outstanding organization, the National Council of Juvenile and Family Court Judges, many pursue continuing education in pediatrics, psychology, and other specialties that amplify their juvenile court capabilities.

I continued as a juvenile court judge two more years, until our county's periodic judicial "rotation" offered me options—stay or move on to the adult courts. I was torn. I was the rare judge who actually wanted to serve in the juvenile division and one of only a few with nonlegal professional experience with children, which enhanced my efforts. But I was exhausted, drained by the cases and bureaucratic battles. And, despite Karen's and my best efforts, serious strain seeped into our family.

During my three years of juvenile court service, Karen and I were concerned about whether and to what extent I should share court experiences with our young sons. Any such sharing, we thought, should be limited and gentle. Thus, as seemed appropriate for Ben, from age six to nine, and Joel, from three to six, I told a few stories about my work. Sometimes they asked questions about kids and cases. Occasionally, I allowed them to visit court

briefly; they played in chambers and enjoyed my doting staff. Karen and I
sensed no distress.

But "children will listen." At dinner one night, while discussing whether
I should leave the juvenile court assignment, Karen and I discovered that,
apparently, our boys had been listening all along. They surprised us. First, they
were quiet (a surprise in and of itself). Then, with Joel nodding in agreement,
Ben said I should leave juvenile court. "Why?" I asked. "Because you're always
so sad."

THE APPELLATE JUDGE

Life, and a Sex Predator

State v. Shawn Schulpius

Vox clamantis in deserto.[1]

Those who rarely encounter America's courts—from attorneys in corporate practice to most people in the public at large—cannot imagine the privations of our justice system. They can be found at every level, and while judges may suffer less than many other professionals, judicial difficulties are particularly revealing if one considers the consequences. I typed my own decisions, walked two flights of stairs to share one copying machine with forty-three other judges, and winced whenever attorneys, calling from their offices, asked, "Could you have your secretary . . ." do something? What secretary? I saw no fat, just the skeletal remains of bone-scraping budgets. During my years in the trial courts, courtroom water coolers sat empty and janitorial services were cut; I carried out our garbage.

But this was not about my convenience. Nor was this only about juvenile courts, where children, politically powerless, could not force funding. In the felony courts, I postponed trials—sometimes for lack of bailiffs to bring defendants from the jail to the courtroom, other times for lack of air-conditioning when summer heat pushed courtroom temperatures over one hundred degrees, making it impossible for jurors to serve.[2]

This was about public safety. I issued warrants for dangerous defendants who jumped bail, only to learn that after being captured in another state, they were released because neither state would cover the cost of transporting them back to our jail. I released dangerous defendants charged with violent crimes for lack of judges to bring them to trial within the constitutional time limit. And sometimes, to avoid such releases, I double-booked, even trying two murder cases at once by starting both the same day (the "speedy trial" deadline), then alternating the trials, morning and afternoon.

These were the criminal courts where I served the next seven years. In big cities, such resource restrictions still set the rhythms of America's "justice" systems. For earnest public servants, the impact is demoralizing; for the public, the injustices are extreme. Indeed, throughout America, communities are endangered as thousands of defendants are locked up while presumed innocent and freed when found guilty.

Locked up while presumed innocent . . . freed when found guilty? Allow me to explain.

In Chicago, litigating the extradition of the nursing home owners, I was working with assistant state's attorney John Glenville, chief of the Cook County prosecutor's "Special Remedies" section. On our way to court one morning, John walked me over to the floor-to-ceiling window at the end of the tenth-floor corridor outside his office. Gesturing toward the sprawling structure below, he explained that we were looking at rooftops of the Cook County Jail. "Guess how many inmates are inside," he quizzed. I had no idea. "Ten thousand," he answered. "And guess how many of them are serving sentences?" "Well," I reasoned, "almost all," except those awaiting trial, unable to make bail.

"One thousand," John answered. "That's our average—10 percent serving sentences; 90 percent awaiting their trials." And, he explained, the nine thousand "presumed innocents" would be released as the choked system finally coughed them up to the courts where almost all actually would forgo trials and plead guilty. Then these newly "found guilties" would be released—released because, by the day of their guilty pleas, most would have been jailed longer than the sentences the judges then would order. *Locked up while presumed innocent; freed when found guilty.*

Thus, from unconscionably (and sometimes unconstitutionally) restricted resources, the injustices flow and the dangers flood. And the politicians pander—while pushing tough-on-crime policies, they babble "trim the fat" nonsense. "No new taxes," they yell at uninformed voters, few of whom want to spend more on a justice system that, most visibly, serves the poor.

But before falling farther into op-ed lamentations, I return to judicial independence. In *S. W.*, I see not only systemic privations, bureaucratic abuse, and judicial acquiescence but also judicial integrity. Consider the Court of Appeals' denial of the Department's challenge to my order. By allowing the contempt order to take immediate effect, three elected appellate judges allowed me to cross over the separation of powers and direct the training of a department of the executive branch.

Might we conclude, therefore, that resource restrictions are less often or less severely corrupting of appellate judges, cloistered and better protected from political pressures? I think so; at least that was my experience in the trial and appellate settings. How meaningful, then, to turn our program's pages and meet the cast's most vilified actor, the sex predator, lurking in both trial and appellate courts. How sobering to see the sex predator, *in the appellate courts*, confined by the corruption of cowardice.

In 1991, Shawn David Schulpius, just a month shy of his eighteenth birthday, was waived to adult court, where he pled guilty to first-degree sexual assault of a four-year-old. This was not his first offense; Mr. Schulpius was a predator. Since age fourteen, he had been molesting children—his six-year-old stepsister, his one-year-old half brother, his biological sister, and other girls in the neighborhood. For this most recent assault, he was sentenced to five years in prison.

But, prosecutors believed, five years proved to be too few. They doubted that he had been rehabilitated; they believed that, once released, Schulpius would assault more children. So in 1995, just before his prison term ended, they petitioned the sentencing court to declare him a "sexually violent person" and lock him up *indefinitely*.

Whoa . . . what? *Indefinitely* . . . what am I saying? That's nuts. Everyone knows that in America, "do the crime, do the time," but not one day more. And besides, judges wear robes and slam gavels, they don't hold crystal balls; they do not diagnose sex offenders and foresee their futures. What's going on here?

What's going on is the sexual abuse of children in epidemic numbers, finally "discovered" by American society. And from that discovery have come the prosecution and incarceration of child molesters.[3] Some, during their imprisonment, declare their desire to strike again. A few, soon after their release, kidnap, rape, and murder more children.

When, a generation ago, such horrific crimes made headlines, the public demanded action to control these predators who, many believed, never should have been freed. When recently released sex offenders murdered a woman in Seattle and mutilated a boy in Tacoma, Washington's state legislators responded. In 1990, they enacted America's first "sex predator commitment" law. By 2007, nineteen other states had followed suit.[4]

Sex predator commitment laws allowed courts to torpedo scheduled releases and lock up sex offenders *indefinitely*—not for punishment or penal purposes but, rather, for "treatment." Under these new statutes, sex predators' time-limited criminal sentences would end, as scheduled, but their indefinite, locked "civil commitments" would begin.

The legal screaming was immediate. Sex offenders now locked up longer than their sentences, joined by many civil libertarians and some criminal justice professionals, stormed the courts. Never in America had anyone ever suggested such a measure; nowhere in the world had any legislature enacted such a law. Within a few years, appeals reached state supreme courts and, soon thereafter, the US Supreme Court.

In 1997, in *Kansas v. Hendricks*, the Supreme Court, five-four, ruled that Kansas's Sexually Violent Predator Act was constitutional. The majority rejected arguments that such laws violate constitutional protections against double jeopardy (second prosecution or punishment for the same crime) and ex post facto laws (after-the-fact designation of conduct as criminal, or newly enacted punishment for previously committed crime). The Court reasoned that these new statutes did not trigger such constitutional protections because they did not generate new prosecutions or additional penalties. After all, the Court explained, these lock-ups were not *criminal* law "sentences" but, rather, *civil* law "commitments." And, like other civil statutes allowing involuntary hospitalization of the mentally ill, these satisfied the constitutional prerequisites for confinement: (1) the individual suffers from mental illness (or an "abnormality" such as pedophilia), and (2) the mental condition renders the individual dangerous. Thus, the Supreme Court concluded, as long as these new statutes set procedural and evidentiary standards to ensure fair hearings, they were constitutional.[5]

In 1995, the year after Wisconsin's legislature enacted chapter 980, its Sex Predator Commitment law (but before the Supreme Court decided *Kansas v. Hendricks*), Judge John A. Franke, an excellent state trial judge, was holding a hearing to determine whether Shawn Schulpius was a "sexually violent person"—a molester suffering from a mental condition that rendered him likely to strike again.[6] Judge Franke found the evidence clear and convincing and, therefore, ordered Schulpius's transfer, at the end of his sentence, from the punishment of a prison cell to the "treatment" of a locked ward.

While Schulpius's locked treatment was indefinite in duration, it also was subject to annual judicial review—a trial, if requested—for consideration of either outright or conditional release.[7] Under the new law, a predator, successfully treated, could qualify for discharge to an unlocked facility or residence, with restrictions such as required counseling and electronic monitoring. Such a supervised "conditional release" would be more than a cosmetic change. While secure "treatment" often entailed little more than a transfer from one prison wing to another,[8] conditional release would provide real freedom.

So one year after his sex predator commitment, Shawn Schulpius returned to court, hoping for release. And he won. Now, the plot thickens.

Judge Franke ordered Schulpius's conditional release to an unlocked facility. But the state Department of Health and Family Services, responsible for such placements, could not find one. Resource realities and community resistance combined to say, "Not in our back yard!" And with that, Schulpius's legal laps lengthened.

With no unlocked facility to take him, Schulpius's confinement continued. So back to court, many times. Judge Franke reiterated his order for conditional release, required implementation "forthwith," threatened and then found the Department in contempt, all to no avail. Time passed, more hearings . . . Schulpius was stuck—stuck in the locked facility Judge Franke had concluded was no longer appropriate for him. Or, viewed from another angle, Schulpius could not come unstuck in order to move to residential treatment, which, Judge Franke had concluded, would best serve him and protect the community.

Predictably, with his continued placement in the wrong place, Shawn Schulpius regressed, emotionally and behaviorally. As a result, prosecutors were left with little choice but to pursue what, no doubt, they deemed a Catch-22 motion for Judge Franke to reconsider his order for conditional release. After all, they argued, even if Schulpius had been ready before, he wasn't now, having mentally deteriorated during his time locked up, languishing, contrary to the court order.

Litigation continued . . . and continued. Before his appeal came to my colleagues and me, Schulpius had been unlawfully locked up four years—that's four years *in addition* to his first year lawfully committed under Judge Franke's first order—four years locked up in violation of Judge Franke's repeated orders for conditional release.

On appeal, Schulpius did not seriously challenge the sex predator commitment law's constitutionality; that had been settled by the state supreme court soon after the statute's enactment, and, by the time his appeal arrived, the US Supreme Court had decided *Kansas v. Hendricks.* He did, however, assert that the state statute was unconstitutional "as applied" *to him.* That is, while conceding that the law had been found proper on paper, he argued that its constitutionality had been shredded *in his case* because of the state's failure to actually implement it. In short, he argued, if court-ordered conditional release simply was not possible, the law simply was not constitutional.

My two colleagues rejected Schulpius's argument. They reasoned that his claim was outweighed by the potential harm to society that would result from his release.[9] I disagreed. Excerpts from my dissenting opinion offer my view (and an example of what often is the sharper tone of a judicial dissent):

> For *more than four years*, . . . the [trial] court ordered Shawn Schulpius' supervised release. During those years, the court repeatedly reiterated its order and: (1) denied the State's motion for reconsideration; (2) concluded, given the

State's assertion of its inability to follow the orders, that Wis. Stat. ch. 980 was unconstitutional as applied to Schulpius; (3) ordered his supervised release "forthwith"; and (4) found the Department of Health and Family Services in contempt. Still, the orders for Schulpius' supervised release were not followed.

Thus, for *more than four years* . . . Schulpius remained confined in violation of court orders. And, throughout that time—and even to the present, as indicated by the Assistant Attorney General at oral argument before this court— the State was and is unable to implement court orders for supervised release of sex predators in Milwaukee County.

In short, Wis. Stat. ch. 980 is the law but, for some, it cannot be enforced. And when it cannot be enforced, individuals remain confined despite court orders to release them. Thus, if one accepts the underlying logic of ch. 980, these sex predators necessarily receive services that are *in*appropriate or, at the very least, *less* appropriate than those the courts have found would provide the best treatment *and* community protection.

Are more than four years of unlawful confinement in violation of court orders "'shocking to the universal sense of justice'"? Does such governmental misconduct "shock[] the conscience" [the appellate standard for measuring whether governmental action or inaction has violated "substantive due process of law"], and thus constitute a denial of substantive due process?

The very questions seem sarcastic. Confining a person in violation of a court order, even for a day, is cause for concern. When unlawful confinement continues beyond a brief time, concern becomes constitutional cause, sometimes even triggering the "great writ"—*habeas corpus*. And that is so even when the unlawful confinement results from an innocent mistake, such as the misinterpretation of a sentencing order or the miscalculation of a release date.

But here, Schulpius' *more than four years* of unlawful confinement did not result from an innocent mistake or misinterpretation. Schulpius' unlawful confinement continued notwithstanding: (1) the State's full understanding of the court orders for supervised release; and (2) the State's claimed inability to implement the orders.

Such governmental conduct is unconscionable; it constitutes deliberate indifference as a matter of law, even absent bad faith by any official. . . .

For Schulpius and others . . . ch. 980 has become an ugly charade. And this charade is performed on what many consider a dimly lit stage. Lest we forget, ch. 980 keeps people confined and/or supervised *after they have completed their sentences*. It is one of the relatively new laws reflecting the efforts of some states to control and treat sex predators *after they have fully paid their penalties*. Powerfully (and appropriately, I believe), these laws respond to the growing body of knowledge about sex offenders, particularly pedophiles, and their virtually certain danger to society long after their sentences have been served. Still, we must recognize that these laws, like none before, seem to say, "Do the crime, do the time, *and then do more time, indefinitely.*"

Understandably, therefore, sex predator commitment laws have raised serious due-process concerns and faced concerted constitutional challenges. Addressing those challenges, courts have sought to balance the rights of sex predators who have completed their sentences and the rights of the communities they endanger.

Balancing the scales, the Wisconsin Supreme Court concluded that, precisely because Wis. Stat. ch. 980 included certain procedural and substantive safeguards, it was constitutional. Reiterating that conclusion, however, our supreme court commented: "As with all enactments, we presume good faith on the part of the legislature. We conclude that treatment is a bona fide goal of this statute and we presume the legislature will proceed in good faith and fund the treatment programs necessary for those committed under the statute."

But betray that good faith . . . destroy those safeguards . . . and the statutory structure falls. . . . [Wisconsin Supreme Court] Justice Ann Walsh Bradley punctuated that very point. . . . She [reiterated] that the constitutionality of ch. 980 derived, in part, from the understanding that the State would not "'simply warehouse'" sex predators. Justice Bradley then noted that she had joined with the majority [upholding the statute in a previous case] "assuming that 'the legislature will proceed in good faith and fund the treatment programs necessary for those committed under chapter 980.'" She then wrote: "We continue to gain experience with the way ch. 980 has played out in the real world. . . . The case law has become rife with examples of the State's inability to provide appropriate placements. The court's assumptions of the State's good faith are wearing thin."

"Good faith [was] wearing thin." Now it is threadbare. If repeated violations of court orders resulting in *more than four years* of unlawful confinement cannot convince our courts to restore the constitutional fabric, individual liberty will no longer be protected from the penetrating winds of governmental cynicism and neglect.

Clearly, Wis. Stat. ch. 980, unenforceable in Schulpius' case, was unconstitutional as applied to him. His *more than four years* of unlawful confinement should "shock the conscience" of all who respect the rule of law and remain dedicated to both civil liberties *and* community protection. And if, as one would reasonably infer from this record and from oral argument, supervised release of predators in Milwaukee County remains nothing more than a charade, the judiciary must respond with speed, wisdom and power.

While to some it may seem poetically just that Schulpius, having uncon-scionably victimized others, has himself been victimized by unconscionable conduct, Wis. Stat. ch. 980 provides for no such *ad hoc* retribution. Where government's unconscionable conduct denies due process of law, courts must fashion appropriate remedies.

So now, what about Schulpius? Years after he was to have been released, he finally was found to be inappropriate for supervised release. The [trial] court, noting the irony, commented, "It would be fundamentally unfair if unlawful confinement were to cause behavior which is then used to justify lawful con-finement." Still, the fact remains that Schulpius, by the time of the final oper-ative order, was no longer appropriate for release. So what is the remedy?[10] . . .

Finally, lest this opinion be misconstrued, I am anything but hostile to legislative efforts to commit sex predators. Notwithstanding the compelling arguments against them, the sex predator commitment laws, properly drawn and applied, are constitutional and, I believe, essential to the protection of the community. . . .

Thus, I need no convincing that sex predators endanger our communities in extraordinary ways and, therefore, that their control requires extraordinary measures. But those measures must be constitutional. A sex predator commit-ment law that, in the most fundamental way, *cannot function as written* cannot stand. . . . This proposition, I trust, is so clear that, I fear, I belabor what should simply be known, without words. And yet, finding that my voice is crying out alone, I persist.

Thus I struggle to state the obvious: if the constitutionality of [the statute] depends on the substantive rights it declares, the unconscionable removal of those rights destroys its constitutionality. I search for metaphors—without strings, a Stradivarius is silent . . . without wings, an eagle dies.[11]

Vox clamantis in deserto. Unanimously, the Wisconsin Supreme Court affirmed my colleagues' conclusion.[12] While embracing one of my points—that Shawn Schulpius had been denied *procedural* due process—the Court allowed indefinite incarceration, in violation of court orders, of sex predators who, like Schulpius, would remain locked up not because courts had concluded they should be but because government was unable to place them anywhere else.[13] First stating the "test"—the standard of review—the Court explained:

The test to determine if the state conduct complained of violates substan-tive due process is [whether] the conduct "'shocks the conscience. . . . '" In addition, when analyzing a substantive due process violation claim, we also consider "whether the government officer's conduct was either a 'deliberate decision[]' to 'deprive' Schulpius of his liberty interest, or reflected the officer's 'deliberate indifference' to that liberty interest. . . ."

. . . [T]here is nothing in the evidentiary record that would lead us to conclude that the failure to place Schulpius on supervised release . . . "was the result of anything but good-faith efforts that did not succeed because of things beyond the control of those to whom the orders were directed. . . ."

We are satisfied that the [Department] made substantial attempts to ensure that Schulpius would be placed on supervised release. It followed court orders to draw up placement plans and contact other counties in search of an appropriate facility. The fact that the . . . efforts were ultimately unsuccessful cannot be characterized as either an intentional or conscious disregard of Schulpius's constitutional rights. When one considers "Schulpius's horrendous history of predatory sexual violence against children," the . . . inability to find an appropriate community placement . . . clearly falls short of the level of a substantive due process violation.

We conclude that the failure to place Schulpius on supervised release . . . does not shock the conscience. Therefore, Schulpius endured no substantive due process violation.[14]

So Shawn Schulpius was stuck; Kafka could not have told a darker tale. Or maybe he could, simply by recounting the judicial charade that then continued. It's not easy to follow, but only because the details seem unbelievable, defying even the most cynical imagination. Here's what happened.

Years had passed before Schulpius's appeal of my colleagues' decision reached the Wisconsin Supreme Court. During that time, the Department still had not located or built a facility for conditionally released predators. Nevertheless, the Court, repeating the words of the decision it had rendered seven years earlier rejecting the constitutional challenge to Wisconsin's sex predator law, reiterated the authority of a trial court to order the Department to do exactly that: "'a court has the authority . . . to order a county . . . to create whatever programs or facilities are necessary to accommodate an order for supervised release.'"[15] But neither the Supreme Court nor any other, on behalf of Schulpius or anyone else, ever exercised that authority. Kafka celebrates.

In its decision affirming my colleagues' conclusion, the Supreme Court, reciting factors reflecting what it deemed the Department's good-faith efforts to find a facility, seemed impressed by the government's "show me the money." The Court declared: "It is significant that the State Building Commission appropriated approximately $1.3 million toward the establishment of a residential facility or dwelling, in order to place individuals committed under Chapter 980 on supervised release in Milwaukee County. Counsel for the [Department] stated at oral argument that, if necessary, the [Department] will request more money in support of this project."[16]

But did the Building Commission ever spend that money? No. In fact, after that oral argument may have faded from memory, the $1.3 million was rescinded—first through the state budgetary process and finally by legislative enactment effectively prohibiting any such expenditure.[17] And now Kafka dances deliriously.

What about the state Supreme Court's invocation of judicial "authority under Chapter 980 to order a county . . . to create whatever programs or facilities are necessary to accommodate an order for supervised release?" Was anyone listening? Seems so. *The legislature revised the statute—to preempt that very authority.* It now provides that no trial court may "authorize supervised release unless . . . the court finds that . . . [t]reatment that meets the person's needs and a qualified provider of the treatment are reasonably available . . . [and a] reasonable level of resources can provide for the level of residential placement, supervision, and ongoing treatment . . . for the safe management of the person while on supervised release."[18]

That's right. In its revised form, the state's sex predator commitment law now provides that the government, by *not* locating, establishing, or funding construction of a facility offering "treatment that meets the person's needs," can preclude the possibility of conditional release. Court orders be damned or, better yet, simply ignored until some judge again attempts to assert authority to ensure compliance. Drunk and smiling, Kafka passes out on the courtroom floor.[19]

Thus, some sex predator commitment laws sit on the books, pages unturned. Predators languish, often untreated, often without any prospect of release. As a result, constitutional challenges percolate. In Minnesota, one recently boiled over. Here's the news:

> In a decision watched by officials in 20 states that hold some sex offenders after they complete prison sentences, a federal judge ruled this week that Minnesota's program for such offenders was unconstitutional.
>
> Judge Donovan W. Frank of the US district court in St. Paul found that the state's program, which holds more than 700 people in two secure facilities for indefinite periods, had failed to release some who no longer met the criteria for being confined.
>
> "The overwhelming evidence at trial established that Minnesota's civil commitment scheme is a punitive system that segregates and indefinitely detains a

class of potentially dangerous individuals without the safeguards of the criminal justice system," Judge Frank wrote.

While Judge Frank's ruling . . . does not directly affect civil commitment programs in other states, officials elsewhere were paying close attention to the outcome, largely because questions about the constitutionality, costs and effectiveness of holding sex offenders beyond their prison terms have long been debated.

Since the 1990s, when Minnesota began involuntarily committing sex offenders deemed to be "sexually dangerous" or to have "sexual psychopathic personalities" to the treatment program after they finished prison terms, no one has been found to have improved enough to be fully discharged. State records show that only three people have been released with tight restrictions.

"The stark reality is that there is something very wrong with this state's method of dealing with sex offenders in a program that has never fully discharged anyone . . . since its inception in 1994," the judge wrote, adding that given the structure of the program and its history, "no one has any realistic hope of ever getting out of this 'civil' detention."[20]

Shawn Schulpius and his Minnesota neighbors were not the only sex predators languishing in lock-ups. New York's bait-and-switch rivals Wisconsin's shell game.

Dozens of sex offenders who have satisfied their sentences in New York State are being held in prison beyond their release dates because of a new interpretation of a state law that governs where they can live.

The law, which has been in effect since 2005, restricts many sex offenders from living within 1,000 feet of a school. Those unable to find such accommodations often end up in homeless shelters.

But . . . the Department of Corrections and Community Supervision, which runs the prisons and parole system, said the 1,000-foot restriction also extended from homeless shelters, making most of them off limits because of the proximity of schools.

The new interpretation has had a profound effect in New York City, where only 14 of the 270 shelters under the auspices of the Department of Homeless Services have been deemed eligible to receive sex offenders. But with the 14 shelters often filled to capacity, the state has opted to keep certain categories of sex offenders in custody until appropriate housing is found. . . .

[T]he situation in New York is now presenting a new twist: The various residency restrictions that have consigned many sex offenders to life as transients are now being interpreted to require their continued incarceration.[21]

So what's the verdict on America's experiment with indefinite confinement of sex predators? In the thirty states *without* predator commitment laws, the consequences are ironic. These states, perhaps contemplating the costs and constitutional complications that come with predator commitment laws, could, instead, simply enact new penalties and promote longer sentences for sex crimes. Indeed, some have done so. After all, lawmakers may reason, why not avoid these conditional release problems by locking up predators longer in the first place? After all, "it's nearly impossible, politically, to object to harsh punishments for perverts."[22]

And in the twenty states *with* predator commitment laws, will judges mandate funding for new facilities? Will they order legislators and governors to pay tax dollars for due process? Don't hold your breath. Look how judges have backed down; look at how the few courageous decisions have fared. In Wisconsin, Judge Franke, an elected state judge, tried; in Minnesota, Judge Frank, an appointed federal judge, tried. So while more constitutional confrontations may come, predators are likely to lose. Shawn Schulpius lost, and he lost despite the ironclad constitutional strength of his legal arguments. Political cowardice consumed judges; appellate courts caved.

In theory, judges, uncorrupted by political pressures or fiscal constraints, uphold constitutional rights, even for sex predators. History, however, rebuts the naïve notion that judges do so easily or as often as they should. Thus, it is noteworthy that, in the many years since the US Supreme Court upheld sex predator commitment laws in *Kansas v. Hendricks*, perhaps the only appellate judges (other than one elected state court of appeals judge, in dissent) to find such a law unconstitutional, "as applied" to an actual sex predator, were federal judges—appointed for life, never subject to election.

In so noting, I mean no disrespect for these federal judges. Not at all—but I do mean to acknowledge the additional challenges for state judges, particularly elected ones. They tend to avoid collisions with their legislative and executive friends across the street. Fiscally dependent on them, state judges abhor ordering anything that would antagonize the other branches. Politically precarious, they watch out for hot buttons—none hotter than one pushed to release a sex predator—and watch their rear-view mirrors for unprincipled political opponents crossing the solid yellow to pass.

Thus, in both state trial and appellate courts, we see the convergence of corrupting factors—emotional revulsion over despicable crimes; political pressure to imprison predators and preserve electability; resource realities that can cause politically problematic confrontations with the legislative and executive branches.[23] Not a pretty picture for an independent judge.

And what about the picture for Shawn Schulpius . . . what about him? He stayed stuck. After the Wisconsin Supreme Court's decision, seven more years passed. Finally, in 2013, more than a decade after Judge Franke first ordered his conditional release, Schulpius was discharged from locked treatment—released with mandatory electronic monitoring, unannounced visits by a probation officer, polygraph tests, and counseling.[24]

"It has become almost axiomatic that the great rights which are secured for all of us by the Bill of Rights are constantly tested and retested in the courts by the people who live in the bottom of society's barrel. . . . Upon the shoulders of such persons are our great rights carried."[25] Or not. After all, at some point they need independent judges to help with the heavy lifting.

THE TRIAL JUDGE

Death, and a Cherished Child

State v. Anthony C. McClain

> One by one [Judge Hidalgo's wife] carried her children up the cliff.
> The cave was a natural one, typical of many in the region. She peered
> inside to be certain it wasn't the den of some wild animal, sat her
> children against its back wall, then, dry-eyed, kissed them goodbye.
>
> —Isabel Allende, *The Judge's Wife*[1]

From 1978 to 1991, Jeffrey Dahmer raped, murdered, dismembered, and can-
nibalized seventeen men and boys, most of them in his Milwaukee home,
walking distance from the courthouse. When, on January 30, 1992, he came to
trial, I was not the judge. Here's why.

"The word 'justice' is not in my job description," Bob Williams declared
to our criminal court judges sitting around a conference table at a lunch-hour
meeting. His words surprised me. I had not read the description, but, given
that only a few years earlier he had been selected for a newly created position,
"Justice System Coordinator," I would have assumed that "justice" appeared
not only in his job title but in the job description as well.

Bob Williams, along with the chief judge, administered the county's many
courts. Thus, it fell to him to find ways for the system to function more
efficiently—from helping judges streamline scheduling to convincing legislators to fund courtroom computerization. His new position, like others in
financially strapped counties throughout the country, was born of caseloads
that had boomed just as tax-cutting advocates were demanding that government, in the slogan of the times, "do more with less."

Some judges resented Bob's involvement. They declined his advice, noting
the irony—creation of one more costly bureaucratic position at the very time
courtroom budgets were being cut. I felt differently. Bothered by courtroom
inefficiencies I had observed as a prosecutor, dismayed by stubborn judges I

was seeing behind the scenes resisting commonsense improvements, and impressed by Bob's insights and energy, I believed we needed him—one shrewd bureaucrat to evaluate the system "systemically" and help us all "do more," and better, "with less."

For me and, I hoped, other judges, "more and better" would mean more time to "do justice." This was not theoretical. Crunching the numbers, I saw real opportunities. My math was simple. If, for example, better scheduling could save even as little as one minute on each case on my daily calendar, then, every day, I could gain the half hour I might need to read a psychological evaluation, study a presentence report, cultivate rather than cut off courtroom comments, or simply "take the time"—the few more minutes to listen and reach out to defendants, victims, witnesses, and others looking to me not only for fair and legally sound decisions but for kindness as well.

So I became a big Bob Williams fan. The more I knew him, the more I liked him; the more I saw his success, the more I respected his work. Thus, I was pleased when, at the end of a long day in felony court, I saw him lingering in the gallery. He asked for a few minutes; I invited him into chambers and was all the more pleased when he asked to learn about my scheduling method. Bob told me that, on the basis of both his observations and statistical study, he believed my method worked well—completing jury trials, reducing adjournments and the resulting costs of police overtime, shortening the time from arraignment to sentencing.

My scheduling method was unusual. Drawing on advice from prosecutors, public defenders, and court clerks, I had devised it with care. Pleased that Bob had noticed, I came to be all the more supportive of his efforts to take such innovations to others. We became friends. How surprising it was when things changed. Here's what happened and, perhaps, why Jeffrey Dahmer and I never met in court.

After almost ten years on the trial bench, I had had enough—the daily diet of abused, sexually assaulted, and murdered victims churning my gut and gutting my soul. I was looking around and nearing an agreement to join the University of Wisconsin Law School full-time faculty. But when the dean departed unexpectedly, my academic plans were postponed. At about that time, Judge Smith, then just recently elected to the Court of Appeals, suggested that I join him there. I was intrigued.

Discreetly, Judge Smith encouraged me to run against the Court's presiding judge, up for reelection the next year. He told me of the incumbent's outbursts and bizarre behavior, details of which were consistent with widespread rumors and with behavior I had seen, both in court and in courthouse corridors. Still, while displeasure ran deep, the presiding judge's powerful personality

and political strength deterred opposition. Believing, however, that he might
be vulnerable, and convinced that replacing him would be a public service,
I decided to run. Besides, I was ready to move on. And, with two years left
in my trial court term, I could be bold but cautious, running for the Court of
Appeals without giving up my trial court seat.

So I announced my candidacy. Shortly thereafter, Bob Williams again visited me in chambers. After chatting briefly, he turned to the topic of my campaign and coyly made an offer so strange that, at first, I did not understand.
Then, in unmistakable terms, he clarified that, as an admirer of my work
and critic of the incumbent, he wanted me to win. He asked that I tell him
"when the time is right" so that he could remove headlined homicides and
other hot cases from the at-random process and assign them to me for front-
page publicity as election day approached.

Shocked, I declined. Incensed, I told Bob that, as he knew, what he was
proposing was improper. I warned that if ever I learned of any such conduct,
I would seek his dismissal. Naïve? Perhaps, but I had never heard of any
attempt, politically motivated or otherwise, to manipulate the very assignment of cases. Now, examining judicial independence and corruption—and
considering the first question, "Who's the judge?"—I'm struck by the importance of case assignments . . . of skewing *the first step* toward an independent
decision.[2]

So later, by the time of the lunch-hour meeting at which Bob Williams
proudly pointed to the absence of "justice" from his job description, we were
at odds. Already suspicious of his motives and moves, I listened as he, softly
sarcastic, invoked this semantic oversight to support one of his efficiency
proposals over the objections of judges who said it would violate statutory
standards.

Thus, behind the scenes, Bob was no help to my campaign. And as a result,
two months before the Court of Appeals election, I was *not* presiding at Jeffrey
Dahmer's jury trial a few hallways away. No luck of the draw for me this time;
as far as I know, Jeffrey Dahmer's case was assigned by the clerk of courts, at
random.

Still, during these years, I presided over other murder trials, each emotionally
demanding and some legally challenging, particularly "two-phase" trials, like
Dahmer's, at which "guilt" and "sanity" are tried separately. One such trial offers
the opportunity to learn about the often misunderstood "insanity defense,"
and about sentencing and its unusual corruptions.

The insanity *defense?* We're getting there, but, it seemed, all the murders
tried before me were insane:

A sunny spring morning . . . a young woman, pregnant, at home caring for her four-year-old son, answered the knock at her door and welcomed a teenage neighbor she knew well. He stabbed them . . . all three dead.

A summer night . . . a young man in his kitchen, chatting with his wife after dinner, then carrying out the garbage only to surprise a burglar in their garage who panicked and killed him.

Seconds . . . lives ended . . . dreams destroyed . . . and now the trials, every autopsied detail described under the bright lights of law. No two trials were alike, facts and legal issues varying widely. But, presiding over each trial, I would have the same, simple, almost silly thought—little more than an impulse, posed as a private question to the defendant: "On what conceivable basis could you ever think that, somehow, you had the right to end the life of another human being?" Thus, falling back into *my* framework, I was, again, grasping for *my* logical life buoy, trying to make sense where none could be made.

Still, some murders can seem motivated by their own twisted *logic* leading, ironically, to the rare circumstances most likely to support an *insanity* defense. As we examine such a case, we would do well to remember that America's legal *systems* do not agree on what constitutes "insanity" and whether, by any psychiatric or legal definition, it may be invoked. Federalism is lurking; some states do not allow any insanity defense at all. In the states that do, procedures vary, but in most of them the trial takes place before one jury in two "burden-shifting" phases.

In the "guilt phase," the jury considers whether the defendant committed the crime. Here, as always in a criminal trial, the prosecution has the burden of proof; the defendant is *presumed* innocent and, therefore, must be found "not guilty" unless the prosecution carries its *criminal law burden* to prove guilt, *beyond a reasonable doubt*, to all twelve jurors. If the prosecution fails, the defendant is acquitted and the trial ends; if the prosecution succeeds, the trial moves to its second phase.

In the "sanity phase" (often termed the "responsibility phase"), the jury considers whether the defendant was sane when committing the crime. In this phase, however, the defense has the burden of proof; the defendant is *presumed* sane and, therefore, must be found responsible for the crime unless the defense carries its *civil law burden* to prove insanity, *by clear and convincing evidence*, to almost all of the jurors (at least nine or ten, depending on the state). If the defense fails to do so, the defendant is found responsible for the crime and will be sentenced within the usual range of penalties. If, however, the defense proves the defendant's mental illness and resulting inability to know right

from wrong at the time of the crime, the sentencing options will be different,
almost always resulting in a commitment for mental treatment in a locked
facility.[3]

In a two-phase trial over which I presided, the jury found Anthony C.
McClain guilty of murdering his ten-year-old son, and found him legally
responsible. Mr. McClain, forty-two, was a single dad doing his best, trying to
make ends meet and raising Tony Jr. A quiet man, cognitively challenged, Mr.
McClain may have misunderstood a caseworker's comment, leading him to
believe that social services might take away Tony. Distressed, possibly drugged
and delusional, he sought to send his son to heaven, where, he believed, they
would reunite. So that evening Mr. McClain engaged Tony in their favorite
game—wrestling on the living room floor, where, as he later confessed, he
applied the "Verne Gagne sleeper," the chokehold named for the champion
wrestler.

When Tony passed out, Mr. McClain slashed his neck with a fish-boning
knife. Satisfied that his son was in heaven, he then turned the knife on himself.
Tony died; he was found in the apartment, his head resting on a sweater, a
rosary around his neck. Mr. McClain survived; he was found outside, near the
apartment, disoriented and covered with blood.

Throughout his trial, Mr. McClain bemoaned his survival; he sat sobbing
between his two attorneys. In a brief first phase, the defense conceded his
guilt. But in the lengthy second phase, Mr. McClain's attorneys offered substantial evidence of insanity—in legal terms, that, at the moment he murdered
Tony, Mr. McClain was suffering from a mental disease or defect such that
he could not distinguish right from wrong and conform his conduct to the
requirements of law.

Three psychiatrists, individually, examined Mr. McClain and testified. The
first two split—one supporting Mr. McClain's insanity defense; the other,
not. Thus, for the jury, it seemed the "tie-breaker" might be the illustrious
third expert—the chairman of the University of Wisconsin Medical School
Department of Psychiatry. In response to questions from Mr. McClain's attorneys, he offered impressive testimony—fair, thorough, and utterly convincing. In my view, it set a firm psychiatric foundation under a perfectly plausible
proposition—that Mr. McClain had suffered a "brief reactive psychosis," causing him to kill the son he loved.

I mused that the prosecutor might forgo cross-examination and concede
that the jury, in all likelihood, had been persuaded by the doctor; that indeed,
in light of his testimony, perhaps even the prosecutor himself might be ready
to accept that Mr. McClain should be committed to a mental hospital, not a
prison. But the distinguished doctor still was on the witness stand when we

reached a lunch break. And the superb, instinctively skilled prosecutor, Steven Licata, had a hunch.

Prompted by either the doctor's written report of his examination of Mr. McClain or by the doctor's testimony, Mr. Licata had his suspicions. He deemed Mr. McClain's account of his thoughts and feelings to be all too conveniently close to the doctor's diagnosis and description of his mental condition. So Mr. Licata headed for the jail where Mr. McClain had been confined since his arrest. In the jail law library, he discovered the attendance log and its circumstantial evidence supporting his suspicion. Just before the doctor's all-important examination, Mr. McClain, who never before had visited the jail law library, signed in six times. Mere coincidence? Perhaps, but the unusual pattern of Mr. McClain's possible "research" was enough to enable Mr. Licata, in brilliant cross-examination, to query whether, possibly, Mr. McClain had misled the doctor. Conceding such a possibility, the doctor retreated somewhat from his diagnostic conclusions.

Was Mr. Licata's theory solid? Hardly; after all, Mr. McClain was intellectually limited, perhaps incapable of devising any such scheme to deceive the doctor or the jury. But Mr. Licata's suggestion could remain speculative. He did not need to prove anything. He simply had to raise questions and plausible possibilities to undermine Mr. McClain's evidence. Remember, in this second phase of the trial, Mr. McClain, not the government, carried the burden of proof. To prevail, his attorneys needed to offer clear and convincing evidence that their theory was correct.

Following hours of deliberation, the jury, voting ten to two, concluded that Mr. McClain was not insane—that, in legal terms, the evidence had not, clearly and convincingly, proved Mr. McClain not-guilty by reason of mental disease or defect; that the evidence had not proved that, at the time of the homicide, he was unable to distinguish right from wrong and conform his conduct to the requirements of law. Thus, he appeared before me to be sentenced for first-degree murder. Legally, my decision was easy. Because Wisconsin was among the states with no death penalty, and because Wisconsin law mandated life imprisonment for first-degree murder, I had almost nothing to decide.[4]

Thus, following my brief pronouncement of the life sentence, the case could have concluded. Indeed, many judges might say that is exactly where such sentencings should end. In homicide sentencings and many others, however, I held a broader view of the judicial role. Therefore, after hearing the attorneys' arguments and eliciting Mr. McClain's remarks (particularly to learn of his possible suicidal intentions), and before ending the hearing, I addressed him directly.

My comments lasted about fifteen minutes. Reading them now, I'm disappointed. My words wander. Some seem inappropriately political, pontifical, and even egotistical, almost as if I were using Mr. McClain's sentencing to express my own rage and reach my own therapeutic needs. While intending to help Mr. McClain in his grief, to help our community in its agony, I may have been tapping into my own. Now reading my remarks in journalists' summaries, I sense a judge overwhelmed, barely maintaining his own emotional balance.[5]

Mr. McClain's case presents circumstances as sad as any I saw during my years on the trial bench. But why dissect it here? It provides the opportunity to learn about the insanity defense, one of the most maligned and misunderstood concepts in criminal law. And it carries us behind the bench to enhance our understanding of sentencing, a judge's most *discretionary* decision.

Early in my judicial career, a juvenile court bailiff offered a gentle critique of my sentencings. "Judge, they're really not listening; just get to the bottom line." (He was, of course, also complaining that my long-winded ways were extending his exhausting days.) I valued his opinion but rejected his advice. While it was true that some of those in the courtroom weren't listening, others were. A wise judge, I believe, knows how hard it is to know the difference. In the courtroom's artificial light, one defendant, intently focused, may be tuning out; another, sullen, may be pondering every word.

How do we know? We don't. Humility helps. More than a century ago, John Wanamaker was said to have quipped, "Half the money I spend on advertising is wasted; the trouble is I don't know which half."[6] The same might be said of sentencing "sermons"—all the more reason to deliver them in *every* case.

"Two burglars walk into a courthouse for sentencing . . ." sounds like the setup for a bad joke. But it's no joke when one strolls out on probation while the other, even when the circumstances are similar, is marched into prison. What, then, are the ingredients of sentencing discretion? And in this most discretionary of judicial decisions, what factors may corrupt independence? From age to gender, race to religion, ego to electoral ambition, ideology to indigestion, the myriad factors that affect judicial discretion may run wild in sentencing.

Sentencing rules are few, legal limits—the minimum and maximum fines and periods of incarceration—easy to follow. As we read in the appellate decision affirming Monica Miller's sentence, the judge's words need only have touched the three bases: seriousness of the crime, circumstances of the defendant, and protection of the community. Substantively, the pronouncement may be modest or profound, but legally, it's a no-brainer. And yet, there's much more.

Imagine a new judge sentencing an armed robber or rapist. Sitting alone, with little experience and only legalistic reference points, what's the judge to do? The prosecutor offers a compelling argument for twenty years; the defense attorney offers an equally compelling argument for probation. Knees knocking beneath the bench, the judge contemplates many options.

Imagine an experienced judge on the same case. Seasoned by hundreds of sentencings but still sitting alone, what's the judge to do? Experience counts, but experience may be both benefit and burden. Over time, judges may form bad habits; they may lock onto unexamined assumptions. "Experience," Thorstein Veblen warned, may be "trained incapacity."[7]

No surprise, then, that the "two burglars" who walk into courtrooms, whether sentenced by rookies or by veterans, may walk out in different directions. The sentence disparities, disturbing to many—courtroom commentators, justice system professionals, students and scholars, and judges themselves—have troubled legislators, too.

For the federal courts, Congress responded, enacting mandatory "sentencing guidelines."[8] Oxymoronically, these guidelines *required* federal judges to sentence within narrow ranges derived from formulas based on sentencing data.[9] Some state legislatures followed suit, but their guidelines were advisory; judges received grids on which to enter a defendant's prior convictions and other data, accompanied by instructions for computing average sentences in similar circumstances. I found such guidelines helpful and used them regularly. Others did, too, but many judges declined, seeing them as encroachments on their discretion.

Many federal judges objected to the mandatory guidelines and what they viewed as the surrender of discretion. They pointed to what they deemed unjust sentences they had been required to order. They protested their reduced opportunity to individualize sentences and, particularly for nonviolent drug offenders, to order less than the required incarceration.

In 2005, in *United States v. Booker*, two appeals of guideline sentences reached the US Supreme Court.[10] The Court concluded that the challenged sections of the guidelines were unconstitutional unless interpreted as advisory, not mandatory. In his cogent commentary, Judge Posner traced the outlines—from no guidelines to mandatory guidelines to advisory guidelines—then linked his analysis to sentencing discretion in areas where strictly "legalistic" direction is unclear.

> Anyone who doubts the pervasiveness of judicial discretion . . . should think back to the extraordinary variance in federal sentences that prevailed before the promulgation of the federal sentencing guidelines, [which] is beginning to creep back into the sentencing process as a result of the Supreme Court's demotion [of the guidelines, in *United States v. Booker*], . . . from mandatory to advisory status. Before the guidelines, the determinants of how severely to

punish a convicted defendant . . . had almost nothing to do with legal analysis;
they depended, rather, on the judge's attitudes toward . . . large, contested,
broadly ideological issues.[11]

Legal analyses of sentencing discretion and guidelines are legion. Many
commentators seem to have thrown up their hands as if to say, "Sentencing—
important, discretionary, difficult. Enough said." Still, drawing on both my
judicial and judicial teaching experience, I offer some thoughts that may advance the analysis.

Sentencing is more art than science, more instinct than law. Judicial agreement on this point, however, offers no consolation for new judges, particularly
state judges without guidelines. They have little idea where, in the wide range
from probation to prison, to locate a "reasonable" sentence. Further, experienced judges' easy acceptance of sentencing "as art" may lead them to Veblen's
"(self)-trained incapacity."

So how do judges learn sentencing? Those who once were prosecutors or
public defenders learned from participating in many sentencings, observing
judges and their approaches. With that, they got a feel for sentencing and the
chance to develop their own philosophies and styles. But judges from other
backgrounds often are embarrassingly insecure, in both sentencing substance
and style. How do they get up to speed?

Judges learn on the job and in judicial education courses.[12] On the job, they
listen to arguments from prosecutors and defense attorneys. Case by case, hearing those adversarial recommendations and, if they have guidelines, compar-
ing them to average sentences, judges catch on. At judicial conferences, judges
choose from many offerings, including sentencing seminars consisting of exer-
cises in which judges offer hypothetical cases and ask participants what sentences they would order and why. Typically, the hypotheticals run from easy
equations (first offender + minor offense = fine or probation; career criminal +
major offense = prison) to hard ones, such as those that present "model" citizens who drink and drive, injure or kill.

On-the-job experience is irreplaceable; classroom hypotheticals are helpful.
Judicial educators, however, consider both incomplete, claiming that they fall
short of cultivating the knowledge and skills essential to sentencing. Surprisingly, the most critical incompleteness comes at the most fundamental levels:
knowing about the crime and the criminal, and understanding the actual impact of a pronounced sentence.

Yes, in sentencing, the most serious source of corrupted independence may
be ignorance. Day after day, case after case, judges do not know much at all
about the crimes, the criminals, or the sentences they're ordering. How can

that be? Well, as a sentencing judge, how *could* I know about the crime and the people involved? If the case had just been tried before me, I learned about them, in detail, from the witnesses. But relatively few cases go to trial; almost all conclude in guilty pleas.

How, then, at both the guilty plea and the sentencing hearings, might I gain information about the crime, the criminal, and the victim? How, for example, would a judge learn about the trauma or degree of injury suffered by a rape victim? How would a judge learn enough about child sexual abuse to evaluate whether a "first offender" really is the rare molester apprehended for an actual first offense or the pedophile who, for years, has been clever enough to avoid arrest? Moreover, how would a judge develop rhetorical skills to sentence with words that reach defendants, victims, and the public? Or, keeping in mind mistakes like mine with Ms. Miller and Mr. McClain, how could an idealistic sentencing judge become sufficiently self-aware to humbly seek and more successfully reach out to those in court and beyond?

And what can be conveyed in a classroom to help judges enhance their sentencing art? That was the question posed by the National Judicial College when it asked me to design a course that would move beyond the conventional, hypothetical case model. We soon found how valuable such an academic product could be but how hard it was to "make the sale."

The Judicial College asked for my help not necessarily because of my reputation as a judge but, rather, on the basis of my reputation as a teacher, growing out of the child sexual abuse lectures I had been offering judges nationwide.[13] The College believed that if I could teach judges about child sexual abuse, I could sell sausage to vegans—or sentencing to judges. I say this not to boast but to set up what I'm about to relate—my sexual abuse courses were well received; my sentencing courses were not. Why? Within the answer we find the corruption of ignorance, tripping judges and causing their sentencing stumbles.

Having seen the limitations of hypothetical case training, Howard Wingren, the National Judicial College academic director, and I tried to create a course to cover (1) the neglected basics—the crime, the criminal, and the actual impact of a pronounced sentence; and (2) the delicate issues—individual philosophies and biases and their sentencing impact. Let's start with the crime—seemingly so obvious; surprisingly, so elusive.

In sentencing, a judge must, of course, understand the nature of the crime—not just its title but also its severity in the specific case. No two robberies are alike; no two rapes are the same. Premeditation, motivation, violence, terror, and trauma vary and should make a difference, often a big difference, in whether an offender goes to prison and for how long. How does a judge learn about the crime? Three ways:

1. Trials. In relatively few cases, defendants go to trial.[14] Victims and witnesses testify; sometimes the defendant does, too, thus providing the judge detailed accounts of the crime.

2. Presentence Reports. In some cases, most often serious ones in which defendants are facing years in prison, a judge may order a "presentence"—a written report, usually prepared by a probation/parole agent or court official, detailing the defendant's background, the crime, and the victim impact.

3. Guilty Pleas. In most cases, defendants plead guilty. In just a matter of minutes, in a plea "colloquy," the judge asks questions to determine whether a defendant's plea is informed and voluntary. Then, usually right after accepting a guilty plea, the judge conducts a brief sentencing hearing. The prosecutor and defense attorney offer their recommendations, the defendant speaks, and, in some cases, the victim and others might be in court to comment.[15]

Thus, in almost all criminal cases, defendants plead guilty, but in proceedings that reveal little about the crime. Could judges find out more? Yes. Without a trial or presentence report, could judges call upon defendants, victims, police, and other witnesses to fill out the picture? Yes. Do judges do so? Almost never. Why? Why wouldn't a judge take the time to learn more about the crime? Three reasons:

First, in big cities, judges have no time. Caseloads are so heavy that judges push guilty pleas and sentencings as fast as possible to preserve precious minutes for time-consuming motions and trials. On a typical day, I was presiding over one jury trial—a single case lasting several days, followed by a single sentencing. But each day of that trial, during brief breaks when the jury left the courtroom, my staff and I stayed. We stayed for defendants, attorneys, and witnesses waiting for me to conduct guilty pleas and sentencings. I would complete as many as possible before resuming the trial, but, in those proceedings, I had little time to elicit more than the minimal, legally required information.

Second, compounding the time crunch is a special disincentive to take the time: when judges ask questions about crimes, guilty pleas unravel. The more a defendant talks (and minimizes), the more likely the prosecution-defense détente dissolves. Their agreements—"plea bargains" by which defendants may gain sentencing benefits in exchange for guilty pleas—sometimes depend on "the less said the better." Indeed, conducting plea colloquies, few judges ever ask the two questions I believe are most important: "Are you pleading guilty because you really did the crime?" and "What did you do?"

Third, avoiding these two questions that can logjam the case flow, judges indulge an unconscionable legal fiction: the *Alford* plea—defendants *pleading guilty while maintaining innocence.* The term comes from *North Carolina v.*

Alford,[16] the appeal in which the US Supreme Court concluded that, in a capital case, a judge may accept a guilty plea from a defendant who maintains innocence.

This is complicated, but so important. To understand the *Alford* plea and feel its judicial rhythms, we stroll out on the courtroom dance floor for the "guilty plea two-step," the "six-step shuffle," and the "seven-step sashay."

First, the everyday favorite—the *guilty plea two-step*:

One. The defendant pleads guilty.

Two. The judge sentences the defendant, no doubt trying to be as fair as possible but within the limits of self-imposed ignorance—ignorance of the crime, the criminal, and the victim.

The judge never asks, "Are you pleading guilty because you really did the crime?" or "What did you do?" The judge does not delve. Instead, the judge relies on prosecutors and defense attorneys, who all know the tune. Together, they sing their song, their lyrics including a "stipulation"—a blink-and-you-miss-it summary of the crime to satisfy legal requirements. The judge sidesteps any questioning that might slow the music.

But what if a more conscientious judge asks the critical questions? Introducing . . . the *six-step shuffle*:

One. The defendant pleads guilty.

Two. The judge asks, "Are you pleading guilty because you really did the crime?" and "What did you do?"

Three. The defendant denies or minimizes the crime, using exculpatory words that do *not* admit criminal conduct.

Four. The judge, appropriately, addresses the defendant and counsel and reiterates that the defendant has the right to a trial and certainly should not plead guilty if innocent.

Five. The defense attorney replies that this is an *Alford* plea, allowing the defendant to claim innocence, concede the prosecution's evidence, and plead guilty to take advantage of a plea agreement that reduces the charges and/or the length of potential imprisonment.

Six. The judge, probing no deeper, joins the prosecutor and the defense attorney in the shuffle they all know so well. Together, they sing "guilty," and the judge closes with the sentencing coda.

This may be the dirtiest of the "justice" system's dirty secrets. Judges are fully complicit. They foster the *Alford* formula, which denies trials, declares defendants "guilty," and sentences them as they stand before the bench maintaining their innocence. And, to accomplish this, judges actively encourage *noncommunication* in court, protecting plea agreements from questions that could undo the deals—the very questions they need to ask to learn about the crime. What, instead, should a principled judge do? What do a few fine judges already do? And what must all judges already do in the few states that, by law, do indeed prohibit *Alford* pleas?[17]

They dance the *seven-step sashay*. Just repeat the six-step shuffle's first five steps, revise the sixth, and add a seventh step:

Six (revised). The judge responds by explaining that, in *Alford*, the Supreme Court allowed a defendant to plead guilty while maintaining his innocence, but in a *capital case*. Why? The defendant insisted on availing himself of the prosecutor's offer: plead guilty and accept life imprisonment rather than go to trial and risk execution. The judge explains that even if, in a capital case, one could justify such a legal sham, this *Alford* "reasoning" does not apply in a noncapital case.

Seven. The judge then allows a brief recess to give defendant and counsel time to consider their options. Shortly thereafter, one of three things occurs:

a. Most often (and frequently in cases before me), the defendant, having reconsidered, pleads guilty—no *Alford*—and admits committing the crime. The judge then is able to ask for details and, now more fully informed, to sentence more fairly.
b. The defendant, having reconsidered, pleads not guilty, goes to trial, and is convicted. The judge hears trial testimony and, now more fully informed, is able to sentence more fairly.
c. The defendant, having reconsidered, goes to trial and is found not guilty. The judge shudders, thinking of countless other judges who would have danced the six-step shuffle, accepted the *Alford* plea, and sentenced this acquitted defendant.

Yes, the seven-step sashay takes time, and, yes, bean counters berate judges who thus burden the system with backlogs. But what could be a more justifiable use of judicial time? If judges would shed the *Alford* sham, announce their revulsion, and declare "no more," they could rechoreograph these last steps. They would sleep better. "Justice" is in their job description.[18]

Sadly, there's more to this corrupting component. If judicial ignorance of the crime were not enough, ignorance of a sentence's actual impact should drain public trust from sentencing. So here's more bad news: most judges don't know what they're doing or, to be precise (we'll need to say this aloud, slowly), *most judges don't know what "what they're doing" actually does.*

Just ask a judge what, for example, "thirty years in prison" really means. Few know. Most do not know how the years recompute to dates of parole eligibility and mandatory release; they do not know how the years they order translate into years actually served.

Informally, I've surveyed prosecutors, defense attorneys, judges, and one more group—incarcerated criminals. Rarely will we find a judge who knows the state's formulas for parole eligibility and mandatory release. A few prosecutors and private defense attorneys know; many public defenders know; and, no surprise, imprisoned criminals can recite chapter and verse, at least to compute *their* parole eligibility and release dates.

Most judges, however, simply have no idea; often, their "guesstimates" are way off. Most are amazed by how little time may be served, even on a "tough" sentence. My point, however, is not that judges should be tougher or, for that matter, softer—just smarter.[19]

Thus, at the Judicial College, we attempted to break away from the conventional course in order to present a seminar to awaken, inform, and challenge judges to address issues of judicial *ignorance*, from the crime to the sentence computation, as well as issues of biases based in race, gender, philosophy, and other factors we'll consider in chapter 13.[20]

So how did we do? With provocative readings, dramatic presentations, and stimulating discussions, I facilitated our seminar for fifty judges. Howard Wingren and I thoroughly enjoyed the week, and we were not alone. Each day, judges gathered around me after class to continue the conversation, several saying the course was the most meaningful in the three-week curriculum. I was elated; Howard was delighted. Then, at week's end, we read the evaluations.

Apparently, the judges surrounding me after class were the only satisfied customers. Many written comments were critical, even harsh. Howard and I took the comments seriously, went back to our drawing board, and made modifications. We did not, however, abandon our premise—judges needed to look at their old approaches and at themselves and develop new sentencing strategies.

So what happened the next year? Pretty much the same—enthusiastic praise from about one-third of the judges, harsh criticism from many others. I'll always remember Howard's concluding advice: "When, after the first year, evaluations are bad, modify the course. When, after the second year, evaluations are bad, modify the evaluation form."

But we didn't do either. And while I continued to present many other seminars to genuinely appreciative judges, I never again taught sentencing. I did, however, further study the evaluations to try to make some sense of their divergent responses. What I found, I think, is important.

Who loved the course? New or less experienced judges, younger judges, female judges. Who hated it? Older, experienced judges, male judges. Why? Why would some judges, including those of the same demographic that embraced my child sexual abuse teaching, reject my sentencing course? The key: judges' perceptions of their very different needs for education on very different subjects. And in the angry comments of some evaluations I found clues to my own insensitivity—insensitivity to what, understandably, was some very thin skin and to what, understandably, may be the delicate judicial soul.

Consider the contrast. I had been warned that teaching courses on child sexual abuse and the treatment of young witnesses in court, and doing so in tandem with pediatricians and psychologists, would be a stretch. I was cautioned that such unconventional "touchy-feely stuff" on unsavory subjects might not work well for judges (many of whom, however earnest, were at conferences for a break from their daily grind). Still, I had been assured that a new approach to sentencing would be well received. So why the opposite?

On child sexual abuse, I was responding to a clearly perceived need. Judges, suddenly seeing abuse cases in court, needed help, and they knew it.[21] Regardless of age or experience, they sensed the gaps in their backgrounds; they welcomed instruction in pediatrics, psychology, and the courtroom treatment of young witnesses. They all were in the same boat, so they felt no shame in admitting their need for education in areas where they all were inexperienced—no resentment of outsiders who conveyed the comforting message: "Of course, this all is new . . . no one would have expected you to know what this class will be covering."

But sentencing was different, so different. What do judges, old and new, do every day? What is their most discretionary decision? What, other than the conventional course hypotheticals, would offer safe turf for teaching?

And how insensitive I was not to realize that, except for the least experienced judges, my "students" would hear an unspoken message: "You've sentenced many defendants. Unfortunately, you've done so without knowing what you've been doing—without understanding the crime, without rejecting *Alford* injustice, without even computing the years of your sentences. Fortunately, I'm here to save you so that, at long last, you can do justice. (And, oh yes, I'm sorry for all the injustice you've done to so many who were unlucky enough to be sentenced by you before you were lucky enough to learn from me.)"

I sentenced both Monica Migliorino Miller and Anthony McClain *after* many years on the bench, *after* sentencing thousands of defendants, *after* teaching sentencing for two years. Yet rereading my sentencing words and reflecting on both cases, I have misgivings about my efforts in both cases. Sentencing—so discretionary and safe from appellate reversal, often so uninformed, always so consequential and conclusive.

During my more than thirty years of judicial service and teaching, I watched America's judiciary change—from a dedicated but self-satisfied, lily-white group of good ol' boys to a more diverse, enlightened, and sensitive assemblage. While some old problems persist, and while new ones emerge, America's judges, now more than ever, constitute an enthusiastic student body, willing to question and ready to learn. Working with them has been among the most gratifying experiences of my life—a few bad apples, of course, but from Gala to Granny Smith, from Akane to Zestar, a delicious group.[22]

10

THE APPELLATE JUDGE

Death, and Three Widows

Wischer v. Mitsubishi Heavy Industries of America, Inc.

to consider soberly, and to decide impartially.

—Socrates[1]

On the sunny afternoon of July 14, 1999, after running lunch-hour errands in downtown Milwaukee, I was walking back to work. A few blocks from the Court of Appeals, I stopped for "Don't Walk" at a busy intersection next to a lot cleared for construction. Suddenly, a fierce wind threw me against the chain-link fence surrounding the site, causing me to grab and hold on while waiting for "Walk."

I thought nothing more of it until evening when I heard that three men had died that afternoon at another construction site a few miles away. They had fallen nearly three hundred feet in the steel "man basket" of a crane above Miller Park, the new $400 million baseball stadium, where they were among the hundreds of workers.

Ironworkers William DeGrave, Jerome Starr, and Jeffrey Wischer were to have bolted one of the stadium's retractable roof panels. Hanging high above the field, they were waiting for the massive panel being lifted by a second crane, "Big Blue," which, at 567 feet (about forty-five stories), was one of the world's tallest. But instead of bringing the panel to their skilled hands, Big Blue, blown by heavy wind, brought them down. Describing the ill-fated lift in his fine book chronicling the most significant cases of Robert Habush,[2] the lead lawyer for the widows, journalist Kurt Chandler wrote:

At 5:13 p.m., from out of nowhere, a sound like a crack of thunder ripped through the air. Workers on the ground scattered for cover. Pitching to the east, Big Blue's long boom suddenly buckled as a gust of wind caught its 450-ton load. The wind tugged at the boom until it crashed through the stadium

114

wall and tumbled like a broken toy to the stadium floor, its load a jumbled wreck.

On its descent, the boom sliced the cable that held the men's basket, sending the three ironworkers plummeting to the infield. As they fell, their screams could be heard by the crane operator . . . over their walkie-talkie radios . . . "get us out of here . . . get us out of here . . . get us out of here!"

A mass of steel, glass, and concrete was strewn across the floor of the unfinished stadium. Lying in the infield, entangled in cables and useless harnesses, were the mangled bodies of the three ironworkers.[3]

The lift never should have happened. That afternoon, sustained winds exceeded twenty miles per hour, with gusts near thirty. But the roof contractor, Mitsubishi Heavy Industries of America, pushed on, violating not only federal safety standards but the crane manufacturer's specifications as well. "The roof was over budget and months behind schedule," and this was the day before the governor was to visit the site. "Mitsubishi supervisors had little patience for delay and little concern for safety. The lift was set, a foregone decision, weather be damned."[4]

Three men died. Three women lost their husbands; six children lost their fathers.

Following fifteen months of trial preparations, six weeks of trial, and three days of deliberations, the jury unanimously found Mitsubishi 97 percent negligent (attributing the remaining 3 percent to the crane manufacturer). The jury awarded the widows $5.25 million for what, in legal terms, were the *compensatory* damages for their husbands' "pain and suffering" and their own "loss of companionship."

The jury also concluded that Mitsubishi had acted "in intentional disregard" of the ironworkers' rights to a safe workplace and, therefore, awarded their widows *punitive* damages.[5] How much? To set that sum, the jury was required to consider three factors: the "grievousness" or malice of Mitsubishi's conduct; the actual and potential damage flowing from Mitsubishi's conduct; and the financial capacity of Mitsubishi to pay.[6] The jury awarded punitive damages of $94 million, the largest jury judgment in state history.[7] Mitsubishi appealed, and, about a year later, a second downtown walk on a sunny day, this one with gentle breezes, came to have unexpected importance.

The appeal brought seven issues to our Court of Appeals. The primary one was whether the $94 million punitive damages award would stand. But, before examining the unusual and unfortunate developments behind the scenes of the appeal, we need to learn the legal and political background of that multimillion-dollar issue.

In the years before Big Blue's crash, many state legislatures had been caught up in battles over "tort reform"—new statutes intended to curtail lawsuits by imposing fixed limits on potential liability. Targeting lawsuits against doctors for malpractice and against manufacturers for unsafe products, such new statutes were generated by their insurers and lobbyists to disincentivize plaintiffs (and their lawyers) by "capping" the amounts that could be recovered. Different state legislatures reached different conclusions, resulting in what the US Supreme Court called "a patchwork of rules representing the diverse policy judgments of lawmakers in 50 states."[8]

Reviewing constitutional challenges to such statutes, I have come to have strong opinions about "tort reform." I believe that in some state legislatures and courtrooms honest and reasonable differences emerge but that, in others, intellectually dishonest political positions pose as legal "reasoning."[9] Here, however, to better understand how judges come to agree or disagree and make their decisions on such hot issues, we would do well to set aside legislative rhetoric and, instead, concentrate on the judicial evaluation of punitive damages, the barely understood and very significant subject underlying the tort reform controversies.

I shall focus on two cases in which judges analyzed punitive damages: *BMW of North America, Inc. v. Gore*, the US Supreme Court's most significant recent decision on punitives, about which I know nothing from behind closed doors; and *Wischer v. Mitsubishi*, the Court of Appeals case from which I shall reveal the disheartening developments from our chambers. But before wading deeper into either, and in order to tease out an intriguing aspect of *BMW* and discern the duplicity of *Wischer*, we must understand the distinct functions of compensatory and punitive damages in American law.

Seemingly simple terminology can be confusing. We begin with "damages" and its triple meaning. First, "damages" are what is suffered—a broken window, a broken arm, a botched operation, a ruined reputation, the reduced value of a VW designed to deceive fuel-efficiency testing. Second, "damages" are the consequential costs of these damages—the glazier's bill for window repair, the hospital charges and income losses resulting from the broken arm, the job loss linked to libel. Third, "damages" are the dollars juries or judges say offenders must pay victims for damages resulting from damages.

Yes, in legal terms, one suffers harm ("damages"), resulting in costs ("damages"), covered by court-ordered payment of dollars ("damages").

In all cases, these court-awarded damages are "compensatory"—money to pay victims for repairs, medical expenses, pain and suffering, income losses, and other consequences of property harm or personal injury. Compensatory damages do not exceed a person's actual losses (unless, in certain areas such as civil rights, a statute specifies that the damages must be doubled or tripled).[10] In cases involving lawsuits like those from the Miller Park tragedy, compensatory damages are enormous and, for all but insurance actuaries and trial jurors, incalculable. In such cases, insurance companies often settle, even paying their policies' full values because the damages from deaths easily exceed the maximum coverages.

In the rare case, the damages juries and judges award may be more than compensatory. They may be punitive—money ordered not to compensate victims for their losses but, rather, to pay them more in order to punish defendants for unconscionable conduct and, thus, "send a message" deterring others from such behavior.[11] Because punitive damages often reach millions of dollars beyond compensatory damages, they have been targeted by many tort-reforming legislators.[12]

Traditionally, punitive damages were unlimited, subject only to reduction at the discretion of the trial judge who, like the jury, knew the evidence and, by law, reviewed the "reasonableness" of a jury's verdict. Thus, traditionally, judges could reduce the punitive amounts juries awarded. But when tort-reforming legislators targeted punitives and, in some states, enacted "caps" limiting the awards,[13] they effectively usurped that judicial function, substituting their policy preferences for judicial case-by-case determinations.

But shouldn't legislators step in if they believe plaintiffs and their lawyers are winning unreasonable awards and that judges are not reducing them enough to protect doctors, manufacturers, and others? Who should decide how much is too much? And how would one measure that? Indeed, how much is too much?

In *BMW*, the Supreme Court answered. In a five-four decision, it reversed a $2 million punitive damages award against BMW in a case involving a bad paint job (there's more to the story, of course) but declined "to draw a bright line marking the limits of a constitutionally acceptable punitive damages award." Instead, the Supreme Court set a less definite standard, prohibiting a jury or judge from awarding punitive damages deemed "grossly excessive."[14]

BMW—a predictable, pro-business decision by the conservative majority of the narrowly divided Court? Not so fast. Justice Antonin Scalia, characterized by many as a conservative ideologue, dissented. He asserted that, historically, "it was well understood that punitive damages represent the assessment by the jury, as the voice of the community, of the measure of punishment the defendant deserved." Therefore, he maintained, the majority's decision, "though dressed up as a legal opinion, is really no more than a disagreement with the community's sense of indignation or outrage expressed in the punitive award."[15]

Justice Scalia may have been suggesting that, precisely because conservatism trusts the marketplace to regulate corporate conduct, jurors, as free-market consumers, should remain free, through their verdicts, to express the public's revulsion toward corporate misconduct. Thus, punitive damages verdicts should be untouched or, at most, modified—but only through "reasonableness" reviews traditionally performed by the trial judges who saw the evidence. Otherwise, Justice Scalia seemed to be saying, "Leave it alone," because a jury's punitive damages determination is an element of the free market's response, not to be altered by legislative fiat or appellate second-guessing.[16]

Justice Scalia's dissenting opinion in *BMW* becomes all the more interesting—and all the more confounding to conservatives who revered him and liberals who condemned him—when we consider the apparent alacrity with which he hurdled precedent. He cited two controlling cases the Supreme Court decided, in 1993 and 1994, conceded that their precedents countered his position, but then declared: "When, however, a constitutional doctrine adopted by the Court is not only mistaken but also insusceptible of principled application, I do not feel bound to give it *stare decisis* [binding precedential] effect—indeed, I do not feel justified in doing so."[17]

And if this was not curious enough, and as if to clarify that, at least on punitive damages, conservatives and liberals can be found where we would least expect them, who else dissented in *BMW*? None other than the Court's liberal leader, Ruth Bader Ginsburg.[18]

So let us indulge; this is, after all, a book about how judges really make their decisions. Having hiked this far off-trail, let's keep searching. Seeing Justice Scalia's dissenting opinion and its intersection with Justice Ginsburg's, let's ask whether friendships matter. Instead of imagining Tony and Ruth as strange bedfellows, ponder whether their operatic bonding helped them harmonize. In 2013, Nina Totenberg, National Public Radio's legal correspondent, reported that the day after the Supreme Court concluded its "epic term," Justice Scalia and Justice Ginsburg "met over a mutual love: opera."

> When it comes to constitutional interpretation, the conservative Scalia and the liberal Ginsburg are leaders of the court's two opposing wings. To make matters yet more interesting, the two have been friends for decades, since long before Scalia was named to the court by President Reagan and Ginsburg by President Clinton.
>
> Ginsburg likes Scalia because he makes her laugh; Scalia likes Ginsburg because she laughs at his jokes; and the two love to spar over ideas. What unites them, though, is opera.

Totenberg went on to report that their friendship and love of opera had become an opera, "Scalia/Ginsburg."[19]

But now, back to the main trail. Whatever their limits, punitive damages are rare. Under what circumstances would a judge be able to consider or allow a jury to consider awarding them? In short, *what would a plaintiff need to prove to justify punitive damages*? That, indeed, was the question facing us in *Wischer v. Mitsubishi*.

The state statute answers: "The plaintiff may receive punitive damages if evidence is submitted showing that the defendant acted maliciously toward the plaintiff or in an intentional disregard of the rights of the plaintiff."[20] But what does that mean? Months passed, briefs were filed; Judge Smith, Judge Michael Jones, and I prepared, conferring at length on this question and six other issues.

At oral argument, so many parties and attorneys would be involved that our courtroom could not accommodate them, the press, and the many spectators expected to overflow the gallery. We arranged to move the hearing to the huge, ceremonial courtroom of the county courthouse, six blocks away. Rather than scheduling the usual hour for oral argument, we set aside a full day.

Preparations were unusually demanding. After reading portions of the trial transcript, studying the many briefs, and trying to untangle the issues, we met weeks in advance to determine what, we believed, would be the best organization and allocation of time at oral argument.[21] We would welcome arguments on all seven issues, but we agreed on a procedural approach that would prove crucial.

We agreed that if Mitsubishi succeeded in its challenge to the punitives, we would reverse the judgment and order a new trial. True to the judicial principle of deciding no more than necessary to resolve an appeal, we also would address only those other issues requiring resolution to guide the trial judge in retrying the case. *If, however, Mitsubishi failed in its challenge to the punitive damages, we would uphold them and, in order to fully resolve the appeal, go on to address all the other six issues.*

Preparing for oral argument, we went on to briefly discuss our preliminary assessments and tentative conclusions. Tentative? Well, not exactly. Judge Smith told us that, on the primary issue, he had made up his mind. For him, it was easy. He deemed the punitives outrageous—grossly disproportionate to the compensatory damages and, therefore, in violation of the *BMW* standard. But Judge Jones and I viewed the issue differently. Less certain, we wanted the attorneys to address Judge Smith's concerns but, based on the briefs, believed the punitives were likely to survive. Thus, Judge Smith seemed certain he would be voting to reverse, while Judge Jones and I seemed likely to affirm unless Mitsubishi could prevail on another issue.

After more than six hours of arguments from several superb attorneys, we adjourned. Judge Smith left immediately. Judge Jones and I lingered, conferred

briefly, then walked together back to the Court of Appeals. Continuing our
conversation on this sunny-day stroll, we found ourselves in agreement; the
arguments had confirmed our tentative conclusion that the punitive damages
would stand. Thus, at least on the primary issue, we knew we would form the
majority.

On our walk, Judge Jones and I also discussed a few other issues. Again, we
agreed. And although we acknowledged that some of them would require
additional research, none seemed likely to require a new trial. We joked about
the months needed to prepare the decision . . . and about his dubious good
fortune—he would be pulling the authorship oar; in our rotation, he was next
up. Judge Jones and his clerk would be completing the research and writing;
I did not expect to see a draft for months.

Surprise! Two weeks later, Judge Jones's draft arrived. And a bigger surprise,
it addressed only one issue—punitive damages. And the biggest surprise, it
concluded that the punitives must be reversed. It reached that conclusion in
a few paragraphs, accepting the very theory Judge Jones and I had discussed
and easily dispatched. It was as if the briefs had never been read, the arguments never heard, the research never done, and the issue never discussed on
our walk back to the Court of Appeals.

So, of course, I went to see Judge Jones in his chambers. "What happened?"
I asked. I had my suspicions, but, with no hint of any change in the interven-
ing weeks, I inquired whether, perhaps, he or his clerk had discovered something we had missed. No, he explained, they had found nothing new—and,
he reassured me, *he had not changed his mind!*

Puzzled, I stammered, "Well, then, what . . . why . . . ?" He explained. No
matter what our decision, the losing party would appeal to the state supreme
court. No matter what we concluded, the "Supremes," as he called them,
would review our decision and address every issue. So why, Judge Jones asked,
should we delay their opportunity to do so? Why should he take the time to
research and write on six other issues when the supreme court's consideration
of the whole case could obviate the need to do so?

His questions, of course, had answers—familiar ones anchored in proper
appellate process and judicial integrity. Even assuming further consideration
by higher courts, we were, by oath and honor, obligated to provide our honest
legal analysis and decision. Indeed, whether affirmed or reversed, intermediate
appellate court opinions may be very helpful to and influential on supreme
court decisions.

While I would have been naïve to think that no other judge had ever so
pragmatically decided an appeal (and, not that it should matter, done so in a
case involving three deaths and millions of dollars), I can say that I never

encountered another judge willing to admit such duplicity. Perhaps I should not have been surprised. I had, after all, been working down the hall from Judge Jones for years. What had I seen?

This is difficult. To accurately describe what I witnessed is to risk readers' skepticism and understandable criticism. Might I be hiding some personal agenda? Is my account exaggerated? Am I unfairly sullying the reputation of a man no longer alive to respond? I concede such concerns but also appreciate that my failure to disclose would betray my mission. After all, this book is about America's judiciary, not an individual judge. While particularly egregious, Judge Jones's conduct in this appeal was not unique; similar underlying problems plague other courts.

"Achieving a sound understanding of judicial behavior," Judge Posner wrote, "is a key to legal reform."[22] To fail to offer this behind-the-bench account would be to conceal an all too common and particularly insidious corruption of judicial independence. Thus, as briefly as possible, I shall try to be candid . . . and respectful.

Judge Jones arrived at court bright and early almost every day. Dapper, cheerful, and consistently courteous, he was, in a pleasant sense, our "hail-fellow-well-met" presiding judge. Administratively able, he contributed to our court's efficiency in some respects and, in the area of municipal law, where he had substantial experience, provided valuable insight. Otherwise, he was problematic—the judge around whom we all had to adjust, law clerks writing his decisions, other judges compensating for his deficiencies. Part of the problem, apparently, was alcohol.

While Judge Jones was at his desk early each morning, he usually departed by about 11:00 a.m. (except for the few days each month we all met to review new cases or hear oral arguments). Then, most days, after returning about 2:00 p.m., he sat at his desk and, for the next few hours, with his chambers door wide open, and in full view of other judges, clerks, and staff, he played computer solitaire. Then, by about 4:00 p.m., he left for the day. In the morning, Judge Jones could meet and converse; in the afternoon, usually, he could not.

When a judge, even one of marginal legal competence, can make a good-faith effort and work well with colleagues, the court soldiers on, often with diligence and grace. But when a judge's deficiencies are complicated by substance abuse, the appellate family may become dysfunctional. In most if not all states, statutes and ethics codes address such difficulties and provide for intervention. In Wisconsin, for example, a statute defines judicial "misconduct" to include "[h]abitual intemperance, due to consumption of intoxicating beverages . . . which interferes with the proper performance of judicial duties,"[23] and the Code of Judicial Conduct provides: "A judge having personal knowledge that another judge has committed a violation of this chapter that raises a substantial question as to the other judge's fitness for office shall inform the appropriate authority. 'Appropriate authority' means the chief judge of an offending judge's district, the director of state courts, the judicial commission, and the office of lawyer regulation."[24]

Although, as I explained in the introduction, I am in unusual circumstances that allow me to share information from behind the scenes, I still am statutorily precluded from divulging any efforts I may have made or any intervention based on such efforts to address any judge's misconduct.[25] Here, however, I hope it helpful to explain that (1) state judiciaries offer confidential resources to respond to such problems, and (2) neither rehabilitative response nor disciplinary intervention is easy, certain, or necessarily successful.

So what happened in *Wischer v. Mitsubishi*? Judge Jones wrote the majority opinion, in which Judge Smith joined. I dissented and, in my opinion, could not reveal that, in fact, Judge Jones agreed with me. Instead, I tried to calmly capture the issue in words signaling our state supreme court to reverse the majority's decision and reinstate the $94 million judgment.[26]

The Wisconsin Supreme Court, tracking my dissent, reversed. I say this not to gloat but rather to emphasize that the legal issue was clear, the proper decision of the "Supremes" virtually certain. Proof of punitives did not require evidence to prove the impossible—that Mitsubishi "intended to cause harm or injury." Proof required only that Mitsubishi's *actions* were "intentional" and in "disregard of the rights" of the ironworkers to a safe workplace. That undisputed legal standard fit the facts exactly.

Thus, the state supreme court confirmed my dissenting view. But then, in an ironic twist, the supreme court bowed out. Instead of addressing the remaining six issues, it remanded them to us (and Judge Jones's authorship) for resolution. Finally—call it bitter irony or poetic justice—after many months passed and Judge Jones finally completed his draft of what was to have become our seven-issue majority opinion, but just before our decision was released, the parties settled. Why?

> "I couldn't take the risk of an unfriendly court of appeals finding some [other] ruling of error [by the trial judge]," says Habush. "So before the appeals court got the chance to take another shot at me, I agreed finally to settle the case." Mitsubishi and its insurance carriers agreed to pay significant additional damages that, when combined with the earlier settlements of $27 million, brought the total monies recovered closer to the jury's verdict. The three widows approved the settlement without hesitation.[27]

"Closer," but how close to the jury's verdict? I don't know; the financial terms of the settlement remain confidential. But doing the math, guided by Habush's words accounting for "the earlier settlements," we may assume that the settlement must have subtracted at least $30 million from the $94 million to bring the final award "closer to the jury's verdict." Thus, Judge Jones's corrupted conduct—whether caused by liquor, laziness, or both—may have cost each widow at least $10 million.

What might we learn from Judge Jones? What might we learn from my colleagues' and my inability to cope with his problems? I offer a few thoughts that may be helpful.

I think it important to understand the intractability of such problems. An appellate court combines individuals, sometimes friends but more often strangers or mere acquaintances, who did not pick one another. Chosen through appointment or election, at different times for different reasons, they come together to address complicated and often emotional issues. They encounter relationship-building pains and pleasures found in many workplaces.

At best, an appellate court offers an atmosphere of intellectual engagement and genuine friendship, somewhat akin to that of a small, fine faculty. At worst, an appellate court intensifies personal, petty, and political differences, thus gutting collegiality that otherwise could have cultivated healthy relationships and sound decisions. Friendships form, enmities develop, alliances ebb and flow. Usually, at least, professional courtesy continues to lubricate the process and the work gets done.

In some appellate courts I've come to know through my teaching, the atmosphere is ideal. Judges, often of diverse backgrounds, and regardless of what may be their limited collaborative experience, listen carefully to one another. Rather than crossing arms over chests and declaring positions at the first opportunity, they find fascination in their differences, try to understand one another, and search for areas of agreement even as they define points of division. They work enthusiastically; they argue often but respectfully; they smile, laugh, and care about one another as well as the people they serve.

In other appellate courts, the atmosphere is dismal. Suffering a variety of afflictions—laziness, nastiness, pettiness, selfishness—judges bring heavy baggage. Add substance abuse, emotional disturbance, or mental illness and the resulting tensions drain both personal pleasure and professional quality from the appellate process.

For earnest, mentally healthy judges, it ain't easy. They can't leave. They can't fire colleagues or force them to find help. They can't breach confidentiality, going to the press or the voters. They can't count on private professional intervention or discipline. So sometimes, instead, they accommodate—circumventing the problems, organizing hours around a judge's illness, doing that judge's work, correcting the most serious errors. Thus, sadly, conscientious judges can become exhausted enablers.

And, in an additional problem peculiar to the appellate process, judges have few alternatives. Because each case is decided by a "panel"—usually three judges—they all share responsibility and must "sign off" before issuing a decision. But what happens when two judges, having received a draft from an ill or incompetent colleague, agree that it is so deficient—not minor matters easily corrected but substantial portions needing complete rewriting—as to be professionally deplorable and legally misleading?

Judge Smith advised me, "It's not *your* case . . . just hold your nose and sign off." But how could I? On what basis would any judge not consider each case *our* case? We—all three—were identified as the deciding judges on the first page of each decision. Authorship assignment to one judge in no way reduces another judge's decision-making responsibility. "But Charlie, it's just the wording," Judge Jones once protested when I declined to approve his draft. But *the wording* was all we had; words, "the right ones in the right order," were our only stock in trade, our only means to guide the bench and bar and, perhaps, as Tom Stoppard wrote, "nudge the world a little" toward justice.[28]

It ain't easy. Throughout my appellate years, several excellent colleagues added invaluable qualities to our efforts. But a few others, in my view, whether due to substance abuse or political ambition or other corrupting factors we will discuss, subtracted so much. I made the mistake of trying to "fix" them or help them with their problems—problems the severity of which I did not initially understand; problems I had little ability to solve and no authority to correct.

Judge Posner wrote, "The interactions between the judge and his colleagues would be an important focus of study . . . a judge's performance can be decisively affected by his colleagues."[29] I agree. From the experiences of my twelve years on the Court of Appeals, I came to see appellate courts less as public bodies and more as private families. I learned that all appellate judges need collaborative communication skills but that all too few are likely to have them; that some are crippled by mental illness or corrupted by substance abuse; that appellate courts can become fatally dysfunctional families.[30]

My consolations were many. Intellectual stimulation was strong, legal challenges profound; the relationships with law clerks and staff were delightful, and the many times my colleagues and I worked well together were wonderful. The opportunities to contribute to lasting law and the many "make a difference" moments remain among the most cherished of my life.

But the damages . . . damages . . . damages . . . my life . . . my wife . . . my children . . . family and friends . . . three widows, and so many more.

II

The Trial Judge
Religion, and White Supremacists

State v. Hollin Lange and Patrick O'Malley

[A judge must be] perfectly and completely independent, with nothing
to influence or control him but God and his conscience.

—Chief Justice John Marshall[1]

"Utterly preposterous"—Assistant District Attorney Norman Gahn used these
words to describe the strange tale Patrick O'Malley had told police. This was
Gahn's opening statement, and it was unusual. In fact, from bomb-sniffing
dogs to police perjury, this trial of a white supremacist would involve little
that wasn't unusual . . . perhaps even the corrupting "influence or control"
of God.

Typically, in an opening statement, a prosecutor, speaking directly to the
jury, offers a summary of the government's evidence. Why? Why not just get
right to it? Call your witnesses; present your evidence. Anticipating such feelings, a good prosecutor employs the opening statement to explain that testimony, witness by witness, and evidence, piece by piece, can be confusing out
of context. A good prosecutor explains that just as the jigsaw puzzle box cover
presents a complete picture to aid in assembling the pieces, an opening statement conveys context to help jurors understand the piecemeal evidence.

Rarely, however, in an opening statement, does a good prosecutor talk
about the defendant's account, preposterous or otherwise. Doing so can cause
strategic problems. Doing so can shift the jury's focus from the government's
evidence, which the prosecutor knows, to what trial attorneys term the "theory of defense," about which the prosecutor can only speculate. Recounting
Mr. O'Malley's statement to police could risk altering the jurors' perspective
on the puzzle box's cover as the government would want them to see it.

Moreover, by forecasting the defense theory in his opening statement,
Gahn gave O'Malley the chance to shift his strategy, adjust his testimony, and

reconsider whether to testify at all. These are choices a defendant and defense counsel can continue to calibrate *after* the prosecutor's opening statement and even *after* the prosecutor's presentation of all the government's evidence.

And these are not the only potential problems a prosecutor invites by referring to a defendant's theory in an opening statement. Legal problems also are possible, some even jeopardizing the integrity of a trial or its outcome on appeal. That is because such an opening statement might seem to be suggesting that the defense should present evidence. But so what? The defense will be doing so, right? Surely, the defendant will be giving "his side of the story."

That, of course, is what the public assumes and the jurors expect. But that is not the law. In every criminal jury trial and in every state, with only minor variations in the verbiage, the judge instructs the jurors: "The defendant need not testify. If the defendant does not do so, you must not speculate as to what the testimony would have been or hold that silence against the defendant in any way. The defendant need not prove innocence; the prosecution has the burden of proof. The defendant is presumed innocent, and you must find the defendant 'not guilty' unless the evidence proves guilt beyond a reasonable doubt."

Thus, for a prosecutor to suggest otherwise at any point in the trial could, in appellate terms, "unlawfully shift the burden of proof" to the defendant and, therefore, "improperly undermine the presumption of innocence." Accordingly, in a prosecutor's opening statement, any indication of the defendant's theory—any words that would imply a defendant's obligation to testify or offer evidence—invites an objection, takes the trial toward a mistrial, or risks reversal of a conviction on appeal.

So why, in his opening statement, would Gahn run any such risks by recounting O'Malley's statements to police? Inexperience? Hardly. A blunder? No. Norman Gahn was a seasoned prosecutor and one of the best trial attorneys among the hundreds who practiced before me. His style was so sublime, in fact, that in trial advocacy courses, I offered him as the model to counter a common misconception among many students—that, like on TV, trial attorneys must be bombastic or dramatic. Norman Gahn was calm. While others raised their voices, he captivated with whispers. While others worked to find *the* way to try cases, Gahn found *his* way—his own honest voice tailoring techniques for each case; his own tempered tone, creating hear-a-pin-drop moments.

So when, in his opening statement, Gahn declared O'Malley's account "utterly preposterous," he did so carefully. He did so standing still, facing the jury from behind a podium, speaking softly and all the more dramatically for his apparent lack of dramatic flair. Still, why would he run risks by referring to O'Malley's "utterly preposterous" account?

Patrick O'Malley and his friend, Hollin Lange, were "skinheads"—self-proclaimed members of one of America's many white supremacist groups.[2] Teenagers, still in their swastika-strutting infancy, they had not yet covered their bodies with racist tattoos. They and other skinheads had come together to live in an old two-story home in a working-class neighborhood on Milwaukee's "South Side." They also were drawing interest from others, including more affluent "North Side" residents and the police.

On a summer night, five students from north suburban Whitefish Bay High School (coincidentally, my alma mater), decided to drive by the skinheads' home. According to their trial testimony, they either wanted to provoke these "prejudiced guys" or "just wanted to see what they looked like." But they did more than drive by. First passing slowly, then driving away, they returned and tossed empty juice bottles at the house "because," one testified, "we thought it might scare" them.[3] They did not know that Mr. O'Malley and Mr. Lange were "sitting look-out" from a second-story window, barricaded by water barrels and armed with rifles. When O'Malley and Lange saw the bottles thrown, they opened fire, wounding two of the students, one seriously.[4]

Questioned by police, O'Malley and Lange claimed self-defense. Preposterous. They said they fired because they feared for their lives. Preposterous. They said they believed the juice bottles were firebombs. Preposterous. They said they believed they might be firebombed because of earlier altercations with Hispanic gang members, including one in which their home was fired upon and Lange was wounded. Preposterous. And they said they were armed and on guard because the police department's gang squad had warned them to be ready that very night for a possible attack.[5] Utterly preposterous!

So at Patrick O'Malley's trial (the defendants were tried separately), Norman Gahn, certain that he would be calling police to testify—to relate O'Malley's claims—knew that *the prosecution*'s evidence would include O'Malley's "preposterous" excuse for firing at the car.[6] Thus, anticipating that the jurors might doubt an apparently unprovoked ambush and concerned that any such doubts might ripen into "reasonable doubt," Gahn decided to inform the jury of the "preposterous" motive O'Malley had claimed. Therefore, in his opening statement, Gahn took the unusual step of framing his case by laying out not only the prosecution's evidence but also the defendant's explanation, thus exposing O'Malley's paranoia and preempting his "preposterous" claims.

But Gahn's clear forecast was clouded. A week later, in closing argument, he retreated from "utterly preposterous" to "legally unsupportable." He had little choice. To his surprise and to the amazement of judge, jury, and everyone else in the courtroom, the "preposterous" proved to be true.

Initially, police officers testified as expected. Yes, they explained, after their arrests, O'Malley and Lange told them that because they believed they were being firebombed, they fired in self-defense. Yes, O'Malley and Lange claimed they believed so because of warnings from police. And yes, the officers testified, such claims were untrue. But then what happened?

During a brief recess in O'Malley's trial, an officer who already had testified informed our bailiffs that he needed to see me immediately. I assumed his urgency related to courtroom security, perhaps a bomb threat or a problem with the metal detector at the courtroom door. I brought the officer and the attorneys into chambers.

Guilt-ridden, the officer told us he was among the police who had obtained evidence of an intended attack on the skinhead home. He was one of the officers who had indeed urged vigilance, warning O'Malley and Lange to protect against a firebombing. Thus, while the bombs proved to be empty juice bottles, the skinheads' split-second surmise was anything but preposterous. Therefore, O'Malley's trial testimony, reiterating his claim to police, was within the arguable range of "feared for my life" self-defense that could have led to acquittal.

Thus, in closing argument, Norman Gahn adjusted his words. Conceding that O'Malley was "fearful and apprehensive" following weeks of harassment and recent police warnings, Gahn argued that the skinheads still had no right to "excise a little part of Milwaukee . . . and declare it a combat zone."[7] Then, a week later, at Lange's trial, now knowing the police confirmation of the defense testimony that was coming, Gahn adjusted his strategy right from the start. He conceded the defendant's understandable "paranoia" but maintained that Lange, like O'Malley, went too far; that their rifled response was too extreme to be "legally supportable."

The juries agreed, convicting each defendant of five felonies: injury by conduct regardless of life, for shooting the most seriously injured student, and four counts of endangering safety by conduct regardless of life, for shooting at the others. Although editorial writers called for me to be "more stern than merciful" and deliver a "stiff judgment,"[8] I concluded that the threats and police warnings were mitigating factors; that the defendants were, as I phrased it at sentencing, "a nuance away from acquittal." Thus, while each defendant faced a maximum of thirty years, I sentenced O'Malley to ten years in prison and Lange to eighteen months in jail and five years' probation.[9]

For me, O'Malley's trial trumped all others in exposing the gap between reasonable expectations and real evidence, between public impressions and juror perceptions. But that gap remained hidden from view beyond the courtroom. The shocking revelation—the veracity of the self-defense evidence that converted certain guilt to possible acquittal—never reached the public, despite daily press coverage.[10]

Often I've been asked for my opinion about a prominent trial. I answer by emphasizing that, not having been in court to hear testimony and see evidence, I'm unable to judge. While many, I'm sure, believe such replies to be diplomatic deflections, they are not. Truly, they reflect in-court experiences and the resulting understanding of how often the "preposterous" proves to be true.

All the more important, therefore, that judges admonish jurors to concentrate on the evidence, unswayed "by sympathy, prejudice or passion." All the more important that judges implore jurors to deliberate by listening to one another and by considering their different interpretations of evidence. And all the more meaningful that judges, jurors, and trial observers—and, for that matter, everyone, whether inside or outside a courtroom—discover the distance between assumptions and facts. Indeed, research shows, the *certainty* of assumptions and beliefs does not necessarily correlate with the *accuracy* of one's conclusions.[11]

Moreover, given America's not-always-so-strict separation of church and state, we would do well to consider another area of, well, we might call it, "dubious certainty." Steeped in religious beliefs, our nation has rendered so-help-me-God courtrooms historically housed in Judeo-Christian values. How important, therefore, to consider the influence of religion on how America's judges really make their decisions. The skinheads caused me to do so.

At their first appearance, O'Malley and Lange asked me to recuse. One of their attorneys, embarrassed (he once had been my student intern and had become a good friend), asked me to step aside because skinheads were anti-Semitic and I, in his words, was "of Jewish persuasion." I denied his motion, noting, perhaps puckishly, that his client couldn't avoid "us"—Jews served throughout all levels of our courts.[12] I regret not thinking of the clever words I would have preferred: "Correction. I am of Jewish *religion* but Constitutional *persuasion.*"

Clever, perhaps, but true? What might be the unlawful impact of religion on judicial decisions? The obvious, of course, is obvious—decisions based on religious beliefs, not law—from refusals, contrary to state law, to even consider death penalties, to denials, contrary to *Obergefell*, of marriage licenses to same-sex couples.[13] But what about the less obvious, the more subtle, and the apparently lawful? After all, an attorney might answer a client's who's-the-judge question with cautious responses such as "Well, he's a devout Catholic," or "Keep in mind, she's a born-again." But why might that matter?

On two occasions—once during my judicial career and, more recently, at a synagogue's "Hot Topics" series—I was asked to speak on the impact of Jewish values on judging. Other than those engagements, and except for cases in which recusal requests came my way (the only other one involved a member of the Posse Comitatus, another white supremacist group), I do not recall religion, Judaism or otherwise, even being mentioned in connection with my work.

But was it a factor? Were the skinheads onto something? Might we find clues in their perception, whatever its perverse source, that being of Jewish "persuasion" might be persuasive? After all, ancient rabbinical practices set our legal template for precedential decision-making; Talmudic principles underlie much of American law. And in case anyone hasn't noticed, Jews heavily populate America's legal profession, law school faculties, and judiciaries.

Neo-Nazis notice. In recent years, white supremacist recruitment and fundraising have been boosted not only by the election of America's first African American president (and his successor) but also by the composition of the US Supreme Court. In the many years preceding Justice Scalia's death, in 2016, the Court evolved from an all-male membership of nine "WASPs" to a racially diverse, gender-mixed membership of six Catholics and three Jews.

Well, then, what might have been the Jewish values factoring in my decisions? At first, I might say "none." Not only am I of Constitutional persuasion, but I never was religiously observant. Forced to suffer through Sunday school, I watched the clock, the minutes moving so slowly, as I awaited release to the bus *delivering* me—taking me home to *my* televised religious observance: the Green Bay Packers. St. Vincent Lombardi ministered my formative years; I worshipped a green and gold winner. Indeed, learning later that the Packers of tiny Green Bay were the world's only publicly owned, nonprofit professional team, I deemed them noble, their success, *miraculous*.

For spiritual inspiration, starting at age nine, I also took to heart the words of my camp director, Lou Ehrenreich (son of the camp founder, a rabbi). "G-O-D," he said, stood for "Great Out Doors." I still feel awkward sitting in a synagogue, unable to understand the Hebrew prayers or recite the English translations with belief or devotion. And yet, a few years ago, my G-O-D confession of paganism only prefaced what I offered as a guest speaker to synagogue congregants expecting, perhaps hoping, to hear of Jewish-judicial connections.

Thus, as I explained, my "Jewish persuasion" proceeded from an indelible memory. In the mid-sixties, sitting in the synagogue my family had attended for generations, I was listening to Rabbi Dudley Weinberg delivering a sermon. He spoke of the open-housing demonstrations in Milwaukee being led by a Catholic priest, James Groppi. He voiced support for Father Groppi's courageous efforts to remove legal and social barriers to tenancy and home ownership for blacks in white neighborhoods. Fist clenched, walking all the way "downstage" where he seemed so near, where he seemed to be glaring at us all and speaking directly to me, Rabbi Weinberg challenged us: "March with Father Groppi . . . you are not a Jew unless you care about civil rights!"[14]

Emotionally full and intellectually powerful, Rabbi Weinberg could "bring it." In fact, I don't think Rabbi Weinberg was capable of *not* bringing it. Bombastic Baptist preachers would have been proud. I was, too. Whatever my religious reticence, I was awed by his intellect, compassion, social consciousness, and dramatic flair.

For me, Rabbi Weinberg and his political activism sealed the deal. Whatever my misgivings, whatever my liturgical ignorance, whatever my deistic doubts, I knew I was a Jew. I realize that, from an early age, embedded in my social consciousness was an excruciatingly painful empathy for others—friends and foes, family and strangers—for anyone, anywhere, suffering pain, poverty, sadness, unfairness. And with that came an insatiable desire to do justice.

Only many years after failing to pay attention in Sunday school do I remember meeting Deuteronomy 16:20, "Justice, justice you shall pursue." And only many years later did I attach added significance to its charge—not to attain but to "pursue." And finally, only in writing this chapter have I recognized what was there for me to see years ago. Without knowing my own connection to Deuteronomy's command, I had been closing keynote addresses with the words, "And if there be a judgment day, the question will be not, 'What did you achieve?' but, rather, 'What did you attempt?'"

Thus, for the synagogue's "Hot Topics" audience, searching for Jewish values that infused my judicial decision-making, I started with Judaism's commitment to social action and advocacy for all those denied justice. I then expanded the list of what I considered the Jewish values that had become components of my judicial consciousness.

Scholarship: I liked that we were "people of the book." Anything but anti-intellectual, Jews seemed to have the curiosity to be continuously searching for questions and answers, guidance and inspiration.

History: I loved our love of history—our own, certainly, but also histories of other peoples and religions, all of which Jews seemed to truly respect. And I was proud of the rabbinical decision-making method at the foundation of American law's allegiance to precedent . . . to *tradition*!

Courage: I aspired to show the stiff-necked determination of my ancestors and children—my grandfather's stowed-away escape from Latvia, in flight from the czar's conscripted service; one son's invocation of that legend when explaining his decision to pursue rabbinical studies in Jerusalem just as an intifada brought bus bombings to the sacred city; the other son's leadership of his high school's LGBT advocacy during times when such efforts incurred risks.

Holocaust heritage: Deep inside, I always felt an unspeakable sadness and suffering. Often, I still lie awake, haunted by early morning images of children and families dragged from their homes, marched into boxcars and gas chambers. For all Jews and others who had been and would be persecuted, I vowed, "Never again!"

Humility and humor: I reached for both, though with limited success. In judicial opinions, I quoted not only law but Twain, Lily Tomlin, and Dr. Seuss. Teaching judges, I sometimes invoked appellate words but often quoted the sign that sat beside the radio in the shoe store where my mother and I shopped: "We're sorry if you have to wait, but when we get to you, you'll get the right fit, too." That radio was broadcasting, and I was looking at that sign, just as we were shopping, minutes after noon, on November 22, 1963.

Integrity: In the Yiddish tradition, my definition was anecdotal . . . just a little story. A member of the British Parliament, interviewed by NPR following Watergate, was asked whether corrupt conduct as serious as Nixon's could ever occur in British government. "Absolutely not," he answered. Asked why, he became flustered, tongue-tied. Exasperated and still stammering, he finally exclaimed, "Well . . . it's . . . *just* . . . *not* . . . *done!*"

Thus, it seems my judicial philosophy came to be infused with these "Jewish" values, all nurturing a sixth sense of what's "just not done"—and what *must be done*. In the words of poet Ruth Brin, it seems many Jews strive to be a courageous people "who continuously file a dissenting report based on the assumption of faith" and who, in the words of Deuteronomy 16:18, try to judge "with righteous justice."[15]

Other faiths, of course, also foster many of these and equally virtuous values. And others, not just white supremacists, may worry about the persuasions of judges of various religious beliefs.[16] Here, however, we are not examining the merits of any particular religion but, instead, asking whether having a religious (or nonreligious) background gives one beliefs and biases that influence judicial decision-making. I can answer only for myself, and only tentatively. Do white supremacists have anything to fear from a Jewish judge driven by desire for "righteous justice"? Would O'Malley and Lange have received different treatment from a judge of a different religion (or no religion at all)?

I do not know, but I ask . . . and I suggest that, in our not-so-strictly church/ state separated society, these questions deserve our attention as we consider the complicated judicial mix—independence, and the religious beliefs that may be unavoidable, may be valuable, may be corrupting.

12

THE APPELLATE JUDGE

Politics, "Out on the Point"

State v. L. C. Clay

He appointed judges in the land . . . and he said to them: "Take care what you do, for you are judging, not on behalf of man, but on behalf of the Lord; he judges with you. And now, let the fear of the Lord be upon you. Act carefully, for with the Lord, our God, there is no injustice, no partiality, no bribe-taking."

—Second Book of Chronicles, 19:5–7

"It's . . . just . . . not . . . done!"—words from an exasperated member of Parliament trying to explain why Watergate corruption could not occur in Great Britain. While we may not know whether the MP's assessment of Britain was naïve, we must concede that conventional "corruption"—bribery, kickbacks, electoral fraud—has a home in America's judicial heritage.

From nineteenth-century legends of Judge Roy Bean and his "Law West of the Pecos"[1] to twentieth-century convictions of Chicago's "Greylords," more than a few American magistrates have lawlessly lined their pockets. Moreover, for those who might make light of fixed parking tickets, the record is clear: throughout our history, some judges have profiteered by altering outcomes in serious cases. And despite long prison sentences for such criminal conduct, judicial corruption continues.[2]

Indeed, it is the twenty-first century that may have given America its most shameful judicial corruption—Pennsylvania's "kids for cash" kickbacks. According to Marsha Levick, deputy director of the Juvenile Law Center in Philadelphia, it was "the most egregious abuse of power in the history of the American legal system" and "the most serious judicial scandal in the history of the United States."[3]

In 2010–11, Wilkes-Barre judges Mark Ciavarella and Michael Conahan were prosecuted for accepting $2.6 million from a real estate developer and an

133

attorney who was a co-owner of two juvenile detention centers. To earn their payoffs, the judges not only contracted with the centers but also filled them, ordering harsh sentences for first offenders and many others whose delinquencies amounted to little more than minor mischief.[4]

In separate trial and guilty-plea proceedings, Judges Ciavarella and Conahan were variously convicted of federal felonies commonly known as mail fraud, money laundering, tax evasion, and racketeering; they were sentenced to twenty-eight and seventeen years, respectively. In related proceedings, the Pennsylvania Supreme Court, concluding that the two judges had violated the civil rights of thousands of juveniles, overturned countless convictions.[5]

But no need to pick on Pennsylvania.[6] My more immediate experience with electorally motivated corruption came closer to home—from the squeaky-clean land of La Follette, behind the chamber doors of the Wisconsin Court of Appeals. No money changed hands, but electoral ambitions altered an outcome, thus denying a rapist the new trial the law required.

For the six months before his capture, twenty-year-old L. C. Clay terrorized a Milwaukee neighborhood with armed robberies and rapes. Most notoriously, he abducted and brutalized a nurse, thus becoming the "St. Joseph's Hospital Rapist." A jury convicted him of many crimes, including nine armed robberies and five sexual assaults. Mr. Clay appealed, bringing four issues to Judge Michael Jones, Judge William Miller, and me. I well remember our reaction. Taking no pleasure in "letting the bad guy go," we were dismayed to discover that one of Clay's claims was solid, requiring reversal of all convictions and a new trial.

While Clay's crimes were brutal, his successful claim was somewhat subtle. Our decision might have been in doubt but for the fact that, just three years earlier, the state supreme court had decided the same issue, thus setting the precedent requiring reversal.[7]

Clay's trial illuminates our trail in two ways. First, further highlighting the "who decides" question, it focuses not on designation of the judge but, rather, selection of the jury. Second, it exposes unlawful conduct by two appellate judges who "sold" their votes—not to a third party for money but, rather, to each other for electoral gain. Let us look at both the law of jury selection and the judicial corruption that denied Clay the process he was due.

THE LAW: SELECTING THE JURY

Selecting a jury in a state court, the judge briefly and the attorneys extensively question prospective jurors in order to choose twelve.[8] More precisely, however, and in a process few outside the courtroom ever see, the judge and attorneys do not "select" twelve jurors so much as they "unselect" others. The procedures vary somewhat in civil and criminal cases, and also from state to state and even county to county, but, with Clay's case as our example, here's how a jury is selected:

Jury duty: Drawn from computer-generated lists of voters or licensed drivers, citizens are summoned to the courthouse, where, for each case, twenty-five are randomly designated as *prospective* jurors. The prospectives are sworn to truthfully answer questions the judge, prosecutor, and defense attorney ask to learn about their backgrounds and whether, for any reason, they would not be suitable jurors for that case.

"For Cause" disqualification: Responding to those questions, prospectives may reveal information disqualifying them "for cause"—an indisputable reason such as a personal relationship with a party or witness, or perhaps a hearing impairment or a religious belief that would preclude service.[9]

"Peremptory" disqualification: Following "for cause" disqualifications (usually only a few), the remaining prospectives (at least twenty) compose the group from which the prosecutor and defense attorney "unselect." Taking turns, each confidentially (their choices known only to each other and the judge) designates four prospectives for "peremptory" disqualification, thus reducing the twenty prospectives to a jury of twelve.[10] Absent unusual circumstances, the attorneys need not give any reason for their designations; they may simply "strike" prospectives on the basis of answers to the questions or their "gut sense" of the jurors they choose to exclude.

But what happens if the attorneys and judge disagree about "for cause" disqualifications? What happens if, for example, (a) the defense attorney believes a prospective should be disqualified and, therefore, moves to strike that prospective for cause; (b) the prosecutor disagrees and, therefore, objects to the defense attorney's motion; and (c) the judge agrees with the prosecutor and, therefore, denies the defense attorney's motion to disqualify that prospective juror? And what if the judge's ruling was wrong? That's what happened at the jury selection for L. C. Clay.

Early in jury selection, the prosecutor asked whether any prospective juror had experienced anything that would "impact in any way" the ability "to be fair and impartial." One man answered that his daughter recently had been sexually assaulted; he feared the experience could affect his consideration of the case. Prudently, so as not to embarrass him or discuss the matter in a way that might influence other prospectives, the judge brought the man and the attorneys into chambers for further questioning.

The prospective juror explained that his daughter had been sexually assaulted by boys who broke into her college dormitory. Consequently, his family had incurred "thousands of dollars for psychiatric treatment" and, he said, "anything

I hear of a person being assaulted, my feelings go toward that person." He continued: "[W]hen the [St. Joseph's Hospital] incident first happened I read about it in the paper. And my feeling went for the victim . . . it just really hit a real tender spot in my heart for the victim. . . . I would say I would rule that [the defendant] would have to do the time."

Additional questions exposed the prospective's leanings. Even after hearing the attorneys' and judge's explanations of the presumption of innocence and burden of proof, he responded, "I would say you [defense attorney] would have to change my mind. The evidence that you would have to present would have to be concrete that he didn't do it." He also commented, "I would say he would have to prove his innocence. I mean that's the way I feel." Then, still in chambers, came these exchanges:

DEFENSE ATTORNEY: Let me ask you this. Do you—you told me that you don't think it's fair that somebody with your mind-set is sitting on a jury where a person is charged with sexual assault, is that right? That would not be fair to him, is that correct?

PROSPECTIVE JUROR: It might not be fair to him.

DEFENSE ATTORNEY: All right. If we're trying to . . . have fairness in this particular trial, would you agree with me that somebody with your mind-set shouldn't be standing in judgment of a person charged with sexual assault if we're trying to be fair?

PROSPECTIVE JUROR: Well I would say yes. I don't think I would make a good juror for him.

DEFENSE ATTORNEY: All right. Knowing how you feel . . . knowing that you feel that in effect you can't be fair, do you think it's right that you should be standing—that you should be passing judgment on him?

PROSPECTIVE JUROR: No, not at this point.

And notwithstanding explanations about a defendant's right *not* to testify, the prospective said he would hold such a choice against Clay.

DEFENSE ATTORNEY: [T]he judge is also going to tell you that my client doesn't have to testify in this case, okay. He's going to say the law says he doesn't have to testify.

PROSPECTIVE JUROR: Okay.

DEFENSE ATTORNEY: Not only the law says he doesn't have to testify but the law says if we chose to do this we could literally sit on our hands and not do anything. I'm talking about the defense.

PROSPECTIVE JUROR: Uh-huh.

DEFENSE ATTORNEY: If we chose not to do that and in other words we chose not to have my client testify and we chose not to put on evidence, do you think that you would hold that against him? Do you think that that would be indication of guilt to you?

PROSPECTIVE JUROR: I would think so.

DEFENSE ATTORNEY: Even though the judge would instruct you that you can't assume guilt from [the] defendant not testifying?

PROSPECTIVE JUROR: Well I say like I said before, he had to prove to me that he wasn't involved in it. That's—that's my feelings. . . .

DEFENSE ATTORNEY: Do you still—would you still require the defense to come forward and prove that he's innocent?

PROSPECTIVE JUROR: No. If the State can't prove he's guilty, you don't have to do anything. Same thing the judge said. If he can't prove anything, he's guilty. State doesn't have to do anything. . . . I'm just speaking my personal feelings toward sexual assaults.

The defense attorney then moved "for cause" to disqualify this prospective. The prosecutor objected.[11] The judge, perhaps revealing possible bias or, at least, inattentiveness to the chambers exchanges, denied the defense request with these marginally coherent words: "I've heard what he said. I've heard the question. I've heard the argument and the court believes that this juror's answer to the question—questions to the extent which would indicate to the court that he would, regardless of his personal feelings, I think he can separate those feelings and be fair and impartial based upon the representations that were made to the court's questions so far as the burden of proof, the responsibility of following the instructions of the court so the court's not going to strike this juror for cause."

Thus, did this prospective become a member of the jury? No. But why? At the next stage of jury selection, the defense attorney used one of his four "peremptory strikes" to remove him. But had the judge ruled correctly, the prospective already would have been disqualified "for cause" and defense counsel would not have needed one of his four peremptories to strike him from the jury. Then defense counsel, like the prosecutor, still would have been able to remove four others.

Such an error, the state supreme court had ruled, required fresh jury selection and a new trial.[12] And in faithfulness to that binding precedent, Judge Jones, Judge Miller, and I, at our review of the month's appeals, concluded that we must reverse Clay's convictions and order a new trial. In the rotation of writing assignments, the decision would be authored by Judge Miller.

THE JUDICIAL CORRUPTION

What then occurred can be understood only with knowledge of the next judicial elections, less than one year away. Judge Miller, a longtime incumbent on the Court of Appeals, was facing a challenge from a politically powerful trial judge; I was running in a primary for an open seat on the state supreme court; and, unbeknownst to me, Judge Jones was planning to enter that same supreme court race.

A few weeks after we met and decided to order a new trial for Clay, I was called to Judge Miller's chambers, where I found my two colleagues having just concluded a meeting on the case. I was surprised, of course, that they had discussed the case in my absence, and even more surprised when Judge Jones informed me that they had decided to affirm the convictions. I asked whether they had found something in the trial transcripts or case law to counter our earlier assessment. They seemed upset by the question; neither offered any explanation.

Within the next few days, I was surprised again—this time learning that authorship had been transferred from Judge Miller to Judge Jones. (In my years on the appellate court, I never had seen a reassignment of authorship unless, of course, in the preparation of an opinion, a judge discovered the need to recuse, or a legal basis for moving from a majority to a dissenting position.) Why? Two law clerks answered. In my contemporaneous confidential notes, I wrote:

> Judge Miller's law clerk informed me that the re-assignment had taken place because Judge Miller had said that although he would "go along" with Judge Jones, he could not, "in good conscience," write the majority opinion. Pressed for further explanation, Judge Miller's law clerk informed me that Judge Jones had convinced Judge Miller to change the decision for two reasons: 1) that Judge Miller, facing a campaign for re-election . . . could not afford to be a judge who reversed the conviction of the St. Joseph's Hospital rapist; and 2) that I, in the . . . supreme court race, could be isolated as the one dissenting judge who had voted to reverse.

Later, I received confirmation. Judge Jones's clerk told me that Judge Jones had told him that, by managing the case this way, he (Judge Jones) and Judge Miller could put me politically "out on the point." Indeed, they could. "An incumbent judge's decisions in criminal cases are easy targets for his opponents in the next election cycle, who can use almost any decision favorable to a criminal defendant, no matter how legally defensible, as grounds for portraying the incumbent as 'soft on crime.'"[13]

What was I to do? What should a judge do in such circumstances? What, ethically, must a judge do (and what must a judge not do) when confronted with such certain, unethical conduct by colleagues? I considered several options: trying to persuade my colleagues to do the right thing; threatening them with exposure of their misconduct; leaking or reporting their misconduct to the attorneys, the press, the chief justice, or the Judicial Commission. I felt conflicted or blocked—by law, confidentiality rules, ethical codes, and relationships with colleagues with whom I would be considering countless other cases.

Searching for an answer, I studied the Code of Judicial Conduct. Confidentially, I sought advice from Frank Tuerkheimer, a professor at the University of Wisconsin Law School and a former Watergate prosecutor, whom I knew as a friend, teacher, and legal ethics scholar. Months later, after further research and reflection, and in a manner consistent with Tuerkheimer's guidance, I reached a conclusion. (Once again, however, I am statutorily precluded from disclosing any action, inaction, or response.)[14]

But while I was agonizing over what to do, the Court of Appeals affirmed Clay's convictions, Judge Jones writing the decision and Judge Miller, "in good conscience," doing nothing more than lending his name and vote to form the majority. I dissented.[15]

But now, once more, the plot thickens. By remarkable coincidence, within the year following our decision *but shortly after the judicial elections*, the identical jury selection issue again came to Judge Jones, Judge Miller, and me, this time in the case of Edward Ramos, convicted of the first-degree murder of his girlfriend's two-year-old child. In Mr. Ramos's appeal, we reached the same conclusion we had initially reached when reviewing Clay's appeal—the conviction must be reversed; a new trial must be ordered.

Coincidentally, Judge Miller again was tabbed to write our decision. This time he did so . . . in his final days on the appellate bench. Judge Miller had lost his re-election bid. Just before leaving office, he authored our decision ordering a new trial for Ramos. Concluding a fifty-year judicial career, Judge Miller decided his last appellate case in "good conscience."[16]

13

INDIGESTION

Food, Mood, and More

Any attempt to account for all the criteria factoring into judicial decision-making, and any effort to discuss all the possible corruptions of judicial independence, would be futile. Both the criteria and the corruptions may be as many and diverse as the cases, their issues, and the judges deciding them. Instead, through intimate accounts of compelling cases, I have tried to feature factors, often overlooked, to expose how judges really make their decisions. Now let us consider others, including race and gender, which also may be among the most important.

FOODS AND MOODS

First . . . back to basketball. I played during lunch hours, then showered, grabbed an apple, and threw on a robe. My staff joked that if I played poorly, no defendant should be sentenced that afternoon, but if I hit the game-winner, felons would walk free. As Judge Posner warns, "Beware the happy or the angry judge!"[1]

Cute . . . but true? Apparently so. Research suggests that it is not only the winning basket or lunch-hour apple that moves the judicial mood but breakfast and snacks as well. Consider "how food-breaks sway the decisions of judges."

> There's an old trope that says justice is "what the judge ate for breakfast[."]
> It was coined by Jerome Frank, himself a judge, and it's a powerful symbol of
> the *legal realism* movement. This school holds that the law, being a human
> concoction, is subject to the same foibles, biases, and imperfections that affect
> everything humans do. We'd love to believe that a judge's rulings are solely
> based on rational decisions and written laws. In reality, they can be influenced
> by irrelevant things like their moods and, as Frank suggested, their breakfasts.[2]

Professor Shai Danziger, of Ben-Gurion University, in Israel, studied more than one thousand parole hearings and decisions by eight judges and correlated them with the judges' workday segments: before and after morning snacks; before and after lunch. Accounting for many variables, merit-based and otherwise (from the seriousness of the crime to the gender of the parole applicant), the research revealed an unmistakable digestive determinant—a prisoner's chance for parole dropped from 65 percent after the judges ate to near zero by the end of their sessions. A good lawyer may help, but to really enhance the chance for parole, go before a nourished judge.[3]

Still, not all judges would agree, at least not completely. Alex Kozinski, formerly a federal appeals court judge, wrote: "[I]f you accept that what a judge has for breakfast affects his decisions that day, judges should be encouraged to have a consistent diet. . . . I am here to tell you that this is all horse manure. And, like all horse manure, it contains little seeds of truth from which tiny birds can take intellectual nourishment."[4]

Brains and Biases

In this era of rapidly advancing brain science and social psychology research,[5] we now can peel previously untouched layers of the judicial onion to uncover biases, subtle but sometimes decisive. No judge is immune. Take me, for example.

Not a racially biased bone in my body? Let's see. I was a teenage civil rights activist. High school officials removed me from the National Honor Society for founding the Student Committee for Education on Race Relations. At Dartmouth, I taught "Social Action in Lily-White Suburbia: White to White."[6] Throughout my career, African Americans have been among my close colleagues. For many years, Spanish language and Hispanic cultures have been among my passions. Good friends have come in all colors.

But when, in 2009, I started teaching "Brains and Biases—Yesterday and Today" at judicial conferences[7] and when, in doing so, I introduced judges to "implicit bias" self-tests,[8] I also took the test . . . and found racial bias in my own psyche. As Charles M. Blow has written, "Basically, our brains have a mind of their own."[9]

This is not to suggest that an "unbiased" upbringing or lifetime has no effect or that the degree of bias may not vary over time. As Nicholas Kristof has pointed out, "Deep friendships, especially romantic relationships with someone of another race . . . seem to mute bias . . . 'If you actually have friendships across race lines, you probably have fewer biases[.]' . . . 'These are learned, so they can be unlearned.'"[10] And this, of course, holds hope for judicial educational efforts to reduce improperly biased decision-making.

Some biases may be brutal; while others may seem relatively benign, they also influence decision-making, albeit in subtle and surprising ways.[11] Moreover, "[d]ecades of cognitive bias research demonstrate[] that both unconscious and conscious biases lead to *discriminatory actions, even when an individual does not want to discriminate.*"[12]

Thus, biases may be broad and diverse. Without elevating one bias over others, it is fair to say that race is particularly potent. Kristof wrote: "The human brain seems to be wired so that it categorizes people by race in the first one-fifth of a second after seeing a face. Brain scans show that even when people are told to sort people by gender, the brain still groups people by race."[13]

Yet gender, of course, also can influence judging, and powerfully so. To elaborate may seem to belabor the obvious, but unrecognized dynamics may be emerging from recent research. Consider, for example, federal judges' decisions in cases of sex discrimination.

> Surveying sex-discrimination suits resolved by panels of judges in federal circuit courts between 1995 and 2002, [researchers] examined whether male and female judges rule alike, and whether the presence of a woman on a panel affects the behavior of her male colleagues. Here's what they found: male judges were 10 percent more likely to rule against alleged sex-discrimination victims, and male judges were "significantly more likely" to rule in their favor if a woman judge was on the panel.
>
> Because [they] were only studying sex-discrimination cases, it's unclear whether their data would hold true in cases where gender was beside the point. Still, [it's] intriguing that male judges rule differently when they're sharing the bench with a woman: it suggests female moral reasoning—if such a thing exists—might be contagious.[14]

The notion of a "feminine jurisprudence," distinct and significant, builds on the work of psychologist Carol Gilligan, whose book *In a Different Voice* maintained that women's moral reasoning is different from men's: "Men, the theory goes, prefer their law with rigid rules, clear lines and neutral principles; women prefer to look at the totality of the circumstances and favor what Gilligan calls an 'ethic of care' over an 'ethic of rights.' So, for example, feminists argue that [Justice Sandra Day] O'Connor's preference for flexible standards regarding abortion . . . reflect a softer, more 'relational' approach to the law, while Justice Antonin Scalia's emphasis on unchanging rules and crisp legal principles is, fundamentally, a guy thing."[15]

Feminists, male and female, find themselves divided. "What best serves the cause of gender equity?" they might ask. Would they want women on the bench who decide cases "just like men?" Or would they prefer women with a distinct decision-making approach?

Such questions may return us to the logic/compassion dilemma. Mixing in gender, however, further complicates an already complicated debate, with judges taking sides less predictably than one might suppose. On our appellate court, for example, we all seemed legalistic and logical, but where that mold did not hold, I was the one more inclined to consider a case's sentimental swirls while a female colleague, ruling against women, children, and other seemingly sympathetic parties, proudly proclaimed, "Too bad, so sad."

Presumably, all agree that the race or gender of a judge should not determine a decision. But, digging deeper, we might consider another possibility: what many term "biases"—race, gender, and at least some other apparently "improper" factors—can convey important insights: "We all view reality from our own peculiar perspective; we all have biases, interests, leanings, instincts. These are important. Frequently, something will bother you about a case that you can't quite put into words. . . . It is important to follow those instincts . . . they can lead to a crucial issue that turns out to make a difference." Such instincts are what many might term "intuition," which, according to Posner, "is best understood as a capability for reaching down into a subconscious repository of knowledge acquired from one's education and particularly one's experiences."[16] Trusting those intuitive instincts may be particularly valuable on appellate courts if the judges, with collegial interaction, welcome the possibility that their "biases" can combine to broaden their views and enhance their judgments.

Identifying and acknowledging one's biases and reaching for the collegial interaction that may follow is not easy. After all, judges are likely to maintain that they are "unbiased," as they understand that term. "Studies show that people tend not to regard themselves as biased and report that they are less biased than others."[17] That's human nature, and, indeed, judges have added incentives to deem themselves pure. Posner asks, "What weight should we give to the fact that many, maybe most, judges would . . . deny that they bring preconceptions to their cases?" He answers, "Very little," and explains: "That denial would reflect in some instances a lack of self-awareness and in others the rhetorical pull, or more bluntly the propaganda value, of the legalist model of judging. Judges want to deny the role of subjectivity. . . . They want to convince people that they wear blinders that keep them from straying off the beaten path. . . . They also want to duck blame for unpopular decisions ('the law made me do it')."[18]

A growing number of judges, however, some assisted by brain science seminars, acknowledge their biases. Many still maintain, however, that they are able to set them aside in order to judge impartially. Can they? Implicit bias tests should soften their certainty. Further, fairness may be compromised not only by unconscious or unacknowledged biases but also by unrealistic confidence in one's ability to avoid their impact.

Sometimes, judicial bias is purely personal, ebbing and flowing emotionally from what may seem the simplest of circumstances—for example, having a daughter. Consider the newfound feminism of a former chief justice.

It was, Justice Ruth Bader Ginsburg later said, "such a delightful surprise."

In a 2003 Supreme Court opinion, Chief Justice William H. Rehnquist suddenly turned into a feminist, denouncing "stereotypes about women's domestic roles."

Justice Ginsburg said the chief justice's "life experience" had played a part in the shift. One of his daughters was a recently divorced mother with a demanding job.

Justice Ginsburg's explanation . . . , though widely accepted, was but informed speculation. Now there is data to go with the intuition.

It turns out that judges with daughters are more likely to vote in favor of women's rights than ones with only sons. The effect, a new study found, is most pronounced among male judges appointed by Republican presidents, like Chief Justice Rehnquist. . . .

In the 2003 decision that so delighted Justice Ginsburg, . . . the Supreme Court considered whether workers could sue state employers for violating a federal law that allowed time off for family emergencies. Chief Justice Rehnquist, who had long championed states' rights, had not been expected to be sympathetic to the idea.

Instead, he wrote the majority opinion sustaining the law. It was, he said, meant to address "the pervasive sex-role stereotype that caring for family members is women's work."

Chief Justice Rehnquist was 78 when he wrote that. . . . In the term he wrote the opinion, he sometimes left work early to pick up his granddaughters from school.[19]

Thus, bias, often so bitter, also may sweetly season the judicial recipe. Now let's peel the next layer off the onion.

PERSONALITIES AND PROFILES

Mystified, people peer into our courtrooms and wonder, "Who *are* those guys and gals" up there on that big bench? Who indeed—patient or abrupt, kind

or harsh, flexible or rigid, industrious or lazy? What personality cloaks that
trial judge looking out on us in open court? What mood envelopes that appellate judge behind closed doors, looking not at us but at judicial peers? And
in that appellate setting, do tempers flare and insults fly? Does collegiality
collapse as judges themselves wonder, "Who *are* these guys and gals?"

Trying to answer, judicial educators have recognized that decision-making,
both trial and appellate, filters through diverse personalities and communication styles. Only in recent years, however, and only in some states, has judicial
education engaged judges to better understand themselves and the impact of
their diverse personalities on their decision-making.

In open court, a trial judge may confront a difficult attorney, lose patience
with a confused witness, or recoil in reaction to traumatic testimony. In chambers, an appellate judge may encounter an obstinate colleague who refuses
to listen, reason, or even discuss a case. But what might develop if, instead of
assuming that others' rough edges were the cause of such friction (although
indeed sometimes they are), judges pondered whether, possibly, the conflicts
came from stylistic differences; whether misunderstandings flowed from
unavoidable personality variables?

Still frustrating, yes; still challenging, of course. But by shifting one's immediate assessment from "bad" to "different," from "wrong" to "interesting,"
judges might give themselves opportunities to better understand themselves,
their colleagues, and the issues they must decide. "[A]ssume positive intent,"
David Brooks counsels. "When in the midst of some conflict, start with the
belief that others are well intentioned. It makes it easier to absorb information from people you'd rather not listen to."[20] And here's the bonus: judges
who follow Brooks's advice find their days less fractious, their work more
fulfilling.

Holding up psychological mirrors for judges is not easy. Judicial educators
use various approaches. Some start the discussion by employing psychological measurements, the oldest, best known, and most popular of which still
may be the Myers-Briggs Type Indicator (MBTI).[21] Other educators may refer
judges to self-help resources, such as the Enneagram,[22] or guide them to confidential, therapeutic support available through state judicial departments and
bar associations.

"Too touchy," judges protested when such initiatives came to judicial
education curricula a generation ago. Since then, however, judges in continuing education programs have become more open, welcoming opportunities to
examine themselves in order to help themselves judge others. Many have come
to accept that even the "'rule of law' often allows for a range of proper answers,"

many of which are "informed" by myriad factors that form personalities.[23] Geyh wrote:

> [W]hen the "correct" answer is unclear, judges must look beyond "law," nar-
> rowly defined, to decide which answer among plausible alternatives is right or
> best. That calls upon judges to make a kind of policy choice that can be
> informed by the judge's upbringing, education, religious convictions, philo-
> sophical perspectives, emotions, and experience (including experience arising
> out of the judge's socioeconomic status, race, and gender). Far from a bad
> thing, exercising judgment and discretion within the boundaries of applicable
> law to the end of achieving results the judge deems best may be the very defini-
> tion of justice.[24]

One need not agree with Geyh, embrace Myers-Briggs, or even endorse innovative education. But to understand how America's judges really make their decisions, one must acknowledge that, in many cases, decisions not only turn on facts and law but spin through complex communication styles and very different personalities.

FRIENDSHIP—GETTING BY WITH A LITTLE HELP . . .

How *independent* is independent decision-making? What about thinking aloud . . . bouncing it off . . . running it by . . . talking it through . . . venting, or seriously conferring with a friend, a relative, or another judge?

I first considered this early in my judicial career at a superb seminar designed by Professor Saul Tauster, of Brandeis University. Judges, with their spouses, explored the ethical and emotional implications of conferring—with each other and with others—about pending cases. Judicial ethics codes left doubt, seminar participants described different practices, and the state's current and recently retired chief justices offered their own opposite opinions. Thus, the judges gained guidance but came to conclusions no more certain than "it depends."

It depends? One would expect, I think, that on an issue as narrow as whether judges may confer with others on pending cases, ethical guidance would be clear. After all, doesn't this go directly to *independent* decision-making? But standards vary from state to state, and practices differ drastically from one judge to the next.

Some judges are absolute. Relying on their interpretation of ethical standards, they never talk with anyone (other than law clerks and appellate colleagues assigned to the same case) about any case. Others seem casual, if not

careless. Relying on their honest readings of these same standards (or on lazi-ness, garrulousness, or need for legal help), they confer. And between these extremes, we see the full spectrum.

Even when disciplinary boards and state supreme courts confront cases of alleged misconduct, the judges judging the judges may disagree. Consider an actual case. An experienced judge had a close friend who was a respected law professor. She asked him for help analyzing dispositive motions in civil cases. She believed that his involvement was permissible. The professor had no per-sonal knowledge of the parties or personal stake in the cases; his only motive was to help the judge. For three years, the professor not only conferred with the judge but actually drafted her decisions in dozens of cases. And from all anyone could tell, the professor's input enhanced the analyses.

The state's judicial ethics code stated: "A judge should not permit pri-vate . . . communications designed to influence his or her decision."[25] The code also set an exception allowing a judge to "consult with other judges or with court personnel whose function is to aid the judge in carrying out the judge's adjudicative responsibilities."[26] (Clearly, therefore, while prohibiting private communication, the code allowed trial judges to rely on law clerks and appellate judges to confer with colleagues assigned to the same case.)

The code also specified: "A judge may obtain the advice of a disinterested expert on the law applicable to a proceeding before the judge if the judge gives notice to the parties of the person consulted and the substance of the advice and affords the parties reasonable opportunity to respond."[27] This judge, however, failed to provide such notice; the parties had no opportunity to respond.

The State Judicial Commission concluded that the judge had willfully vio-lated the code; it recommended that she be suspended for six months. In the appellate reviews that followed, court of appeals judges divided two-one, and supreme court justices divided five-two, differing on whether the judge's con-duct was improper. Ultimately, the judge was not suspended but was publicly reprimanded.[28]

This case presents not only an interesting ethical issue but also another encounter with our old friend "Who decides?" To be impartial, must a trial judge decide alone? Is merely conferring with another person a corrupting invasion of independence? And within these questions we find one more: How does an independent judge most effectively gather information, deliber-ate and decide, and, at the same time, preserve the appearance of fairness?

It depends—and it's not always clear. In this case, the supreme court dis-senters declared: "[T]he question is: where are the lines drawn? Who can be a law clerk/intern? What are the parameters of utilization?" They presented nine sets of questions exposing practical problems of implementation and enforcement and concluded, "The questions posed, and not answered by any rule, regulation, or guideline, leave all judges . . . in a legal and ethical quandary."[29]

And yet we find far less "ethical quandary" in the obvious misconduct committed by many judges every day—in their consultations with spouses and other judges. My wife is a psychotherapist who, for years, specialized in marital and family therapy. Should I, while serving in juvenile court, have shielded myself from her opinions or restricted our conversations to the theoretical? And what about other judges? Particularly during my first weeks in each new assignment or when considering what, for me, was an unfamiliar area of law, should I have shielded myself from their thoughts?

Many judges maintain that accommodation is possible. They believe they may "confer" with one another but without reference to a specific case, phrasing questions hypothetically. Still, others argue, such an approach is awkward and pretextual—and prohibited. Reasonable judges, it seems, may reasonably disagree.[30]

More than fifty codes and countless approaches continue to yield "it depends." The most interesting result may be how these questions expose delicate dilemmas. If law requires judges to avoid "thinking aloud," "bouncing it off," "talking it through," venting or conferring with spouses, what are the costs—to thoughtful decision-making *and* to fulfilling marriages? To be impartial, must judges impose isolation on themselves and their colleagues? To ensure independence, must judges accept their own analytical limitations—limitations that could have been overcome with a little help from their friends?

SHOW-OFF RAPISTS—STRESS, BURNOUT, COMPASSION FATIGUE, AND ERROR

On a thank-goodness-it's-Friday afternoon, a young woman left her suburban office and drove downtown to meet friends at a restaurant. Still during daylight, and in the city's statistically safest area, she parked in a shopping mall garage. Exiting her car, she was accosted by a man and a boy, twenty-eight and fourteen, who wrestled her into their car and drove off. For the next seven hours, they sexually assaulted her in ways almost unimaginable.

But they weren't done. In the early morning hours, just before tavern closing time, they drove from bar to bar, coaxed the last customers outside, and opened the trunk to display their bloodied, naked trophy. Then they drove off and dumped her. Media named them "the show-off rapists."

Somehow, she survived. Supported by family, sexual assault counselors, college health services, and courage, she testified at two trials. Perhaps most remarkable, she asked for the chance, right after sentencing, to meet her fourteen-year-old attacker in jail to tell him the impact of his attack. Asking for that opportunity, which I granted, she explained that while she held no hope for the older assailant, she believed that, at fourteen, the younger one might be salvageable. She hoped her words would help.

Weeks before that sentencing day, in the motions before trial, the prosecutor and the defense attorney had informed me that the assaults were so horrific that I should review the details to determine what should be excluded from evidence. They actually agreed—agreed that certain descriptions and photos should be excluded not because they were legally inadmissible but, rather, because they were so horribly graphic that some jurors, unable to stomach the facts, might become ill or so upset that they would be unable to continue, thus resulting in a mistrial.

So together, the attorneys and I dissected the evidence. Despite years as a prosecutor and judge, after working with hundreds of battered women, and even after watching the autopsy of a woman I tried to protect, I never had been so immersed in such gruesome details of an assault. In the weeks and months that followed, while flashbacked images distracted me, I felt fine. I was functioning normally, both at work and home . . . but with one exception. From the day I reviewed the evidence, and for the following six months, I was impotent. I could neither touch nor be touched by Karen without flashbacks filling my mind and consuming my mood.

Sharing these experiences in "Healing the Healers," programs Karen and I facilitated for social workers and police officers, nurses and doctors, lawyers and judges, we relieved our listeners' tension with gentle touches of levity. But, dead seriously, Karen explained the dynamics of posttraumatic stress disorder and distinguished PTSD, stress, burnout, and compassion fatigue.[31] I then asked: "If, at trial, months after the fact, distant from the scene, protected by bailiffs beneath bright lights, I—not the victim, not the victim's parent, not the first responder or investigating officer, not the victim's social worker or counselor or advocate—if I, a prepared professional, suffered a psycho-physio-sexual reaction lasting six months, what might you expect . . . and what should you accept in your own reactions to your work with sexual assault victims?"

These "pin-drop" moments were revelatory and often tearful. Karen and I heard exhalations from many and watched relieved expressions from some who seemed to say, "So it's normal; it's not just me." We stayed after each session to console a few, understanding these dedicated men and women who, for many different reasons, had committed themselves to these heartbreaking careers. In what became our most fulfilling professional collaboration, we helped them gain the knowledge they needed to continue their work, or to recognize why and when to modify or conclude their careers.

Judges were not immune. Though relatively removed from the scenes and victims, many were deeply touched; some were haunted. For years, such trauma, certainly in judicial circles, went unacknowledged or denied; stress, burnout, compassion fatigue, and PTSD remained undifferentiated and untreated. We've come a long way. Still, while in recent years much has been studied and written, and while some judges have been helped, such progress does not really reach our immediate question: How does secondary trauma—whether resulting in stress, burnout, compassion fatigue, or PTSD—affect judicial decision-making? Consider America's immigration courts, where judges see asylum seekers who fear life-threatening persecution if ordered back to their countries of origin.

> Surging caseloads and a chronic lack of resources to handle them are taking a toll . . . leaving [immigration judges] frustrated and demoralized, a new study has found.
>
> . . . The survey found that the strain on them was similar to that on prison wardens and hospital physicians, groups shown in comparable studies to experience exceptionally high stress.
>
> . . . [R]eport[ing] anonymously, the judges spoke of an overwhelming volume of cases with insufficient time for careful review, a shortage of law clerks and language interpreters, and failing computers. . . .
>
> . . . In 2006, [the United States Attorney General] reported serious problems with overload *and flawed rulings*.[32]

And, as reported seven years later: "Experts say the conditions that immigration judges work under—fast paced, high pressure and culturally charged—make some *misjudgments all but inevitable*."[33]

While again our attention is drawn to grossly insufficient resources, here, most critically, we consider the connections among (1) the gravity of asylum or deportation; (2) the loss of bare-minimum minutes to decide; (3) the resulting "flawed rulings" and "misjudgments"; and (4) the physical, psychological, and emotional exhaustion and demoralization of judges. And stepping from federal immigration courts to state courts, we must remember the judges who, every day, absorb the conflict from our civil courts, feel deeply for the children in our juvenile and family courts, and meet the show-off rapists in our criminal courts.

Judges, whether calling out through journalistic accounts from federal immigration courts or through my accounts from state courts, are not bellyaching about too much work. They are describing the *impossibility* of doing what the people have hired judges to do. They are imploring us to learn why and to see the consequences—for those abroad, improperly deported; for those at home, horribly harmed.

Our judges are not complaining of their own pain. Professionally proud, most suck it up and suppress their suffering. But knowing of the emotional impact they feel is part of understanding how they judge—impartiality eroded by emotion, independence corrupted by secondary trauma. Thus, how incomplete it would be to describe decision-making without recalling the show-off rapists, recounting my reaction, and relating the agony of other judges behind the bench.

Judges, Posner explained, experience "the natural anxiety that decent people feel when they find themselves exercising power over other people and therefore want very much to think that their exercise of that power is just."[34] Judging, therefore, under ideal circumstances, is difficult; judging life and death issues is excruciating. Judging with depleted resources, real and emotional, is self-destructive and dangerous for all. The resulting inevitability of injustice is, for judges and all those they serve, devastating beyond words—beyond all the words shouted here, on this midnight ride sounding the alarm.

And now, Mr. Revere, if things weren't bad enough . . .

Part Three

VANISHING INDEPENDENCE

14

JUDICIAL CAMPAIGNS
Declarations and Contributions

Chapter 12 described how, for electoral gain, two of my colleagues denied a rapist the new trial they knew the law required. Less blatantly but far more prevalently, how do electoral ambitions corrupt judicial decision-making? We now consider the two most serious sources of such corruption—campaign declarations and campaign contributions. We ask whether, in light of four recent Supreme Court decisions, America's elected judiciaries can ever be independent.

DECLARATIONS

When I first ran for judicial office, I could say nothing about actual cases coming before me and almost nothing about issues likely to arrive. The Wisconsin Code of Judicial Conduct stated:

> A judge who is a candidate for judicial office shall not make or permit others to make in his or her behalf promises or suggestions of conduct in office which appeal to the cupidity or partisanship of the electing or appointing power. A judge shall not do or permit others to do in his or her behalf anything which would commit the judge or appear to commit the judge in advance with respect to any particular case or controversy or which suggests that, if elected or chosen, the judge would administer his or her office with partiality, bias or favor.[1]

Twenty years later, altering settled laws and traditional practices, the Supreme Court changed the rules. Today, almost no holds are barred—a judicial candidate can address any issue, pandering at will, sometimes surrendering even the pretense of independence. What happened? To see, please join me on the judicial campaign trail.

Like many judges, I came to the bench by a chain reaction of vacancies and appointments. A state supreme court justice retired, the governor appointed a trial judge to fill the vacancy, and I applied to fill the resulting trial court vacancy. The governor's staff interviewed applicants, reviewed references, and narrowed the field. The bar association's "merit selection panel" then screened the finalists and forwarded five to the governor, who appointed me in June 1982. I took office a few weeks later, and, as required by state law, faced election the following April. So I started campaigning right away, trying to pre-empt opposition. No such luck; I drew an opponent.

Campaigning was exhausting. Following full days on the bench, I ate drive-through dinners on the way to civic gatherings—a wonderful world of union and political party meetings tucked inside the assembly halls of bowling alleys and old taverns.[2] I enjoyed it, my candidacy allowing entry to members-only meetings with people and problems outside my experience. Best of all, on Friday nights, I raced from church to church, greeting voters at fish-fry dinners where I handed out thousands of small calendars containing my brief bio and, more important, the upcoming season schedule for the pennant-winning Milwaukee Brewers.

But what I did not do was state my opinions—on abortion, or gun control, or school choice, or any other issue. Our state code of judicial ethics prohibited me from doing so. And although, as I've mentioned, state judicial ethics codes came in many varieties, on this point they were consistent.[3] In fact, every night as I campaigned, I found that the voters, except for a few, politely accepted my silence; they seemed to have been civically schooled to understand that *judicial* candidates could not comment.

Indeed, voters seemed to believe that such silence was golden, essential to the preservation of judicial independence.[4] Moreover, their belief was widely shared by judges, regardless of political philosophy. Consider the rationale for campaign silence as expressed by two eminent jurists at opposite ends of the political spectrum—federal appeals court Judge Diane S. Sykes and Supreme Court Justice Ruth Bader Ginsburg. Relating the rationale "deeply rooted in our history," Judge Sykes wrote:

> [O]ne of the most important qualities we look for in a judge is the mental discipline to avoid prejudging a case or legal issue until all the facts are in, and the law has been argued and analyzed in the context of the facts. Only then have the parties . . . received . . . their "day in court."
>
> This is the essence of fairness, and one of the reasons that longstanding rules of judicial ethics . . . prohibit judges and judicial candidates from . . .

engaging in campaign rhetoric about cases or legal issues that may come before them. The reason for this is obvious: how can the public or a person with a lawsuit expect a fair hearing from a judge with an agenda, a judge who has committed himself or herself to a particular position on a case or legal issue during the course of a campaign?[5]

No less emphatic, Justice Ginsburg wrote:

When a judicial candidate promises to rule a certain way on an issue that may later reach the courts, the potential for due process violations is grave and manifest. If successful in her bid for office, the judicial candidate will become a judge, and in that capacity she will be under pressure to resist the pleas of litigants who advance positions contrary to her pledges on the campaign trail. If the judge fails to honor her campaign promises, she will not only face abandonment by supporters of her professed views, she will also "risk being assailed as a dissembler" willing to say one thing to win an election and to do the opposite once in office.[6]

Who would argue otherwise? Not I. Bolstered by both rationale and rationalization, I came to consider campaigning a calling—for the advancement of both my electoral ambitions *and* the voters' "silence is golden" civic schooling. After all, as Justice Kennedy has written, "Judicial elections are no exception to the premise that elections can teach."[7] So, on the stump, I exchanged greetings, talked about my professional background, proclaimed my proud (and local) family heritage, acknowledged the difficult issues coming to our courts, and preached the importance of *not* offering my opinions lest they compromise my impartiality.

But while almost all accepted their electoral silence, some judges and judicial candidates rebelled. Driven by personal beliefs and political interests, they searched for and sharpened their campaign edge, speaking out on controversial issues. A few then found themselves in court, fighting disciplinary prosecutions of their alleged ethics violations. Thus, invoking the First Amendment, they challenged ethics code restrictions on free speech.

For the courts, the dilemma was difficult. Judge Posner, exposing the tangled "roots . . . deep in our constitutional heritage," explained: "Two principles are in conflict and must, to the extent possible, be reconciled. Candidates for public office should be free to express their views on all matters of interest to the electorate. Judges should decide cases in accordance with law rather than with any express or implied commitments that they may have made to their campaign supporters or to others."[8] Reconciliation was difficult; indeed, different federal appellate courts reached irreconcilable conclusions,[9] resulting in US Supreme Court review.

In 2002 the challengers prevailed. In *Republican Party of Minnesota v. White*, the Supreme Court invalidated the "announce clause" of Minnesota's Code of Judicial Conduct, which, like many other state codes, foreclosed judges and judicial candidates from "announcing" or in any other way stating their views on issues during their campaigns.[10]

The call was close, five-four. The justices' opinions offer well-reasoned reflections on whether and how judicial ethics codes and campaigns could preserve judges' independence without breaching their First Amendment rights. Their differences are rather nuanced; each opinion merits careful reading. None doubts or disputes the irreplaceable value of judicial independence.[11]

While I find the dissenters' arguments particularly persuasive, my purpose here is not to take sides but, rather, to recognize that, with *White*, things changed dramatically. As never before, judges and judicial candidates calibrated their campaign comments for political gain. They navigated partisan seas, risking that their statements could oblige them (or be perceived as obliging them) to decide cases in keeping with their campaign comments or, possibly, to recuse in some cases. As never before, judges filtered (or were perceived as filtering) politically sensitive decisions through the campaign declarations that helped elect them.[12]

How can judicial independence survive? It can't. As Judge Sykes wrote: "[J]udges cannot correctly and credibly carry out their core constitutional functions if the pressures of politics push them to carve out positions on cases and legal issues in order to get elected."[13]

CONTRIBUTIONS

In 2002, with *Republican Party of Minn. v. White*, the Supreme Court, for the first time, unharnessed judicial campaign declarations. Then, from 2009 to 2015, with two or possibly three other decisions, the Supreme Court, as never before, gave judicial campaigns full political rein. Why and how are these decisions destroying judicial independence?

The answers arise from our judicial history, comprehensively recounted in Professor Jed Handelsman Shugerman's extraordinary work, *The People's Courts: Pursuing Judicial Independence in America*.[14] Here, building on this historical foundation, I shall examine what I consider the transformative time when political/judicial battles proved pivotal. Then I shall concentrate on actual election experiences to show judges spinning away from independence, propelled by the centrifugal forces of all four Supreme Court decisions.

The story begins as one of political determination. More than fifty years ago, conservative activists, after a long and restless sleep, awoke to see that many of the issues that concerned them most—abortion, capital punishment, civil rights, flag burning, school prayer—while debated in legislatures, were being decided in courts. Judges, it seemed, had become the most important players. So why, these activists asked, should they pound the pavement in legislative and executive races but ignore judicial campaigns?

Why indeed. Thus, in the sixties, when President Lyndon Johnson's War on Poverty gave birth to liberal lawyers fighting entrenched powers (and, most offensive to some, bringing tax-financed lawsuits against government itself to compel civil rights enforcement), conservative lawyers pushed back. But they lost, consistently. In case after case, the legal-services lawyers won, persuading judges that poor people's constitutional rights were being violated, often brazenly—from western farm fields where migrants worked without drinking water, to eastern cities where people lived with discriminatory limits on housing and employment, to southern towns where blacks exercised voting rights at their peril.

In groundbreaking cases, poor people prevailed, most prominently in farmworkers' appeals to the California Supreme Court.[15] Energized by such success, left-wing lawyers continued their march. But then right-wing activists, becoming more legally experienced and strategically astute, arrived at a crossroads and turned. They figured that if judicial cops kept road-blocking their interests, well, then . . . "fire 'em" and hire new judges to patrol the old roads and pave new routes.[16]

Within a decade or two, judicial elections had morphed—from polite affairs, with almost all incumbents running unopposed, to contested campaigns, with respected jurists running scared; from yawners, drawing only attorney interest, to screamers, drawing heavy voter turnout. Moreover, as Texas Supreme Court Chief Justice Thomas R. Phillips noted, "What clearly is new, and what has caused so much attention to be focused on how problematic judicial elections are, is the amount of resources that interested persons and groups are willing to expend to influence the results."[17] And he wrote that in 1998, a decade before the Supreme Court opened the financial floodgates.

In almost all thirty-nine states in which judges were elected, in both partisan and nonpartisan systems, judicial campaign contributions started flowing like never before. Heavy advertising, promoting tough-on-crime candidates rather than fair-for-all jurists, misrepresented the very nature of the judicial role. And the misrepresentations masked what Shugerman identified as the real reason for many of the newly energized campaigns. As he explained, while campaign advertising focused on "crime and the death penalty," it actually was "most often a front for the tort wars between trial lawyers and business interests."[18]

Still, "tort reform" was rarely enough to drive voters. But death penalty appeals ignited judicial campaigns, defeating California Supreme Court Chief Justice Rose Bird and two of her colleagues in 1986[19] and Tennessee Supreme Court Justice Penny White in 1996.[20] Interestingly enough, such campaigns also helped launch the career of the man who would control conservative strategies for thirty years. As Shugerman explained, the "transformation" of judicial elections "is illustrated by the end of Rose Bird's judicial career in California and by the beginning of Karl Rove's political career in Texas and Alabama judicial races."[21]

Soon, other issues—most prominent, marriage—came to America's courts, drawing intense political involvement. In 2010, voters replaced Iowa Supreme Court Chief Justice Marsha Ternus and two of her colleagues after their votes helped overturn Iowa's ban on same-sex marriage (five years ahead of the US Supreme Court's decision in *Obergefell*). The *New York Times* headlined, "Ouster of Iowa Judges Sends Signal to Bench," and reported:

> An unprecedented vote to remove three Iowa Supreme Court justices who were part of the unanimous decision that legalized same-sex marriage in the state was celebrated by conservatives as a popular rebuke of judicial overreach, even as it alarmed proponents of an independent judiciary.
>
> The outcome of the election was heralded both as a statewide repudiation of same-sex marriage and as a national demonstration that conservatives . . . are able to effectively target and remove judges who issue unpopular decisions.[22]

While similar efforts in other states failed to defeat some incumbents, the conservatives' won-lost record, in my view, was far less important than the wind-chilling effect of their campaigns on all elected judges.

Ousting the three Iowa incumbents was not easy; the campaign to do so was not cheap. Even in uncontested judicial electoral systems like Iowa's—the so-called Missouri Plan states in which incumbents run for "retention," unopposed, and citizens vote "yes" or "no" to retain or reject them[23]—spending exploded. And in all thirty-nine states that elect judges, whether by retention elections or contested elections, the unprecedented campaign spending was catalytic.

To better understand the enormous impact of the *new* political investments in judicial elections (particularly by those with thinly veiled interests in "tort reform"), we would do well to compare something *old*—trial lawyers' investments in judicial elections. "Trial lawyers were one of the most important sources of money in judicial elections for most of the twentieth century."[24] That continues to be so. Lawyers contribute to state judicial campaigns at a rate approximately ten times that of the overall voting population.[25]

In 1982–83, when I ran for the judgeship to which I had recently been appointed, my campaign raised $20,000 from friends and relatives and, mostly, attorneys who appeared before me.[26] But I *never* asked an attorney to contribute; the judicial conduct code barred such solicitation. Instead, code compliant, my state-regulated campaign volunteers made the calls and sent the fundraising letters, signed by a bipartisan group of prominent attorneys and community leaders. Still, I wrote the "thank you" notes. I knew who contributed—and who did not—and the attorneys knew I knew.[27]

Twelve years later, running for state supreme court, needing a much bigger budget, I met the sad reality of my ideals. Against my media consultant's advice, I refused to allow "tough" or other such terms in any ads. And, against my treasurer's advice, I refused to raise money the way my treasurer said she and a supreme court justice recently had solicited contributions, and successfully so.

Our confrontation came at our first fundraising meeting, sitting at the kitchen counter of my treasurer's home. She handed me a long list of attorneys' names and phone numbers, along with the amounts they had contributed to the supreme court justice's campaign. Time to start "dialing for dollars," she said. Surprised, I protested that I was prohibited from doing so. My treasurer, an attorney, recounted her knowledge of the code and said we would comply by teaming in two ways: (1) she would call and say, "I'm sitting here with the judge," make the pitch, obtain the pledge, then hand me the phone for a "thank you"; (2) I would call, request permission to use the attorney's name in campaign advertising,[28] then hand her the phone to raise the money. I refused, saying that such teaming probably violated the letter of the law and certainly violated the spirit.[29]

I tried to take the high road. Concerned about what I deemed the ethical deterioration of judicial campaigns, I took the approach, both strategic and sincere, that I had used in my first campaign for the Court of Appeals. To every attorney, I sent a biographical brochure accompanied by a statement, "Campaign Standards: A Pledge to Wisconsin Lawyers," stating:

> I share the concerns that many of you have about the misleading and negative nature of some judicial campaigns of recent years. In *Electing Justice: The Law and Ethics of Judicial Campaigns* (1990: The American Judicature Society), Loyola University Law Professor Patrick M. McFadden wrote:

Judicial campaigning is problematic, and its problems are growing worse. . . . Advertising in judicial campaigns has grown progressively more negative. Today's judicial candidates are more likely to eschew campaigns based on their own records as judges and attorneys, and instead engage in attacks on their opponents. Campaign literature and television spots have become increasingly misleading, distorting not only the records of opponents, but the nature of the judicial office and the decisions judges make. . . . These developments are cause for deep concern.

I agree. Accordingly, as I have done in my three previous judicial campaigns, I pledge to conduct this campaign in a manner consistent with the highest ideals of the judiciary. Despite media or political demands to do otherwise, I shall campaign without politically pandering soundbites; without negative attacks. I shall maintain consideration and respect for other candidates. I shall base my campaign on a serious and positive presentation of my judicial credentials.

This brochure attempts to offer such a presentation. Please understand, however, that it is written not only for lawyers, but also for many outside the legal profession. Therefore, because it may not address questions of importance to you, I encourage you to contact me. If you have concerns, would like to meet, or would like to evaluate examples of my published works or appellate decisions, please call me at home, evenings or weekends [phone numbers listed].

No one called. And although I promoted this statement at each of my many interviews with editorial boards statewide, none ever mentioned it.[30]

I campaigned hard and, in a seven-candidate race, won almost all editorial and organizational endorsements. But I campaigned without "getting tough" or "dialing for dollars." Underfunded, I was the only candidate without TV advertising. I was trounced, not even surviving the primary.

No big deal. After all, the public might say, that's just politics, and politics is part of judicial life. But such casual comment is uninformed, and so historically incomplete as to be mostly meaningless. To see how judges really make their decisions, we look deeper. To sense the new pressures judges feel from campaign financing, we probe the entangled relationship between campaign dollars and judicial decisions. And we do so with my own admissions as background for the three Supreme Court decisions we must consider.

While I would want to believe that my ethics embodied impartiality—that my independence was strong enough to never judge under the influence of donors—what was really taking place? I tried to be true. Usually that was easy.

After all, hundreds of attorneys contributed; almost all, one hundred dollars or less. Still, as a trial judge, I recognized some of the donor-attorneys as they and their clients walked in the courtroom. As an appellate judge, I read their names on the briefs. And when amounts were big enough to stand out, I remembered. Sometimes, when deciding against big donors, I couldn't help but feel some regret.

Equally important, regardless of my actual impartiality, what were the appearances? How did it look when a big donor-attorney came before me? The ethical standard is explicit: "A judge shall avoid impropriety and *the appearance of impropriety*."[31] As Justice O'Connor explained, "Even if judges were able to refrain from favoring donors, the mere possibility that judges' decisions may be motivated by the desire to repay campaign contributions is likely to undermine the public's confidence in the judiciary."[32] And, as the public may astutely discern, judges themselves might not know for sure whether contributions tipped their scales. Inadvertently, might they let a thumb touch a balance pan?

Attorneys come to assume the value of contributing to judges' campaigns. True, many make their contributions on merit; in faithfulness to good government, some attorneys do indeed promote judicial quality.[33] And, paradoxically I suppose, they understand that independent judges are those for whom campaign contributions make no difference. But even for these fine judges, might *close* cases be at risk of turning less on law, and more on mood . . . and gratitude?

Are these reflections just one way to say that judges are human . . . that money matters and friendships, real or imagined, are felt? Maybe so, but if my experience counts for anything, it confirms that attorneys' contributions are influential. At the very least, they promote the public *appearance* of corruption. But might such contributions be an avoidable, "just say no" excisable source of corruption? Easier said than done.

In each of my campaigns, I wrestled with the possibility. I really wanted to refuse contributions from attorneys, or at least from those appearing before me. But three factors dissuaded me. First (and, yes, I admit, I took this into account), without them, I would have been almost certain to lose. Second, implementation would have been impossible—what about contributions from an attorney's spouse or children, some with different last names; what about contributions from associates, partners, and staff members at the attorney's firm? Third, refusing such contributions would have been "above the law." Proclaiming myself "holier than thou," I would have been elevating *my* ethical standards over the code's specific allowances for such contributions and, further, implicitly impugning the integrity of judges who "merely" complied.

Part of the dilemma reached the US Supreme Court in 2015. Let's tune into NPR:

STEVE INSKEEP: Here's a constant question when we talk about big money influencing campaigns. It's whether spending money equals free speech. A ruling by the Supreme Court answered a related question. It's whether public officials asking for money equals free speech. The court yesterday ruled that states can bar judicial candidates from personally soliciting campaign contributions. Here's NPR legal affairs correspondent Nina Totenberg.

NINA TOTENBERG: The unexpected outcome in the 5-to-4 ruling came for one reason. Chief Justice John Roberts jumped the fence on the issue, siding with the court's liberal members instead of the conservatives as he has in the past on campaign finance issues. Nonetheless, he wrote a narrow decision emphasizing the importance of public confidence in the independence and impartiality of the courts. Bert Brandenburg, executive director of the nonpartisan group Justice at Stake, was relieved by the decision.

BERT BRANDENBURG: More and more people are realizing that the courts can't be fair if the judges are not insulated from political pressure. And that insulation is getting eaten away by money.

NINA TOTENBERG: In the last election cycle, some $33 million was spent on judicial elections, according to Brandenburg. Thirty-nine states elect some or all of their judges and almost all of those have a rule barring judicial candidates from personally soliciting money for their campaigns. The case before the court came from Florida where the canons of ethics allow committees to raise money for judicial candidates but do not allow the candidates to personally solicit contributions.

Lanell Williams-Yulee, a candidate for the trial bench in Hillsboro County, mailed and posted online a signed letter to potential contributors soliciting funds. For this, she was reprimanded and fined. She then challenged the ban on personal solicitation as a violation of her free speech rights. At the time her case reached the court, several appeals courts had already struck down similar bans in other states. But the Supreme Court did not agree.[34]

The case was *Williams-Yulee v. The Florida Bar*. Writing for the majority, Chief Justice Roberts declared: "Judges are not politicians, even when they come to the bench by way of the ballot. And a State's decision to elect its judiciary does not compel it to treat judicial candidates like campaigners for political office. A State may assure its people that judges will apply the law without fear or favor—and without having personally asked anyone for money."[35] But only that—*personally* asking for money—was at issue. Indeed, in *Williams-Yulee*, the Supreme Court was weighing the *personal* solicitation of campaign contributions on the scale of Florida's judicial ethical standard (modeled on the ABA's Model Code of Judicial Conduct): "A candidate, including an incumbent judge, for a judicial office that is filled by public election between competing candidates shall not personally solicit campaign funds, or solicit attorneys for publicly stated support, but may establish committees of responsible persons to secure and manage the expenditure of funds for the candidate's campaign and to obtain public statements of support for his or her candidacy."[36]

Thus, such standards leave open the door to others soliciting campaign contributions on the candidate's behalf. And when a campaign "committee" makes the calls, such standards do nothing to prevent judges and candidates from learning who answers "yes" and the amounts they donate. Attorneys know that; they calculate accordingly, deciding whether to contribute (sometimes even to competing candidates) and how much.

Some states, however, limit the amounts. In *Williams-Yulee*, the Supreme Court, noting Florida's "additional restrictions" limiting donations to $1,000 for a trial court candidate and $3,000 for a supreme court justice,[37] hastened to declare: "Although the Court has held that contribution limits advance the interest in preventing *quid pro quo* corruption and its appearance in political elections, we have never held that adopting contribution limits precludes a State from pursuing its compelling interests through additional means. And in any event, a State has compelling interests in regulating judicial elections that extend beyond its interests in regulating political elections, because judges are not politicians."[38]

What "additional means"? Future appeals may answer. Here, I'm intrigued by what, under other circumstances, might seem little more than a rhetorical grace point. For the second time in a single opinion, Chief Justice Roberts declared that "judges are not politicians."[39] And in her concurring opinion, Justice Ginsburg, quoting Chief Justice Roberts, echoed those very words.[40]

Repetition, in America's Judeo-Christian tradition and particularly in matters of justice, may add more than emphasis. Biblical scholars have considered the importance of repetition of "justice" in the various versions of Deuteronomy 16:20, "Justice, justice you shall pursue."[41] Am I stretching too far? Perhaps, but we might consider whether Chief Justice Roberts and Justice Ginsburg, often philosophical foes, came together here to repeat and shout words of desperate reaffirmation—words the public and many judges themselves no longer believe—as if by proclaiming that "judges are not politicians" they might make it so.

But if a judge campaigns like a politician, addresses political issues like a politician, and raises money like a politician (or directs a campaign committee to do so), might that be a duck waddling up to the bench?

Still, notwithstanding the fifty-plus judicial codes that variously allow and disallow contributions, might all at least reach consensus on how much is too much? Might all at least agree on what fails the smell test, effectively converting a judicial campaign contribution into a bribe? That was the question for the Supreme Court in *Caperton v. A. T. Massey Coal Co., Inc.*,[42] a complicated case, but one we need to consider carefully in order to understand the future of America's judicial independence.

First, we meet the players and their case's procedural progression:

1. Hugh M. Caperton, president of Harmin Mining, sued Massey Energy and its CEO, Don Blankenship, alleging Massey's illegal business conduct "in utter disregard" of Harmin's rights. Caperton won; in the trial court, a jury awarded him $50 million.
2. So Blankenship and Massey Energy appealed to the West Virginia Supreme Court, where they won, thus reversing the $50 million judgment.
3. So Caperton and Harmin Mining, challenging the West Virginia Supreme Court's decision and trying to win reinstatement of the $50 million judgment, then appealed to the US Supreme Court.

Next we add the most important foundational facts—with thanks to Shugerman for his summary: "In 2002, a West Virginia jury hit Massey Energy, a West Virginia coal company, with a $50 million verdict for using illegal and fraudulent tactics to force a smaller company, Harman Mining, out of business. As Massey appealed this verdict . . . , its CEO, Don Blankenship, recruited Brent Benjamin, a former state party treasurer with no judicial experience, to run against [West Virginia Supreme Court] Justice Warren McGraw." Why, while challenging the $50 million judgment before the West Virginia Supreme Court, would Blankenship recruit a candidate, Brent Benjamin, to run against Justice McGraw, and how would he promote his campaign? Shugerman continued:

> Blankenship spent $3 million—the lion's share of the funding for Benjamin's campaign—to defeat Justice Warren McGraw. Most of Blankenship's money financed "And for the Sake of the Kids," an organization created just for this election which blitzed the state with television advertisements attacking McGraw for being soft on crime and dangerous to children. The most prominent ad alleged:
>
> > Supreme Court Justice Warren McGraw voted to release child-rapist Tony Arbaugh from prison. Worse, McGraw agreed to let this convicted rapist work as a janitor in a West Virginia school. Letting a child rapist go free?

To work in our schools? That's radical Supreme Court Justice Warren
McGraw. [The word "radical" flashes onto the screen in red over
McGraw's grainy picture.] Warren McGraw. Too soft on crime. Too
dangerous for our kids.

The McGraw campaign lacked the resources to overcome these attacks. Benjamin beat McGraw 53 percent to 47 percent and became the deciding vote to
overturn the jury verdict in 2007. Later, photos surfaced of a second justice,
Spike Maynard, vacationing with CEO Blankenship in the French Riviera
soon before he heard the case and also ruled in favor of Massey Energy. Under
pressure, Maynard recused himself from the 2008 rehearing. . . . But again
Benjamin refused to recuse . . . , and again cast another deciding vote against
the jury verdict.[43]

But justice was coming for Caperton. The US Supreme Court, concluding that due process required Justice Benjamin's recusal, explained, "Under
our precedents there are objective standards that require recusal when 'the
probability of actual bias on the part of the judge . . . is too high to be constitutionally tolerable.'" Accordingly, Justice Benjamin should have stepped
aside—not necessarily because he could not be fair (the Court specified that it
was *not* saying that)[44] but, rather, because, having accepted $3 million from
Blankenship to finance his candidacy, he could not ensure the *appearance* of
fairness. Thus, given the contribution amount, Justice Benjamin should not
have decided Massey's appeal of the $50 million verdict. Seems obvious? It was
a close call, five-four.

What about these circumstances required recusal? What rendered "the
probability of actual bias . . . too high to be constitutionally tolerable?"[45]
Given the settled proposition that "[n]ot every campaign contribution by a
litigant or attorney creates a probability of bias," what made this the "exceptional case" requiring recusal?[46] It was, the Supreme Court explained, a matter
of timing and amount.

The timing—the "temporal relationship between the campaign contributions, the justice's election, and the pendency of the case"—was "critical."[47]
The Supreme Court majority detailed the sequence and, in particular, the
procedural history of Blankenship's appeals.[48] By the time he recruited a candidate to oppose Justice McGraw's reelection, Blankenship knew the state
supreme court's three-two votes on several issues, leaving him certain that
Justice McGraw would cast the deciding vote against him in the ultimate state
appeal. So, with $50 million at stake, Blankenship was willing to spend $3 million to bankroll a candidate against McGraw.

And the amount—the US Supreme Court was impressed. Justice Kennedy, writing for the majority, explained how a big financial backer can circumvent campaign contribution limits: "In addition to contributing the $1,000 statutory maximum to Benjamin's campaign committee, Blankenship donated almost $2.5 million to 'And For The Sake Of The Kids.' . . . Blankenship spent, in addition, just over $500,000 on independent expenditures—for direct mailings and letters soliciting donations as well as television and newspaper advertisements. . . . To provide some perspective, Blankenship's $3 million in contributions were more than the total amount spent by all other Benjamin supporters."[49] This combination of timing and financing, the majority ruled, crossed the constitutional line:

> We conclude that there is a serious risk of actual bias—based on objective and reasonable perceptions—when a person with a personal stake in a particular case had a *significant and disproportionate influence* in placing the judge on the case by raising funds or directing the judge's election campaign when the case was pending or imminent. The inquiry centers on the contribution's relative size in comparison to the total amount of money contributed to the campaign, the total amount spent in the election, and the apparent effect such contribution had on the outcome of the election.[50]

The majority emphasized that "[a]lthough there is no allegation of a *quid pro quo* agreement, the fact remains that Blankenship's extraordinary contributions were made at a time when he had a vested stake in the outcome."[51]

For the four dissenters, Chief Justice Roberts protested that the majority drew no "clear line between when recusal is constitutionally required and when it is not."[52] He then went on to phrase forty groups of eighty-three questions as "only a few uncertainties that quickly come to mind" when attempting to apply the majority's standard of "significant and disproportionate influence." The majority conceded as much, acknowledging, "It is true that extreme cases often test the bounds of established legal principles, and sometimes no administrable standard may be available to address the perceived wrong."[53]

Still, in *Caperton*, the Supreme Court, however imprecisely, tried to answer the question, "How much is too much?" But more exactly—and the difference is critical—*Caperton* responded to a much more specific question: In a judicial election, when a party involved in an appeal contributes money to the campaign of one of the judges who, at that very time, is on the appellate panel deciding the case involving that contributor, how much is so much that the judge must recuse?

Does the answer matter? Or is the *Caperton* situation so exceedingly rare that it is unlikely to come up again? After all, for such a situation to arise: (1) a party in an appeal would have to contribute to the campaign of an appellate judge (or candidate); (2) the amount of the contribution would need to be so high as to have a "significant and disproportionate influence" in electing the judge; (3) at that time or soon thereafter, the judge would need to be reviewing an appeal involving that party; and (4) notwithstanding appearances of impropriety, the judge would need to have accepted the contribution and not recuse. Thus, while other similar circumstances are possible, the timing, the multi-million-dollar amounts, and the blatancy of the *Caperton* conduct make their occurrence highly improbable.

Probability analysis, however, misses the more important point. After all, in *Caperton*, the extreme circumstances the Supreme Court considered formed only the iceberg's tip—campaign contributions by a litigant to a judicial campaign to *directly* influence a judicial decision. But now, lying just beneath the surface are increasingly common circumstances—campaign contributions by non-litigants to judicial, legislative, and executive campaigns to *indirectly* influence judicial selection and judicial decisions. What are the deeper dangers and how might they depend on whether judges are elected?

Helping us answer such questions, Frank Sullivan Jr., a professor at the Indiana University School of Law who served for two decades as a justice of the Indiana Supreme Court, recounts the substantial contributions to supreme court campaigns in Illinois, Ohio, and Michigan from, among others, personal injury lawyers and insurance companies, while their multimillion-dollar jury verdicts were on appeal. "Unlike our neighbors to the west, east, and north, the justices of the Indiana Supreme Court do not rely on campaign contributions and television advertising to obtain their seats. We have instead a merit selection system" helping to "assure that people of integrity, impartiality, and intelligence are appointed."[54] Moreover, Sullivan maintained, throughout his many years of judicial service and notwithstanding his and his colleagues' partisan backgrounds, such impartiality prevailed in *every* case, resulting in nonpartisan, independent decisions.[55]

Such independence now is endangered and, in light of *Citizens United v. Federal Election Comm'n.*, soon may be extinct.[56] But how can that be? *Citizens United*, explicitly, does not deal with judicial elections. And yet, as I shall explain, to understand the exponential growth of financial influences on judges, we now must open our lens to focus not only on *Caperton*, a case that specifically addresses judicial elections, but also on *Citizens United*, a case that specifically does not.

Citizens United has become so hot politically that, like *Dred Scott* or *Roe v. Wade*, its familiar name alone now sizzles the daily news. It has generated both careful commentaries and passionate polemics, even drawing President Obama's very controversial criticism, six days after its issuance, in his 2010 State of the Union address. But to understand how it might have anything to do with judicial independence and corruption, we must move beyond the headlines, set aside the slogans, and consider *Citizens United*'s treatment of financial "free speech" in non-judicial campaigns.

What was the case about? Citizens United, a politically active nonprofit corporation, challenged certain provisions of a federal law—the McCain-Feingold Bipartisan Campaign Reform Act of 2002 (BCRA)—that regulated campaign contributions from corporations, unions, and political action committees. Why the challenge? In early 2008, Citizens United had released a ninety-minute film, *Hillary, the Movie*, that was critical of Hillary Clinton, then a candidate in the Democratic presidential primaries. Citizens United wanted to increase the movie's distribution through video-on-demand.[57] But, according to the Federal Election Commission, the agency responsible for administration of the BCRA, such distribution would violate a provision of the law making it a felony for any corporation to broadcast electioneering communications within thirty days of a primary or sixty days of a general election.[58] Zephyr Teachout explained: "According to [Citizens United's] lawyers, [*Hillary, the Movie*] was a documentary, it was not offered over broadcast, and BCRA did not apply. According to the government, it was a ninety-minute ad designed to hurt Mrs. Clinton in the primaries, the distribution counted as broadcast, and BCRA did apply."[59]

The Supreme Court's decision was mixed. It upheld certain BCRA provisions regarding disclaimers and disclosures, thus supporting transparency in political advertising.[60] But, in its five-four decision, the Supreme Court also concluded that the BCRA's "outright ban" on the film's distribution leading up to the election, "backed by criminal sanctions," violated the First Amendment.[61]

But this all flowed from a presidential primary election. In *Citizens United*, the Supreme Court did not address any such restrictions in *judicial* elections. And remember, "judges are not politicians." Further, four years later, in *Williams-Yulee*, Justice Ginsburg wrote that *Citizens United* "should not hold sway for judicial elections." She maintained:

> [E]ven if one agrees with [the decision in *Citizens United*, it was] geared to elections for representative posts, and should have "little bearing" on judicial elections. "Favoritism," *i.e.*, partiality, if inevitable in the political arena, is disqualifying in the judiciary's domain. . . . Unlike politicians, judges are not

"expected to be responsive to [the] concerns" of constituents. Instead, "it is the business of judges to be indifferent to popularity." . . . *States may therefore impose different campaign-finance rules for judicial elections than for political elections.*[62]

Still, notwithstanding Justice Ginsburg's opinion about the reach of *Citizens United*, and alongside repeated declarations like hers and Chief Justice Roberts's—that "judges are not politicians"—we need to dig deeper into the decision.

Citizens United, while not dealing directly with judicial elections, referenced *Caperton*, which did, and *Citizens United* contended that "*Caperton's* holding was limited to the rule that the judge must be recused, not that the litigant's political speech could be banned."[63] Further, in *Citizens United*, four justices, all concurring in certain aspects of the majority's decision but dissenting from others, and without excluding the judiciary, declared that the majority's decision "threatens to undermine the integrity of *elected institutions* across the Nation." They warned:

[T]he consequences of *today's holding will not be limited to the legislative or executive context.* The majority of the States select their judges through popular elections. At a time when concerns about the conduct of judicial elections have reached a fever pitch, the Court today unleashes the floodgates of corporate and union general treasury spending in these races. *Perhaps [recusal] will catch some of the worst abuses. This will be small comfort to those States that, after today, may no longer have the ability to place modest limits on corporate electioneering even if they believe such limits to be critical to maintaining the integrity of their judicial systems.*[64]

Further, as Shugerman explained, "Some states had not limited corporate spending in the first place, so *Citizens United* has little effect there, but in states that had been trying to contain the flood, the U.S. Supreme Court possibly has accelerated corporate and union spending, and [*Republican Party of Minn. v.*] *White* probably *prevents states from treating the financing of judicial elections differently from the financing of other elections.*"[65]

Complicated . . . oh so complicated. These details, fascinating for a few, must be confounding for so many more. But let's not miss the big picture. After two hundred years of barely breathing in the direction of judicial elections, the US Supreme Court has made four unprecedented decisions that recast and intensify concerns about judicial independence and corruption:

2002 / *Republican Party of Minn. v. White*—In judicial campaigns, judges and candidates can announce their positions on issues likely to come before them; under the First Amendment, ethics codes cannot prohibit them from doing so.

2009 / *Caperton v. A. T. Massey Coal Co., Inc.*—In judicial elections, when a campaign supporter with a case pending or likely to be pending contributes an "extraordinary amount" creating the "probability of actual bias," the contribution still may be lawful (depending on that state's limits on contribution amounts),[66] but, if the amount has a "significant and disproportionate influence" on the election, the judge must recuse.

2010 / *Citizens United v. Federal Election Comm'n*—In legislative and executive branch elections, virtually unlimited campaign contributions from corporations (profit and nonprofit), unions, and their political action committees are lawful; the constitutional status of such contributions to *judicial* campaigns is uncertain.

2015 / *Williams-Yulee v. The Florida Bar*—In judicial elections, judges and judicial candidates may solicit contributions through campaign committees or, if state laws allow, may do so directly and personally, even from attorneys appearing in their courts. States, however, may prohibit such personal solicitations.

And finally, despite their repeated protests that "judges are not politicians," these decisions, taken together, provide substantial support for the conclusion that states may not be able to treat the financing of judicial elections differently from the financing of legislative and executive elections. And even if states can find some limited ways to do so, these decisions, taken together, subject America's elective judiciaries to unprecedented political pressures.[67] Therefore, historians, jurists, and policymakers, regardless of whether they agree with the Supreme Court's constitutional reasoning, now must come together to answer how, in light of these decisions, America's judicial independence can survive.[68]

15

BEGGING THE QUESTION

Elective or Appointive?

Under some [state] constitutions the judges are elected and subject to
frequent reelection. I venture to predict that sooner or later these
innovations will have dire results and that one day it will be seen that
by diminishing the magistrates' independence, not judicial power only
but the democratic republic itself has been attacked.

—Alexis de Tocqueville, *Democracy in America*[1]

Thus, a Tocqueville tweet: "judges . . . elected . . . dire results . . . sad." The
evidence is overwhelming. Supreme Court rulings, notwithstanding what may
be their constitutional correctness, have unleashed political beasts that, every
day, threaten or destroy the independence of America's elected judges—the
actual independence of many and the *appearance* of independence of all. Last
gasps that "judges are not politicians" are unavailing.

The "dire results" have come. No-holds-barred brawls of campaign declarations and contributions subject our judiciary to political influence as never
before—"the democratic republic itself has been attacked." Even judges who,
like me, once lauded our elective judicial process for its "profoundly invigorating . . . visceral experiences" and the "subtle understanding" gained from campaigning now call for reform.[2] It's not that campaigning no longer educates
and sensitizes voters and judges; it's that these campaign values now are eclipsed.
Judges become less independent as they sit in the shadow of their colleagues'
electoral defeats; as they contemplate their own electoral risks. Indeed, their
electoral vulnerability grows even when, and often because, their decisions are
courageous and constitutionally correct.

Justice O'Connor understands. Following her retirement from the Supreme
Court, in conjunction with the University of Denver Institute for the Advancement of the American Legal System, she dedicated her "legacy project"
to a nationwide effort to convince states to jettison judicial elections and
adopt merit-based appointive systems.[3] Years earlier, in three disarmingly calm

sentences of her concurring opinion in *Republican Party of Minn. v. White*, she captured the essence: "We of course want judges to be impartial, in the sense of being free from any personal stake in the outcome of the cases to which they are assigned. But if judges are subject to regular elections they are likely to feel that they have at least some personal stake in the outcome of every publicized case. Elected judges cannot help being aware that if the public is not satisfied with the outcome of a particular case, it could hurt their reelection prospects."[4] Moreover, she emphasized, "Even if judges were able to suppress their awareness of the potential electoral consequences of their decisions and refrain from acting on it, the public's confidence in the judiciary could be undermined simply by the possibility that judges would be unable to do so."[5]

Compelling evidence confirms the consequences—even deadly ones. Again, Justice O'Connor: "[J]udges who face elections are far more likely to override jury sentences of life without parole and impose the death penalty than are judges who do not run for election."[6]

Studies show that timing may mean everything: "the shorter the average term of judges in a state, the more likely they are to impose the death penalty."[7] Indeed, "judges seeking re-election start ruling differently as Election Day approaches."[8] For an elected judge, "ignoring the political consequences of visible decisions is 'like ignoring a crocodile in your bathtub.'"[9]

But I shower (and I judged in a state without the death penalty). So, while not ignoring the crocodile, I step away from the tub . . . at least far enough for safety while sizing up this croc by history's measures. Might history caution us merely to pause, not panic? Although elections may erode independence, might history disabuse us of any easy notion that merit-based appointed judiciaries should be the answer?

Shugerman conceded that "[c]ountless scholars describe judicial elections as a 'threat to judicial independence'"[10] but pointed to corruption in America's appointive judiciaries as well. He identified five historical periods and described the forces, primarily economic, that moved America's judicial systems back and forth between appointive and elective. Neither ensured independence. In fact, while the founders opted for appointed federal judges[11] and many states followed suit, the pendulum started swinging in the early nineteenth century when *reformers* "defined judicial independence as insulation from . . . the partisan patronage politics of appointments."[12] "At each stage, reformers focused on separating the courts from an immediate set of evils, but separating the judges from one set of interests often left them vulnerable to the next."[13]

Historically, then, where are we now? Would advocates for judicial independence invoke history to offer reassurance or to raise alarm? Shugerman answered: "[M]odern America has shifted to an era of judicial plutocracy, not necessarily a judiciary of the wealthy, but a judiciary shaped by the massive campaign spending by lawyers, litigants, and interest groups. . . . Today, judicial elections have reached their own crisis point of corruption and special interest excess. . . . America is now at a crossroads."[14] Crossroads, indeed. For more than two centuries, America's crossing roads of appointive and elective systems, rocky or repaired or rerouted, remained predictably unpredictable.[15] Whether appointive or elective, contested or retentive, partisan or nonpartisan, selection systems rendered both independent judges of integrity and corrupt judges of pandering politics. No longer. America's state elective judiciaries are, for the first time, predictably, politically corrupt—if not in fact, then certainly in appearance.

While allowing for individual judges unmoved by political pressure, history forecasts three trends intensifying as the result of the Supreme Court's decisions on judicial campaign declarations and campaign contributions. Generally, and predictably: (1) appointed judges will be more independent than elected judges (though variations, of course, will occur for reasons ranging from presidential preferences and power at the federal level to judicial term lengths at the state level); (2) nonpartisan judges will be more independent than partisan judges; and (3) incumbent judges facing retention elections will be better insulated and more independent than those facing contested elections[16] but, more than ever, they also will be vulnerable to high-financed, unprincipled political opposition.[17]

History teaches that political considerations have always played and will always play a part in judicial selection, appointive or elective. And, granted, political considerations are not necessarily bad; indeed, balanced by other legitimate criteria, they may be good and wholly compatible with independence. But political considerations now have pushed judges way off balance, toppling the scales of justice. Elective state judiciaries, always leaning under some political pressure, now have fallen from the weight of *White, Caperton, Williams-Yulee,* and *Citizens United.*

Now generating American history's most dramatic transformation of judicial campaigning, these Supreme Court decisions, whatever their First Amendment merits, are leaving our judges politically vulnerable and ethically compromised as never before. While contagions consuming thirty-nine of our state judiciaries would be cause enough for alarm, the actual percentage of America's judges so infected—that is, the percentage of judges in elective system states—nears ninety.[18] Thus, today, nearly 90 percent of America's judges find their independence on life support. If these states choose to continue electing their judges, their independence cannot recover.

Shugerman wrote, "We could walk away from this historical tour of American courts shaking our heads cynically and conclude that judicial selection just doesn't matter." After all, as he conceded, "Politicization and corruption are inevitable, and reformers are often biased, manipulative, and disingenuous." Thus, he acknowledged, "A number of political scientists and hard-core legal realists believe that law is nothing but politics by other means" and, therefore, that "judges should play by the same rules as other politicians."[19]

But in Shugerman's opinion, and mine, such cynics, while not entirely wrong, are mostly so. They are inattentive to the historical record of (1) courageous judges who, regardless of political pressure or professional gain, have made unpopular, principled decisions, and (2) concerned citizens who, civically schooled in the values of judicial impartiality and supportive of independence, have understood that judges, by constitutional oath, sometimes must make decisions with which they—the voters, and even the judges themselves—strenuously disagree.

The cynics have not been behind the bench to feel the difference between a secure, appointed judge with long-term or lifetime ownership and an insecure, elected judge with a short-term lease. The cynics have not been in chambers to discern the decisive difference between an appointed judge, focusing on facts and law, and an elected judge, glancing at the rearview mirror and seeing political opponents approaching.

I've been there; I have seen such foes and felt such forces, perverse and politically potent. Again, there's that crocodile. As a California Supreme Court justice wrote: "There's no way a judge is going to be able to ignore the political consequences of certain decisions, especially if he or she has to make them near election time. That would be like ignoring [the] crocodile. . . . You know it's there, and you try not to think about it, but it's hard to think about much else while you're shaving."[20]

Thus, while understanding the cynics and acknowledging the modest merits of their critique, and while respecting the invaluable lessons learned on the judicial campaign trail, I now echo Justice O'Connor's arguments and Professor Shugerman's invocation of the warning voiced at a state constitutional convention in 1877: judicial elections are the "'route to hell.'" Only by replacing them with merit-based appointments will we find the "plausible path back to judicial independence."[21]

Will reform of judicial selection end all corruption and restore independence? Of course not. As Teachout wrote, "Corruption cannot be made to vanish, but its power can be subdued with the right combination of culture and political rules."[22] We must reinvigorate that "culture" and institute those "political rules" of judicial selection. We must institute the new rules of merit selection now desperately needed to ensure independence—independence being buried under new Supreme Court standards; independence suffocating in the smog of political pollution; independence vanishing, perhaps forever.

The Supreme Court has spoken; the constitutional standards have shifted. Now, only ignorance, complacency, and a little more time are needed to drive the last nails into the judicial coffin. More than two centuries of democracy brought much success . . . and much too much relaxed confidence. As Teachout warned, "democracy, without constant vigilance against corruption, is an unstable, unmoored thing, subject to great gusts of whimsy, and likely to collapse."[23]

The collapse of judicial independence has come. In the history of the American judiciary, today is unlike any other. To fail to recognize the unprecedented, qualitatively transformed conditions created by the new rules of judicial campaign declarations and contributions is to ignore the overwhelming evidence . . . and to ignore Tocqueville's spot-on warning of "dire results" that, "sooner or later," would come from an elective judiciary. As he wrote, "not judicial power only but the democratic republic itself has been attacked." Our politically corrupted judiciary no longer will have the independence to protect America.

"Reform! Reform! Aren't things bad enough already?"[24] Guess not. So, Mr. Revere, saddle up for one more midnight ride.

AFTERWORD

Fathers and Grandfathers

Life is painting a picture, not doing a sum.

—Justice Oliver Wendell Holmes Jr.[1]

In my introduction, I suggested that "while focusing on *America's* judges, we would do well to glance away occasionally, broaden our view, and gain insights from abroad." Now, in closing, let us do so again.

I was mugged in Moscow, not Beijing, and I know nothing about Chinese law. But on inauguration day 2017, as I was writing this book, my attention was drawn to a headline, "China's Chief Justice Rejects an Independent Judiciary, and Reformers Wince."

Chief Justice Zhou Qiang, China's top judicial official, is hardly a radical reformer. But to liberal-minded watchers of the country's evolving court system, he has nonetheless been an encouraging figure.

In recent years, he has spearheaded an effort to make China's judiciary, which is subordinate to the ruling Communist Party, more professional. He has pushed to weed out poorly trained judges and to raise the pay of those with formal legal training, which often includes a heavy dose of Western jurisprudence.

So when the chief justice used warlike language . . . to denounce the idea of an independent judiciary and other cherished liberal principles, warning judges not to fall into the "trap" of "Western" ideology, observers in China and abroad were shocked and dismayed.

"We should resolutely resist erroneous influence from the West: 'constitutional democracy,' 'separation of powers' and 'independence of the judiciary,'" Chief Justice Zhou, the head of the Supreme People's Court of China, said in a speech to legal officials in Beijing. "We must make clear our stand and dare to show the sword."[2]

To many Americans, judicial independence may seem theoretical, its prominence in the revolutionary cause and constitutional formation largely forgotten. While casually respected, judicial independence is hardly an ideal around which we would expect the masses to rally and "dare to show the sword." But not so abroad—not so in China or Chile or Russia or Poland or Hungary,[3] or in Germany, where, a few years ago, I was a Fulbright fellow at the University of Giessen, teaching at Justus Liebig Law School.

I was hosted by the law school's wonderful director, Professor Walter Gropp. In World War II, his father fought for the German army; mine served in the US Army Air Corps. Walter and his wife, Inge, took Karen and me to quiet sites, including a churchyard where many martyred nuns were buried, remembered for their righteous resistance. By coming together in true friendship, in both teaching law and pausing at these graves, Walter and I felt we were honoring not only these brave women but our beloved fathers as well.

In Germany, many memorials recall what happened when judicial independence died. But in America, it seems, we allow our memories to dim, as if we want to pretend that *that* could never happen here. So we ignore our history of judicial corruptions and acquiescence, from Japanese American internment[4] to African American mass incarceration,[5] and we have yet to recognize or respond to today's unprecedented evisceration of judicial independence.

John Marshall cautioned that a corrupt judiciary is "the greatest scourge an angry Heaven can inflict," and Alexis de Tocqueville warned that the loss of judicial independence brings "dire results" to "the democratic republic itself." Their words now resound, ringing tragically true.

Marshall and Tocqueville were warning of political corruption—the corruption now most immediately threatening our elective judiciaries. But, as we have seen, other corruptions, affecting all judges, also can be so very consequential. While systemically they may seem less significant, such corruptions, case by case, judge by judge, also erode independence and vitiate justice. They are contagious. They leave judges susceptible to unconscionable betrayals, emboldening the worst in us and the worst judges among us.

"Remember, half the judges in your audience take bribes on a regular basis; the other half worry about their lives because they don't." Insights from abroad; corruptions, closer to home, some political, others so personal. Judges are, after all, just people—powerful people, principled and perverse, virtuous and vulnerable, with their own families and frailties; just people doing their best, trying to be fair.

I tried. I did not always succeed, but I really tried to deflect political pressures, recognize and repel personal corruptions, and uphold ideals of independence. I tried to remain true to Lincoln's "unimpassioned reason" while believing, with

Justice Blackmun, that "compassion need not be exiled from the province of judging." But sometimes I came to excruciatingly close calls, challenging my best efforts to apply law and divine justice. Sometimes, even as I exhausted my search for the legal line, arguments still divided evenly and issues ended in equipoise. What was I to do? Do any judges really believe *the* legal line always can be located? Do some just trust their gut?

My gut gave me my own methods, two of them spanning the generations I treasured. For all my work, I found daily motivation from the question I imagined, coming early in my career, when Ben and Joel, sleeping so sweetly, might have awakened as I kissed them: "Dad, what did you do today to make the world better?" I worked hard to bring home good answers.

And for the closest calls, whether deciding alone on the trial bench or with colleagues in appellate chambers, I imagined my own three-judge panel. Grampa Charlie and Grampa Ben—I was so proud to have been named for them—both of modest education, immigrant values, absolute integrity, and profound kindness, were as wonderful and wise as anyone I've ever known. There they were, one on each side, steadying my shoulders. I'd make my tentative decision, then confer—run it by them, listen and learn, and feel forever grateful that they held the majority.

Judges, so strong, so fragile; independence, so vital and threatened. "Life," Justice Holmes wrote, "is painting a picture, not doing a sum." I wonder about that. But judicial life? That, I know—reason *and* compassion . . . many sums, and paintings, too.

Acknowledgments

A memoir that would presume to be a legal treatise requires an unusual author—bold, or at least quixotic. It needs an astute editor, perhaps a bit quixotic as well, but better able to distinguish giants and windmills. Its success depends on the candid critiques of careful readers and the commitment of a fine publisher. Fortunately, this memoired treatise has been guided by them all. Wherever it stumbles, the falls are my own. Where it rises, it is lifted by others who contributed their valuable time and invaluable insights.

The first feedback came from Michael Schudson. As a professor at the Columbia University School of Journalism and a recipient of the MacArthur Prize, he was a heavyweight in the academic ring. As my big brother, he was incapable of pulling punches. After reading the manuscript, he emailed: "Well, I think you have something terrific here . . . a fine, powerful book, which means I have only six single-spaced pages of critique. If you want only praise, do not open the attachment!"

Mike also warned that my work, flying back and forth over memoir/treatise borders, might not enjoy a soft landing on the publishing runway: "[T]he university press might see it as not sufficiently scholarly and the commercial press as not sufficiently popular." He reassured me, however, "It will find its publisher. . . . I don't know which editor at which publisher is going to fall in love with it, but he or she is out there."

I can't say whether she fell in love, but Gwen Walker, executive editor of the University of Wisconsin Press, was enticed. She bet on a bold book and, for two years, shared her superb instincts and imparted insightful, steady direction. Thank you, Gwen, for your kindness, wisdom, and trust.

This book matured thanks to the lovingly blunt feedback of friends and relatives and to the sound advice of professional colleagues. For their early readings and cogent comments, I thank Professor Steven Barkan, University of Wisconsin Law School; Judge Leonard Edwards, California Judicial Council; and Steven Engel, Debra Greenfield, Ellen Henak, Benjamin Sperber, and Bonnie Stern Miller. I also gratefully acknowledge those I am unable to name, including three anonymous peer reviewers who evaluated the manuscript and offered thoughtful suggestions.

This book approached final form with help from Madeline Schmid, my excellent legal editor, who provided a painstaking review of every verifiable fact and legal proposition; and from Kathy Hinderaker, my dear lifelong friend who, as always, responded to my request for her uncommon common sense and artistic sensitivity. Finishing touches were applied by senior editor Sheila McMahon, copyeditor Jeri Famighetti, and indexer Carol Roberts. Thank you, Maddy and Kathy; Sheila, Jeri, and Carol.

As mentioned in the final note to chapter 4, wherever appropriate and possible, to ensure accuracy, I consulted individuals directly involved in the cases I've described. I welcomed their input, respected their privacy, and, I hope, honored their lives. I acknowledge their contributions and thank them.

As intimated in chapters 7, 10, and 13, despite my best intentions and "family first" philosophy, I could not prevent my career's tension and sadness from entering our home. Now, allow me to acknowledge more.

Trying to find words to capture my love for Karen, I probably revised the dedication more than any other passage. Still not satisfied, I want to express so much more but here only add thanks for her devotion during many difficult times, and for helping me understand difficult people and dysfunctional systems so that I might pursue justice in the midst of them all.

Thirty years ago, I dedicated my first book to our children, Ben and Joel. They formed the core of my life and the conscience of my career. They still do. Even as adults, they remain foremost in my heart and touch me as only one's children can. Someday, perhaps, they will consider their judgments, reflect on Stoppard's prefatory words, and ponder whether my life's "poem" will be worthy of their own children.

I've mentioned my brother's encouragement of this book but said nothing about his role in my life. Mike created stories for me with our toys on his bedroom floor, turned us into Lewis and Clark for expeditions along the Lake Michigan bluffs, and introduced me to lifelong loves—birds, hiking, history, and literature. My loyal companion, he has always been everything, truly everything, a loving brother can be. And Hod, the brother we lost, infuses these pages with his artistic passion and fierce determination.

Appreciation for my brothers, Mike and Hod, Tom and Steve (no one could be closer), merges with the gratitude I feel for great and gracious parents and grandparents; remarkable Mona; marvelous aunts, Audrey, Pat, and Ruth; my amazing uncle, Marvin, who, with humor and grace, personifies our family's highest ideals and maintains my magnificent mother's spirit in our lives; devoted cousins, Ann, Ellen, Mark, and many more; sweet nieces and nephews; Enid, Julia, Tracie, and all my "in law/in love" sisters and daughters; and of course, my (just ask me about 'em) grandchildren.

I offer a loving salute to my father, who would have celebrated his one hundredth birthday the year I completed this book. No father worked harder, served his country more honorably, or exuded greater pride in his children. And because no man ever loved his four years in Madison more, it is with a hug to him that I feel particular pride in seeing this memoired treatise come from the press of the University of Wisconsin.

A decade before my father's birth, William Howard Taft wrote, "The meanest man in the world is the man who forgets the old friends that helped him on an early day and over early difficulties."[1] I have not forgotten. Wanting to acknowledge them here, I prepared a list of all who helped me "on early day[s] and over early difficulties" and others who have helped ever since. As the list lengthened from dozens to hundreds, I conceded the futility of doing so. Still, I thank you, Eagle, my best man forever; Walt, my wise friend and counselor; and Bonnie, Chris, Christy, Deb, John, Steve and so many others as dear as any bloodliners could be. Thank you all for joining me on my many adventures. I whisper your names as I embrace you from between these lines.

To those I gratefully acknowledge, I must add cherished teachers. Among my superstars: Evelyn Fefer, Sally Hanna, Jackie Seidler, Helen Thompson, and Esther Jane Hoffman at Richards Elementary School; Ervin Nowicki at Whitefish Bay High School; James Cox and Robert Russell at Dartmouth College; Ralph Ellison at New York University; Frank Remington at the Wisconsin Law School. Thank you for your brilliant teaching and for your faith in my future. Add to my writing mentors—Mary Maren in high school, Alan Gaylord and Roger Masters at Dartmouth, and Joe Zeka at the *Wisconsin Law Review*—thank you for the "comeuppances" I deserved. You were direct; I was thin-skinned. You were right; finally, I understood. Thank you for conveying the importance of fresh eyes and the pleasure of almost endless rewriting.

Fostering my career were many mentors, first among them, District Attorney E. Michael McCann and Governor Lee Sherman Dreyfus. With pure motives and independent actions, they exemplified the highest virtues of public service. I thank them for giving me the opportunities to serve. And in recent years, for their inspiring dedication and for the continuing opportunity to serve, I thank Rick Baldauf, Peg Cook, Al Cornell, Frank and Carol Wirkus, Mike and Susan Vitek, Spence, and, truly, our entire Verde Search and Rescue team.

An iconoclast, I might be among the least likely authors to acknowledge institutions, but I have benefited from exceptional ones. A summer camp and a college, Kawaga and Dartmouth, were wonderful; they challenged and mentored me. Marquette University and the University of Wisconsin, through innovative assistant deans, Peter Rofes and Kevin Kelly, believed I had something special to offer law students and, for many years, gave me the chance to try.

Law schools abroad hosted me as their "scholar in residence," enabling me to see America's judiciary through international lenses, teaching me as I taught their students. I thank my gracious hosts at Universidad Diego Portales in Chile, Justus Liebig Universitat in Germany, and Pontificia Universidad Católica in Perú. And I thank the US State Department for a Fulbright fellowship, which supported much of my international teaching from 2010 through 2014.

Both before and during the development of this book, other organizations gave me the chance to test drive my ideas with law students, judges, and professionals of many disciplines. The National Judicial College, the National Council of Juvenile and Family Court Judges, the National Association of State Judicial Educators, and state judicial colleges throughout America sponsored my teaching, and the Chautauqua Institution allowed me to introduce portions of my manuscript to adult learners, lay and professional. Thank you to all who facilitated these opportunities.

Bjorklunden Seminars, an extraordinary adult education program, gave birth to this book. For many years, Bjorklunden, Lawrence University's beautiful retreat center along the Wisconsin shores of Lake Michigan, has allowed me to play—to let my imagination run wild, creating classes in diverse subjects. In 2012 Bjorklunden hosted "In Chambers—Behind the Bench of America's Justice System—Classic Issues/Current Conflicts." Featuring authors from Isabel Allende to Leo Tolstoy, and legal scholars from James Madison to Cousin Vinny, the seminar drew enthusiastic students. Midweek, one exclaimed, "You should write a book." And so . . . in 2015 I offered "Judges, Judgments . . . and Justice? America's Courts in the New Age of Political Pressure." Again, students were not shy, this time helping to harvest the first fruits from my early drafts.

To Bjorklunden's superb staff and spirited students, thank you. To Bjorklunden's delightful director, Mark Breseman, thank you for your leadership and trust. And to Lawrence and Bjorklunden, thank you for your dedication to interdisciplinary education—helping musicians learn law, scientists read literature, writers watch birds, doctors trek trails, engineers recite poetry; and for teaching judges to paint pictures, too.

Miguel de Unamuno wrote: "No basta curar la peste, hay que saber llorarla. ¡Sí, hay que saber llorar!"[2] Thank you to those judges everywhere who embrace independence and often weep, inside and out, as they seek justice. Thank you, judicial educators and talented teachers everywhere, who help hearts throb and eyes twinkle, who invite serious souls to laugh and sad souls to smile. Thank you all for accepting Unamuno's challenge.

And thank you, dear readers, for joining me on this journey and for dedicating yourselves to the world we will never see, the children we will never know. With your help, may they grow to care for our planet, and to care deeply for justice.

Notes

INTRODUCTION

1. Speaking in the US House of Representatives in 1802, Representative John Rutledge Jr., of South Carolina, son of the recently deceased US Supreme Court Chief Justice John Rutledge, was describing the "shield" of the judiciary. See Irving R. Kaufman, "Maintaining Judicial Independence: A Mandate to Judges," *American Bar Association Journal* 66, no. 4 (1980): 470–72.

2. Addressing Virginia's constitutional convention in 1829, and opposing "a proposal that would have permitted Virginia's legislature . . . to repeal a law establishing the superior courts and to thus end the tenure of those holding judicial office," US Supreme Court Chief Justice John Marshall expressed his belief "in the absolute necessity of maintaining a judiciary not vulnerable to inappropriate influences." California Chief Justice Ronald M. George, "John Marshall Award Acceptance Speech," American Bar Association John Marshall Award, California, San Francisco, August 22, 2017.

3. My sponsors were working together under the auspices of the Central and East European Law Initiative (CEELI). Following the fall of the Soviet Union, CEELI was established by the American Bar Association to provide American judges, law professors, and other consultants to emerging European democracies that had requested assistance in developing new constitutions and legal systems. When, about five years later, Russia requested CEELI's assistance, the US Justice Department joined in the project. In 1996, I was a member of CEELI's first teaching team in Russia.

4. See Joseph J. Ellis, *The Quartet: Orchestrating the Second American Revolution, 1783–1789* (New York: Knopf, 2015), a superb study of the efforts of Alexander Hamilton, John Jay, James Madison, and George Washington to replace the Articles of Confederation with the Constitution.

5. Zephyr Teachout, *Corruption in America: From Benjamin Franklin's Snuff Box to Citizens United* (Cambridge, MA: Harvard University Press, 2014), 217.

6. "The judicial Power of the United States, shall be vested in one supreme Court, and in such inferior Courts as the Congress may from time to time ordain

and establish. The Judges, both of the supreme and inferior Courts, shall hold their Offices during good Behaviour [*sic*], and shall, at stated Times, receive for their Services, a Compensation, which shall not be diminished during their Continuance in Office." US Const. art. III, § 1.

7. For my mixed feelings, I am indebted to Jed Handelsman Shugerman's wonderful work *The People's Courts: Pursuing Judicial Independence in America* (Cambridge, MA: Harvard University Press, 2012). At the time of its publication, the author was an assistant professor of law at Harvard University Law School; since 2016, he has been an associate professor of law at Fordham University School of Law.

8. Although America's judicial history holds more than a few political battles over federal court appointments, no era rivals the most recent, extending, at the Supreme Court level, at least from Robert Bork to Clarence Thomas to Merrick Garland and, at the federal district and circuit levels, to the Trump administration. See "Trump's 87 Picks to Be Federal Judges Are 92% White with Just One Black and One Hispanic Nominee," *USA Today*, February 14, 2018.

9. Teachout, *Corruption in America*, 245; *Citizens United v. FEC*, 558 U.S. 310, 447–49 (2010) (Stevens, J., *concurring and dissenting*).

10. Such numbers may seem inflated, but similar statistics are familiar in big jurisdictions. During my trial court years, I averaged twenty-five cases per day; calculating five-day workweeks and correcting for vacations, the ten-year total would be 58,750 cases.

11. For ten years, 1982–92, I served as a trial court judge in Milwaukee County. My first three years were in the juvenile division, hearing cases of "delinquency" (misdemeanor and felony); "waiver" (whether children would be prosecuted and sentenced as juveniles or adults); and civil issues (abuse and neglect, custody and care, and termination of parental rights). My next seven years were in the adult criminal divisions, misdemeanor and felony.

12. For twelve years, 1992–2004, I served as an appellate judge on the Wisconsin Court of Appeals, where my colleagues and I reviewed diverse issues of state law, both civil and criminal.

13. These intermediate appellate courts are relatively new additions to America's legal systems. All states, with their founding, provided trial courts and supreme courts to review trial court decisions. But only starting in 1891 did the federal and approximately forty state systems create intermediate appellate courts—to both expedite appeals for litigants, and to reduce burgeoning caseloads for supreme courts. See Charles Gardner Geyh, *Courting Peril: The Political Transformation of the American Judiciary* (New York: Oxford University Press, 2016), 32. Geyh is the John F. Kimberling Professor of Law at the Indiana University Maurer School of Law.

14. The percentage of litigants appealing trial court outcomes is higher in the federal courts. Of all cases filed, approximately 10 percent are appealed, and of all cases going to judgment, approximately 20 percent are appealed (including approximately 40 percent of those going to trial). Theodore Eisenberg, "Appeal Rates and Outcomes in Tried and Nontried Cases: Further Exploration of Anti-Plaintiff Appellate Outcomes," *Journal of Empirical Legal Studies* 1, no. 3 (2004): 659–88.

15. Concerned about that, I devised ways to keep people close. I did not delegate review of transcripts; I touched the pages, read the words, and tried to feel people between the lines. I did not assign writing of published decisions to law clerks; I labored over them, draft after draft, trying to understand not only the law but emotions as well. I formed a stylistic habit, starting each decision, "_____ appeals," adding the name of the person or party bringing the appeal. While other opening words also would have been appropriate, none, in my view, punctuated the point: every case starts with someone calling out for help.

What is a "published" decision? In appellate courts, almost all decisions are written, printed, and disseminated to the parties in each case (and now, in many states, made available electronically to all). But only "published" decisions are printed and issued to the public for potential use in future cases. These are decisions by courts of appeals, which are printed in their entirety and, along with supreme court decisions, "published" in the "official reports"—the impressively bound books covering the walls of law firm libraries and judicial chambers.

In almost all intermediate appellate state courts (the "Court of Appeals" in Wisconsin and most other states), the judges decide which few of their many decisions will be published (usually about 10 percent). The publication process is hidden and almost unknown outside the world of appellate lawyers and judges. The mechanics are simple. In confidential and untranscribed meetings or conference calls, the judges periodically review their most recent decisions. They evaluate which merit publication, selecting those that cover new ground—"set precedent"—and thus guide lawyers and judges in future cases. Those they choose become law for their state, with precedential authority equal to that of the state's supreme court decisions.

Thus, the difference between published and unpublished decisions can be consequential in courts every day. The published decisions are law, controlling or at least influencing attorneys' arguments and judges' decisions; the unpublished decisions, depending on the state or federal jurisdiction, cannot even be mentioned, or can be cited only as "persuasive," not "binding," authority. See Diane Slomowitz, "Watch Your Step with Unpublished Opinions," *Wisconsin Law Journal*, September 28, 2010; see also Federal Rules of Appellate Procedure 32.1. The significance of the distinction even reaches into academic research. Astute scholars appreciate the limited scope of their view into appellate decision-making: "Even in countries with good case databases, there are potential biases if one considers only published and not all judicial decisions." Julio Ríos-Figueroa and Jeffrey K. Staton, "An Evaluation of Cross-National Measures of Judicial Independence," *Journal of Law, Economics, and Organization* 30, no. 1 (March 1, 2014): 110, n.5.

Published decisions, by both intermediate and supreme appellate judges, are called "common law"—law created not by legislatures, in the form of statutes, but by appellate judges, in the form of their written decisions on actual cases. On the issues presented in an appeal, each published decision sets the precedent, or at least advances the analysis, *for that state* (or federal circuit, if issued by federal appellate judges). Judges must abide by the precedents of their state's appellate courts. Judges also may consider decisions of other states' courts, but they need not follow them, and they must not follow any in conflict with their own state's precedents.

Thus, to summarize: trial judges, acting alone and deciding issues in the cases before them, never set precedent for any other case or court. But appellate judges, both intermediate and supreme, acting in groups of three or more, resolve issues on appeal from trial courts and publish decisions, setting statewide precedent.

But if some intermediate and all supreme appellate decisions are published in the same books and have equal, statewide precedential power, do they differ in any way? Yes. A state's supreme court can affirm, reverse, or modify decisions of the state's intermediate court of appeals. Still, the clout of the intermediate appellate courts continues to increase. Because they consider every appeal, even their small published percentage usually adds up to more published decisions than the state supreme court's total. Indeed, the intermediate state courts of appeals have become "the courts of last resort in virtually all cases," thus "elevat[ing] the political profile of their work." Geyh, *Courting Peril*, 6.

16. Most state supreme courts hold oral arguments regularly. In state intermediate appellate courts, however, the situation is very different. Practices vary widely. In some states, the intermediate appellate court conducts oral arguments in almost all cases and, as a result, hosts so many that, according to many judges, the arguments are perfunctory and of little value. In other states, intermediate appellate courts almost never hold oral arguments. (Each month in the appellate district where I served, my colleagues and I reviewed about fifty appeals. Each month, however, on average, we held oral argument—often lengthy and very meaningful—in only a few cases.)

17. Brutus XI (January 31, 1788), and Brutus XV (March 20, 1788). The author, believed to have been the anti-Federalist Robert Yates, was a New York judge who had served as a delegate to the Constitutional Convention. Writing anonymously as "Brutus," he provided sixteen essays addressed to "the Citizens of the State of New York," published in the *New York Journal*, 1787–88. (Brutus was one of Julius Caesar's assassins, credited with helping to prevent him from overthrowing the Roman Republic.)

18. Richard A. Posner, *How Judges Think* (Cambridge, MA: Harvard University Press, 2008), 120.

19. And might I also do so in chapter 2, where I relate lessons learned during my years as a prosecutor that linked to my judicial life? My assignments as a prosecutor were unusual; some gained notoriety. Honestly described, they include certain failings but also reflect some successes, accurate descriptions of which advance our analysis but, perhaps, immodestly so.

20. See also, e.g., Wisconsin Code of Judicial Conduct, Wis. SCR 60.04(4)(m) ("A judge may not disclose or use, for any purpose unrelated to judicial duties, non-public information acquired in a judicial capacity").

21. See, e.g., Wis. SCR 60.05(2) ("Avocational Activities. A judge may speak, write, lecture, teach and participate in other extra-judicial activities concerning the

law, the legal system, the administration of justice"). As Robert M. O'Neil, former law professor, president of the University of Virginia, and director of the Thomas Jefferson Center for the Protection of Free Expression, explained:

> Judges have not always been so severely constrained. . . . "[T]he level of tolerance shown judicial speech since the birth of the United States has fluctuated depending upon the passion of the speech, the popularity of the speaker, and the power of those against whom the speech was directed." . . . [P]ublic confidence in and support for the bench "will only decline unless the public understands some details of the constraints under which judges must adjudicate. . . . [J]udges must take the forefront in actions to educate the alienated." . . . There are, and should continue to be, special limits on judicial expression—restraints that are necessary to preserve both the fact and the appearance of objectivity in our courts. Yet, such vital interests do not require that the people who are most expert about, and often best able to demystify, the workings of our courts, need be kept silent.

Robert O'Neil, "Assaults on the Judiciary," *Trial* 34, no. 9 (1998): 54–65 (quoting former ABA president Talbot "Sandy" D'Alemberte, and Professor Erwin Chemerinsky, dean of the University of California–Irvine Law School).

22. And not for lack of interest. Journalists, perhaps frustrated by their limited success in getting behind the bench to dissect decision-making, have had little choice but to concentrate on blatant bribery and exposed scandal, both rare, or to pursue tangential theories. Consider, for example, a recent attempt to tally travels and speeches of US Supreme Court Justices in order to draw decisional inferences from the number and nature of such engagements and their sponsors: Adam Liptak, "Justices' Calendars Full, and Hard to Check," *New York Times*, June 2, 2015.

23. See, e.g., Benjamin N. Cardozo, *The Nature of the Judicial Process* (New Haven, CT: Yale University Press, 1928); Jerome Frank, *Law and the Modern Mind* (1930; repr., New York: Tudor, 1936). As Judge Posner notes, "judges on judging" is "a neglected literature." Posner, *How Judges Think*, 256. Why? This "literature" remains neglected because it is so theoretical as to be of little practical value. It offers "little understanding of how cases are actually decided, where the judges who decided a case were coming from, and what *really* made them alter existing doctrine as distinct from what they said made them change it" (219). Thus, as Judge Posner wrote, "how unrealistic are the conceptions of the judge held by most people, including practicing lawyers and eminent law professors, who have never been judges—and even by some judges" (2).

24. Posner, *How Judges Think*, 112.

25. Posner, *How Judges Think*, 121. See William Shakespeare, *King Lear* (New York: French, 1967), act 1, scene 1.

26. Posner, *How Judges Think*, 2–3, 6.

27. Posner, *How Judges Think*, 6.

28. Posner, *How Judges Think*, 217–18.

29. Irving R. Kaufman, "Judges Must Speak Out," *New York Times*, January 30, 1982. Similarly, Supreme Court Justice Hugo Black observed that "an enforced silence, however limited, solely in the name of preserving the dignity of the bench, would probably engender resentment, suspicion, and contempt." *Bridges v. California*, 314 U.S. 252, 270–71 (1941).

30. "Some of the most thoughtful and careful commentary on secrecy in democracies . . . finds secrecy in government suspect on its face but nonetheless justifiable in many circumstances." See Michael Schudson, *The Rise of the Right to Know: Politics and the Culture of Transparency, 1945–1975* (Cambridge, MA: Belknap Press of Harvard University Press, 2015), 23. It may be noteworthy that courts are not under the jurisdiction of the Freedom of Information Act. Schudson, *The Rise of the Right to Know*, 35.

31. Open doors should not invite open season on judges or other individuals involved in the cases to be considered. I am trying to enlighten, not embarrass or insult. Accordingly, as appropriate and possible, while using many real names throughout this work, I have changed others so as to reduce the risks to privacy. The aliases are not coded in any way but merely correlated to an individual's order of appearance in the narrative and, in order, the most common first and last names in the United States.

Chapter 1. Who's the Judge?

1. Richard A. Posner, *How Judges Think* (Cambridge, MA: Harvard University Press, 2008), 1.

2. See, e.g., Wis. Stat. § 971.20. "Substitution," sometimes called "peremptory disqualification," is available under the statutes of approximately twenty states. See *State v. Holmes*, 106 Wis. 2d 31, 63 n.29, 315 N.W.2d 703, 718 (1982). See also Charles Gardner Geyh, *Courting Peril: The Political Transformation of the American Judiciary* (New York: Oxford University Press, 2016), 105, n.25, 152.

3. See Reid J. Epstein, "Trump Attacks Federal Judge in Trump U Case," *Wall Street Journal*, May 27, 2016. See also Matt Ford, "Trump Attacks a 'Mexican' U.S. Federal Judge," *The Atlantic*, May 28, 2016.

4. "[M]any lawyers have long been reluctant to seek disqualification of judges, who are unlikely to second-guess their own impartiality and who may take umbrage at the suggestion that their impartiality is in doubt." Geyh, *Courting Peril*, 123. Not only might they "take umbrage," but savvy or suspicious judges may believe that such requests for recusal are "strategically motivated" to soften them up. Geyh, *Courting Peril*, 151.

Reasons for recusal, while usually clear, still can be controversial. In 2016, the US Supreme Court decided the appeal of a death row inmate, Terrance Williams, who contended that former Pennsylvania Chief Justice Ronald D. Castille should have disqualified himself from a previous state supreme court appeal because, before becoming a judge, he had been the supervising district attorney in Williams's case and had authorized seeking the death penalty. In a five-three decision, the US Supreme

Court agreed, remanding the case to the Pennsylvania Supreme Court for reconsideration, without Justice Castille. See Adam Liptak, "Court Counters Judge on a Call Not to Recuse Himself," *New York Times*, June 10, 2016. See also Michael Mechanic, "This Supreme Court Case Shows the Perils of Appointing Prosecutors as Judges," *Mother Jones*, March 8, 2016.

5. Substitution has been controversial. In *Holmes*, Wisconsin's trial judges challenged the state's substitution statute. *State v. Holmes*, 106 Wis. 2d 31 (1982). Contending that the statute violated the separation of powers, the judges argued that the legislature, by enacting such a law, had usurped the judiciary's authority to administer the courts. The state supreme court rejected the judges' challenge. Nevertheless, in Wisconsin and elsewhere, the controversy has continued. See, e.g., Steve Schultze, "[Legislator, Chief Judge] Offer Ideas to Cut Judge-Shopping by Defense Lawyers," *Milwaukee Journal*, September 6, 1989; Patrick Jasperse, "Judges Split on Substitution," *Milwaukee Journal*, October 10, 1989. Some states "level the playing field" by also allowing prosecutors to substitute. In such systems, supporters say, substitution then not only shields defendants from judges who may be unduly harsh but also protects the public from judges who may be too lenient. See, e.g., Alex Kozinski "Criminal Law 2.0," *Georgetown Law Journal* 103 (2015): xxxviii–xxxix ("This tactic [of filing peremptory challenges] can be used en masse to effectively preclude a judge from hearing any criminal cases"). [Alex Kozinski, an esteemed federal judge on the US Court of Appeals for the 9th Circuit for many years, retired in December 2017, amid allegations from several women, including former law clerks, that he had behaved inappropriately. See Matt Zapotosky, "Federal Appeals Judge Announces Immediate Retirement amid Probe of Sexual Misconduct Allegations," *Washington Post*, December 18, 2017; see also Dara E. Purvis, "When Judges Prey on Clerks," *New York Times*, December 13, 2017; Editorial, "Who Will Judge the Judge?," *New York Times*, December 15, 2017; Adam Liptak, "Court Must Better Police Themselves on Harassment, Chief Justice Says," *New York Times*, January 1, 2018.] Geyh sees substitution in a much broader context, viewing its possible spread to more states as a useful component of the new "legal culture paradigm" he recommends. See Geyh, *Courting Peril*, 152.

6. For a fascinating analysis of how federalism emerged, see Joseph J. Ellis, *The Quartet: Orchestrating the Second American Revolution, 1783–1789* (New York: Knopf, 2015). Under the Articles of Confederation, "Each state retain[ed] its sovereignty, freedom, and independence" (6, quoting the Articles of Confederation). Replacing the Articles and trying to correct for their many deficiencies, the Constitution still preserved much state autonomy. See US Const. amend. X ("The powers not delegated to the United States by the Constitution, nor prohibited by it to the states, are reserved to the states respectively, or to the people"). Moreover, as Ellis explained, the Constitution said almost nothing about America's federal judiciary and nothing about state judiciaries, thus leaving "judicial authority . . . infinitely negotiable in the future." Ellis, *The Quartet*, 172.

While legally, morally, and politically problematic, federalism has advantages. Consider federal Judge Frank Easterbrook's praise for "a federal republic where local differences are cherished as elements of liberty, rather than eliminated in a search for national uniformity." *Friedman v. City of Highland Park*, 784 F.3d 406, 412 (7th Cir. 2015).

7. The statistical reality was not quite so stark. During my first two years serving in the juvenile courts, my substitution rate ranged from 4 percent to 16 percent. Moreover, because the juvenile division had only two other judges, substituting "against" me gave any defendant a fifty-fifty chance of substituting "into" a court of first choice. Later, however, in the adult criminal courts, serving with six other judges, my substitution rate rose substantially. See Eldon Knoche, "Substitutions May Force Transfer of Schudson," *Milwaukee Sentinel*, September 7, 1989; Eldon Knoche, "Judge Transferred over High Substitution Rate," *Milwaukee Sentinel*, September 28, 1989.

8. Chuck Kahn also was one of two trusted attorneys I had appointed as court commissioners. "Commissioner" may be confusing; in the federal and many state systems, "magistrate" is the more common title. In some states, they may be full-time, publicly employed attorneys exercising quasi-judicial authority in bail hearings, divorce mediations, and a host of other matters preceding a judge's review. But "Commissioner" also may be the honorary title of attorneys who, while still in private practice, receive such appointments from judges. In Wisconsin, the designation allows them to perform weddings and invoke the title for professional prestige. Chuck, a friend since law school, was an astute attorney. I trusted his advice—*never* sought on a case but sometimes requested on issues of bench/bar politics and judicial administration. In any case in which he or a member of his firm appeared before me, I disclosed the relationship and offered to recuse.

9. See James Gribble, "[Schudson] Plans to Retain 'Innovative' Image," *Milwaukee Journal*, October 22, 1989, describing me as "controversial"—an "innovator," a "maverick," and, to the surprise of friends familiar with my liberal leanings, one with a "classically conservative legal philosophy." Gribble explained, "A believer in the letter of the Bill of Rights when it comes to protecting rights of the accused, he also is a believer in stern punishment when the occasion demands it." Innovation may seem at odds with precedential fealty, but it also may be integrated into the art of judging. As Judge Posner explained: "[I]nnovative judges challenge the accepted standards of their art, just as innovative artists challenge the accepted standards of their arts. As there are no fixed, incontestable criteria of artistic excellence, so there are no fixed, incontestable criteria of judicial excellence. And in law as in art, the innovators have the greater influence on the evolution of their field." Posner, *How Judges Think*, 12–13. Further, "Norms govern the various art genres, just as norms govern judicial decisions—and in both cases the norms are contestable" (63).

10. "If I am right in thinking that the judges in our system have a large measure of discretion, the exercise of which is bound to be influenced by personal experiences, character foibles, and so forth, biographical details may help to explain a judge's decisions." Posner, How Judges Think, 217.

11. Posner, *How Judges Think*, 97.

CHAPTER 2. THE PROSECUTOR'S PERSPECTIVE

1. "With few exceptions, judges are lawyers: State law demands it; and in the federal system, no nominee for an Article III judgeship could survive the confirmation gauntlet without a law degree." Charles Gardner Geyh, *Courting Peril: The Political Transformation of the American Judiciary* (New York: Oxford University Press, 2016), 84.

2. Although some state judges were former federal prosecutors, such a professional progression is relatively rare. Federal prosecutors, also known as "assistant US attorneys," are responsible for prosecuting violations of federal civil and criminal laws in federal courts. They are selected by each federal district's US attorney, appointed by the president. With more manageable caseloads, higher compensation, and stronger pensions than their state counterparts, federal prosecutors more often see their positions as careers, not stepping stones to private practice or judicial posts. Still, in high percentages, federal court judges come from the ranks of federal prosecutors, and that's so regardless of the political persuasions of the presidents appointing them. For example, 40.8 percent of President Reagan's appointees to the federal bench and 45.7 percent of President Obama's first-term appointees had once been federal prosecutors. See Bob Egelko, "Obama Nominations Heavy on Ex-Prosecutors," *SF Gate*, February 3, 2013. See also Josie Duffy Rice, "Former Prosecutors Shouldn't Be Judges: Here's Why," *Daily Kos*, April 27, 2016 ("[W]hile there are no official numbers, research indicates that a significant number of state judges are also former prosecutors").

3. Counting is complicated. Do state courts include village and municipal courts? Do federal courts include adjudicative venues for employment discrimination suits, immigration and deportation conflicts, tax disputes; do they include military tribunals or tribal courts? Thus, depending on the categories one counts, my 90 percent estimate, more impressionistic than precise, is on the very conservative side. According to data cited by Geyh, in 2010 the federal courts handled 361,323 cases; the state courts, 103.5 million. Geyh, *Courting Peril*, 26.

4. See, e.g., Comment to Wisconsin's ethical standard, *Special Responsibilities of a Prosecutor*, stating, in part: "A prosecutor has the responsibility of a minister of justice and not simply that of an advocate. This responsibility carries with it specific obligations to see that the defendant is accorded procedural justice and that guilt is decided upon the basis of sufficient evidence. Precisely how far the prosecutor is required to go in this direction is a matter of debate and varies in different jurisdictions. Many jurisdictions have adopted the ABA Standards of Criminal Justice Relating to Prosecution Function, which in turn are the product of prolonged and careful deliberation by lawyers experienced in both criminal prosecution and defense." Wis. SCR 20:3.8 comment (1).

5. For my discussion of criteria underlying such decisions, see Billie Wright Dziech and Charles B. Schudson, *On Trial: America's Courts and Their Treatment of Sexually Abused Children* (Boston: Beacon Press, 1991), 36–39.

6. *The MacNeil Lehrer Report*, #799-4079, October 19, 1978 (re-broadcast December 22, 1978); Charles B. Schudson, "The Criminal Justice System as Family:

Trying the Impossible for Battered Women," *Battered Women: Issues of Public Policy: A Consultation Sponsored by the United States Commission on Civil Rights, Washington, D.C., January 30–31, 1978* (Washington, DC: The Commission, 1978).

7. See *State v. Collins*, No. 1975CF005829 (Milwaukee Co. Nov. 17, 1976).

8. Historically, the reason is revealing. In the period leading to Congress's creation of Medicaid (Title XIX of the Social Security Act, enacted in 1965–66), lawmakers considered whether to monitor the millions of dollars Medicaid would be paying to the professionals providing care. As things turned out, Congress approved the program, but not the monitoring; Medicaid *recipients* would be watched and often prosecuted, but, lawmakers assumed, *providers*—particularly doctors—could be trusted. Years passed before Congress attacked provider fraud, establishing state-based "Medicaid Fraud Control Units" in 1977 and enacting the Inspectors General Act of 1978. See Helane Morrison, "Joint Attack on Medicaid Fraud Set," *Milwaukee Journal*, August 4, 1978. See also Michael Schudson, *The Rise of the Right to Know: Politics and the Culture of Transparency, 1945–1975* (Cambridge, MA: Belknap Press of Harvard University Press, 2015), 239. Part of the attack started in San Diego and Milwaukee with the "cross-designation" of a few state and federal prosecutors in order to give them authority to share investigative information, coordinate federal/state/local law enforcement, and select from both federal and state statutes and courts according to their relative strategic advantages. See Carla DeDominicis, "The Two-Court Prosecutors," *National Law Journal*, January 11, 1982.

As one of three cross-designated prosecutors in Wisconsin, I served as an assistant Milwaukee County district attorney, a special assistant Wisconsin attorney general, and a special assistant US attorney. See Bill Hurley, "3 Forces Join in Probe of Health Aid," *Milwaukee Sentinel*, April 27, 1977. Nice résumé builders, to be sure but, of importance for our purposes, these three roles allowed me to investigate through both federal grand juries and state "John Doe" proceedings, and gain experience in both federal and state courts. And wearing these three hats, I saw politics at its best. District Attorney McCann, a Democrat (and perhaps a Socialist at heart), initiated the investigations. With our discovery of widespread fraud, he reached out to Wisconsin Attorney General Bronson C. La Follette, an elected Democrat, and US Attorney William F. Mulligan, a Republican presidential appointee. All three must have seen political plums hanging from a low branch, but they never exhibited any turf-protecting tendencies. They realized that such sizable fraud exceeded the grasp of any one office and that success and credit could be shared. For years, complete cooperation followed. I experienced only one act of political jockeying and that, regretfully, was my own premature disclose of an indictment. See Mary Zahn and Dan Patrinos, "Charges Due in Overbilling to Medicaid," *Milwaukee Sentinel*, November 10, 1978.

Our efforts led to convictions and imprisonments, huge monetary recoveries, and, for the three cross-designated prosecutors, the US Justice Department Award for Superior Performance. See United States Department of Justice press release, July 31, 1980. But "shucks, we were just doing our job." While complicated in some respects, our job had been relatively easy because the crooks had been clumsy. Devising their schemes long before anyone was watching, they seemed to have assumed that no one ever would look. We needed only to find cooperative witnesses, then do the math to prove fraudulent billings, some for days that exceeded twenty-four hours.

9. In writing "not ready for prime time," I run the risk of perpetuating the common misunderstanding that often results from the traditional felony/misdemeanor hierarchy, inextricably connected to the daily life of young prosecutors. State statutes divide crimes into felonies and misdemeanors. While statutory schemes differ, many define a felony as any crime punishable by more than one year in prison, a misdemeanor as any crime punishable by one year or less. Practitioners and the public, therefore, presume that felonies are serious and difficult to prosecute, misdemeanors less so. DA office status stratification follows; seasoned prosecutors handle felonies while less experienced or respected ones labor over misdemeanors. But such separations render ironic results. Some nonviolent felonies—forgery or caught-in-the-act burglaries, for example—are at the less serious end of the spectrum and almost always end in guilty pleas. But some misdemeanors—drunk driving, for example—are deadly dangerous; others, such as battery to a woman or resistance to a police officer, are violent and difficult to prove, often resulting in jury trials.

10. I do not denigrate alternative schools or social work services. Indeed, in arguing that some doctors and agency directors should be imprisoned (and not coddled with the "probation and restitution" often granted white-collar criminals), I emphasized that their crimes threatened the continuation of Medicaid coverage for legitimate social services. Sentencing one of the agency executives to prison, Judge Marvin C. Holz echoed that theme: "Perhaps the saddest aspect of the crimes which you have committed is directed to those who would benefit by such programs. Psychotherapy is not accepted by everyone. There are many who doubt that it has any place in treatment. I happen to be one of those who thinks it does. But when there are abuses such as . . . occurred here, such programs are first to be touched by the budgetary ax." *State v. Cook*, July 14, 1978, transcript at 8.

11. Interestingly enough, in 2015, the John Doe suddenly swirled in political controversy. The *New York Times* editorialized and, I believe, correctly explained:

> Gov. Scott Walker of Wisconsin . . . signed a bill to protect public officials like himself from [the John Doe law,] an effective and well-established tool for rooting out political corruption. . . .
>
> Mr. Walker has been a target of two John Doe investigations in recent years. The first, which looked into misconduct by his aides or associates while he served as Milwaukee [C]ounty [E]xecutive, led to six convictions. The second involved allegations of illegally coordinated fund-raising between Mr. Walker's campaign for governor and conservative political groups. . . .
>
> Under the new law, which passed on party-line votes in the Republican-controlled Legislature, neither of these investigations would be permitted. Bribery, official misconduct, campaign-finance violations and many other election law offenses—all are now exempt from a law that has served Wisconsin well, and without controversy, since the mid-nineteenth century.

For years, the John Doe law has been crucial in combating political corruption in both major parties, but because Mr. Walker was a rising conservative star, there were predictable howls from right-wing forces. . . .

The law will continue to apply in cases involving violent or drug-related crimes. Where it will not apply is corruption cases against politicians, for whom the new law carves out an unexplained and unjustified exception.

See The Editorial Board, "The Revenge of Scott Walker," *New York Times*, October 27, 2015. Prosecutors appealed the Wisconsin Supreme Court's rejection of their challenge to the new law's exemption for political corruption cases but, in 2016, the US Supreme Court declined to consider the case. Matthew DeFour, "US Supreme Court Rejects John Doe Appeal," *Wisconsin State Journal*, October 4, 2016.

12. This section is adapted, in part, from Charles B. Schudson, Ashton P. Onellion, and Ellen Hochstedler, "Nailing an Omelet to the Wall: Prosecuting Nursing Home Homicide," in *Corporations as Criminals*, ed. Ellen Hochstedler (Beverly Hills: SAGE, 1984), 131–45.

13. In most states, "coroners" or "medical examiners" have authority, independent of police and prosecutors, to investigate causes of suspicious deaths and to recommend whether to file criminal charges. They conduct their investigations through "inquests"—public hearings at which witnesses testify under oath.

14. Charging a "corporate partnership"? For a white-collar-crime prosecutor, the controversy brought about by Mitt Romney's 2012 campaign comment—that a corporation is a "person"—was silly. Politically, as things turned out, his words were imprudent, but legally, his remark was unremarkable. Throughout statutes and appellate law, a corporation is a "person" or "party," able to sue and be sued. That opens the legal door to valuable prosecutions of business entities. In the absence of a "smoking gun" in anyone's hand, that may be the best a good prosecutor can do and, by disgracing a corporation and recovering millions in restitution and fines, such a case can do justice. Still, prosecutors know that behind almost all such crimes are executives who made decisions that destroyed lives. When it is not possible to identify them and prove their knowledge and conduct, prosecution of their corporations may be the only option. When, however, such prosecutions become the first or most frequently used option, they may lead to the lazy avoidance of more tenacious pursuit and prosecution of executives, who then come to view restitution and fines as affordable "costs of doing business." Moreover, some prosecutors, attracted to the easier option, may not cultivate the investigative instincts and courtroom skills to prosecute executives who deserve to be jailed, and whose incarceration would offer stronger deterrence. See Ellen Hochstedler, ed., *Corporations as Criminals* (Beverly Hills: SAGE, 1984). See also Jesse Eisinger, *The Chickenshit Club: Why the Justice Department Fails to Prosecute Executives* (New York: Simon and Schuster, 2017); Jesse Eisinger, "What Enron Taught Robert Mueller," *New York Times*, July 16, 2017.

15. See, e.g., Carl Hulse, "A G.O.P. Problem: 'Repeal and Replace,' but with What?," *New York Times*, January 16, 2017. In 2018, the unsavory mix of profit motives and human services emerged again with President Trump's termination of

David Shulkin, secretary of the Department of Veterans Affairs. See David J. Shulkin, "A Move That Will Hurt Veterans," *New York Times*, March 30, 2018.

16. See Thomas Heinen, "Home's Ex-Boss Convicted: Jury Finds Negligent Homicide in Patient Death," *Milwaukee Journal*, November 14, 1981.

17. By 1985, according to the study of "chronically deficient" skilled-care nursing homes presented to the US Senate Committee on Aging, of thirty-five states reporting on their problematic facilities, Illinois and Wisconsin had become two of the three best. See "Elderly Care: 'Thousands Warehoused,'" *USA Today*, May 22, 1986.

18. But immodest confidence was not always with me. Months before filing charges, in a memo to Deputy District Attorney Herman John, a wonderful colleague and Mr. McCann's top aide, I confided:

> The case is the most difficult I've ever had. The defendants are among the most powerful nursing home owners in the country. Although we have succeeded in piercing the conspiracy, the case is fragile. . . . The evidence flows from so many witnesses, and the theory of the case has never been tried before. I try over and over again to simplify and narrow the focus (after all, twelve strangers have to understand it) but so often it jumps at me in unpredictable ways. Each time I dive into financial records, I feel so inadequate and wonder if I am falling into a trap that the defendants' accountants have so carefully set.
> . . . As you know, I grew up very close to my grandparents, and was blessed to have all four of them alive and well even through my college years. . . . As I work this case, I feel their presence, and I see the faces of the hundreds of nursing home residents I have seen during the last two years. I feel these helpless people depending on me, and I see the future of so many other people who will become nursing home residents—a future, the quality of which might relate to the quality of this case. In short, hopefully without being overburdened by any unrealistic sense of self-importance, I am burdened by the importance of this case. . . . I realize that my background is inadequate and I am trying to compensate with passion and perspiration.
> Of course I believe we will be successful—resoundingly so. And, of course, I know that the vigilance of the state, as reflected by the very fact of thorough investigation, already provides a significant public service. But, short of total success, I am looking for no consolation. For the word must go out to nursing home owners and administrators: "You shall not squeeze your dollars from the bodies of our elderly and helpless. And if you do, you will share their fate of long incarceration."

19. I testified before a legislative committee (see, e.g., "Senate Human Services Committee/Statement of Charles B. Schudson," March 7, 1979), addressed a conference of nursing home owners and administrators, advised prosecutors in other states, and authored or contributed to published works on the case (see, e.g., John Pray, "State v. Serebin: Causation and the Criminal Liability of Nursing Home Administrators," *Wisconsin Law Review* [1986]: 339–66). District Attorney McCann wrote that I had "most successfully plowed virgin territory with this prosecution,"

and that he had "marveled" at the "ingenuity in developing this concept of neglect and admired the painstaking patience with which" I had "sedulously [gone] about investigating this matter." Following the administrator's sentencing, *Newsweek* reported that the Glendale administrator was "the first . . . ever to be sentenced to prison for the death of a patient under his care" and that it took me "five dogged years . . . to investigate the case and pursue the legal possibilities." "Reckless Homicide in a Nursing Home," *Newsweek* 99 (1982): 66.

20. See, e.g., "Nursing Home Case May Take Years," *Milwaukee Journal*, July 18, 1979; John Fauber, "Extradition Battle May Set a Record," *Milwaukee Sentinel*, December 13, 1982; "Man [Henry Gully, liaison between the Chicago owners and their Milwaukee administrator] Guilty in Nursing Home Case," *Milwaukee Sentinel*, April 26, 1986; "Care Home Agent [Gully] Pleads Guilty," *Milwaukee Journal*, April 27, 1986; John Fauber, "Delays Keep Chicago Men from Appearing in Case," *Business Journal*, April 6, 1987; Eldon Knoche, "3 Enter Pleas in 13-Year-Old Case," *Milwaukee Sentinel*, October 26, 1988.

21. Although the Glendale case caught Governor Dreyfus's attention, I believe three other factors eventually led to my selection from a field of forty-four applicants. First, Dreyfus had decided not to run for re-election. Thus, he had nothing to lose and no need to placate political allies who might have been troubled by my liberal leanings. Second, unknown to me until the last stage of selection, one of my references, Ben Barkin, a family friend, also was the governor's lifelong friend, and one on whom he had regularly relied for advice. Third, when religion came to be a possible factor in the governor's decision, I wrote Ben, as well as another supporter, Max Karl, two of the most prominent members of Wisconsin's Jewish community. My letter read, in part:

> I understand that Governor Dreyfus has asked you to meet with leaders of the Jewish community, and make a recommendation for a judicial appointment. To those who meet with you, please convey these thoughts.
>
> I have serious misgivings about any process that renders a choice of a "Jewish judge." . . . I am concerned that competitive pressures have imposed terms that . . . should have no impact on a judicial appointment. If leadership in the Jewish community is to be a credential for the judiciary, who defines it? If leadership is family power and influence, I do not have it. If it is measured by wealth or contributions, I do not have it. Yet, I believe I am a leader according to terms and traditions that emphatically state that an *outstanding* judge, not a "Jewish judge," is what Jews should most fervently desire.
>
> . . . I maintain sensitivity to a very real religious concern. I appreciate that only sixty-five years ago, Harvard President Lowell sent the White House an anti-Brandeis petition and, even after Brandeis was confirmed, Justice Reynolds refused to sit beside him. I suggest . . . that my appointment will be best for the Jewish community precisely because it will be best for the whole community . . . because I will bring to the judiciary . . . independence, scholarship, creativity, and compassion.

I sent a copy to Dreyfus. When, months later, at my investiture, we met for the first time, he told me that this letter had convinced him to appoint me.

22. "[A]bout half of the states and the District of Columbia have no minimum-age limits for trial and appellate court judges. And of the states that do . . . , nine set the age limit at a mere 18 for trial court judges in some or all of their courts. That begs another question: Have states decided to entrust the administration of justice to teenagers and 20-somethings? Not exactly. Most states have requirements [for years of licensed legal experience] in place to keep that from happening." Mark DiVincenzo, "Open Court: How Young Is Too Young to Be a Judge?," National Center for State Courts, *NCSC Connected Community*, February 18, 2018, http://connected.ncsc.org.

CHAPTER 3. THE DECISION-MAKING IDEAL

1. Socrates, "Four things belong to a judge: to hear courteously, to answer wisely, to consider soberly, and to decide impartially." Franklin P. Adams, *FPA Book of Quotations; a New Collection of Famous Sayings, Reflecting the Wisdom and the Wit of Times Past and Present and Including the Virtuous, Humorous, and Philosophic Commentary on Life by Men and Women of Every Age, Together with Riches from the Profound Wells of the Bible, Proverbs, and Anonymity* (New York: Funk and Wagnalls, 1952), 466.

2. See, e.g., Lee Epstein, *Oxford Handbook of U.S. Judicial Behavior* (New York: Oxford University Press, 2017), a valuable volume of thirty-eight academic considerations of judicial conduct and decision-making in a variety of contexts. For other excellent entry points to the history and literature of judicial independence, both in America and abroad, see the studies of David S. Law, Washington University Charles Nagel Chair of Constitutional Law and Political Science, including his fine summary, "Judicial Independence," in *Britannica*. Charles Nagel, *Encyclopaedia Britannica*, 8th ed., s.v. "Judicial Independence" (Chicago: Encyclopaedia Britannica, 2009). See also "Judicial Independence Resource Guide," National Center for State Courts, http://www.ncsc.org/Topics/Judicial-Officers/Judicial-Independence/Resource-Guide.aspx.

3. See Julio Ríos-Figueroa and Jeffrey K. Staton, "An Evaluation of Cross-National Measures of Judicial Independence," *Journal of Law, Economics, and Organization* 30, no. 1 (March 1, 2014): 128.

4. Laurie L. Levenson, "Book Review of The People's Courts: Pursuing Judicial Independence in America, by Jed Handelsman Shugerman," *Journal of Legal Education* 62, no. 4 (May 2013): 631–39; Paul Friedman, "Taking the High Road: Civility, Judicial Independence, and the Rule of Law," *New York University Annual Survey of American Law* 58, no. 2 (2001): 187–202. Similarly, as Supreme Court Justice Antonin Scalia explained, a single definition of "impartiality" may be equally elusive. See *Republican Party of Minnesota v. White*, 536 U.S. 765, 775–78 (2002).

5. See Ríos-Figueroa and Staton, "An Evaluation of Cross-National Measures of Judicial Independence." The authors conclude, "In light of its latency, scholars ought

to be creative in their efforts to identify the ways in which independent judicial behavior is likely to manifest" (128).

6. See Ríos-Figueroa and Staton, "An Evaluation of Cross-National Measures of Judicial Independence," 105–6.

7. In full, "A judge shall uphold and promote the independence, integrity, and impartiality of the judiciary, and shall avoid impropriety and the appearance of impropriety." ABA Model Code of Judicial Conduct Canon 1.

8. Charles Gardner Geyh, *Courting Peril: The Political Transformation of the American Judiciary* (New York: Oxford University Press, 2016), 21. That "pivotal role," Geyh explained, "evolved against the backdrop of an ancient and pervasive understanding, reflected in folktales, plays, biblical passages, novels, poems, polemics, and historical accounts" (5).

9. See *Adams, FPA Book of Quotations*, 466 (quoting Socrates).

10. Abraham Lincoln, *Abraham Lincoln: Mystic Chords of Memory* (New York: Book-of-the-Month Club, 1984).

11. Lincoln, *Abraham Lincoln: Mystic Chords of Memory*, 14.

12. Doris Kearns Goodwin, *Team of Rivals: The Political Genius of Abraham Lincoln* (New York: Simon and Schuster, 2012), 53.

13. "We the People of the United States, in Order to form a more perfect Union, establish Justice, insure domestic Tranquility, provide for the common defence [*sic*], promote the general Welfare, and secure the Blessings of Liberty to ourselves and our Posterity, do ordain and establish this Constitution for the United States of America." US Const. Preamble.

14. John Kaminski, Director of The Center for the Study of the American Constitution, University of Wisconsin, at page 15 of "The Origins of the Independent Judiciary" (a participant handout for Professor Kaminski's presentation at the 2003 Annual Meeting of the Wisconsin Judicial Conference, October 15–17, 2003) (quoting Fisher Ames letter to Dwight Foster, June 2, 1806). Ames (1758–1808) was a member of the first United States Congress, elected over Samuel Adams from the First Congressional District of Massachusetts. He served several terms, distinguishing himself as an orator and Federalist leader.

15. Sam J. Ervin Jr., "Separation of Powers: Judicial Independence," *Law and Contemporary Problems* 35, no. 1 (1970): 108–27. Sam J. Ervin was a senator from North Carolina and the chairman of the United States Senate Select Committee on Presidential Campaign Activities (the "Watergate Committee").

16. In the Declaration of Independence, Thomas Jefferson, listing grievances, wrote that King George "has made Judges dependent on his Will alone, for the tenure of their offices, and the amount and payment of their salaries." Declaration of Independence (US 1776).

17. See, e.g., Wis JI-Criminal 460 Closing Instruction; Wis JI-Civil 190 Closing: Short Form; see also other concluding instructions judges read to juries just before their deliberations; Manual of Model Criminal Jury Instructions 3.5 ("A reasonable doubt is a doubt based upon reason and common sense"); California Civil

Instruction CACI 5000 ("You must not let bias, sympathy, prejudice, or public opinion influence your decision").

18. Paul Krugman, "Ideology and Integrity," *New York Times*, May 1, 2015 (emphasis added).

19. Joseph J. Ellis, *The Quartet: Orchestrating the Second American Revolution, 1783–1789* (New York: Knopf, 2015), 152 (emphasis added).

20. Ellis, *The Quartet*, 218. Ellis continues: "Like wise parents," the founders allowed us, their "children," to "maximize our own moments for ourselves within the capacious republican framework they designed" (219). And with powerful implications for America's judiciary, Ellis closes his wonderful work thus: "Jefferson spoke for all the most prominent members of the revolutionary generation in urging posterity not to regard their political prescriptions as sacred script. It is richly ironic that one of the few original intentions they all shared was opposition to any judicial doctrine of 'original intent.' To be sure, they all wished to be remembered, but they did not want to be embalmed" (220).

21. Noah Feldman, "When Arrogance Takes the Bench," *New York Times*, June 11, 2009.

22. Countless examples could be cited and, in chapter 12, we will see some recent ones. But for a particularly interesting older example, consider Timothy Egan's fine work and his fascinating history of "the furious buying and selling of legislators, judges, and newspaper editors" and its tragic consequences throughout the western copper wars of the late nineteenth century. Timothy Egan, *Lasso the Wind: Away to the New West* (New York: Knopf, 1998), 157–65.

23. See *Citizens United v. FEC*, 558 U.S. 310, 447–49 (2010) (Stevens, J., *concurring and dissenting*).

24. Patrick Radden Keefe, "Corruption and Revolt: Does Tolerating Graft Undermine National Security?," *New Yorker*, January 19, 2015, 30.

25. Keefe, "Corruption and Revolt," 30.

26. *Webster's New Collegiate Dictionary* (Springfield, MA: G. & C. Merriam), 1977, 256. See also *Citizens United*, 508 U.S. 310 (Stevens, J., *concurring and dissenting*) ("When private interests are seen to exert outsized control over officeholders solely on account of the money spent on (or withheld from) their campaigns, the result can depart so thoroughly 'from what is pure or correct' in the conduct of Government, Webster's Third New International Dictionary 512 (1966) (defining "corruption"), that it amounts to a 'subversion . . . of the . . . electoral process'").

27. Robert Klitgaard, "International Cooperation against Corruption," *Finance and Development* 35 (1998): 3–6.

28. Keefe, "Corruption and Revolt," 30.

29. See *Citizens United v. FEC*, 558 U.S. 310, 450 (2010) (Stevens, J., *concurring and dissenting*).

30. See, e.g., Wisconsin Code of Judicial Conduct, Wis. § SCR 60.03 ("A judge shall avoid impropriety and the appearance of impropriety in all of the judge's activities"). According to the Comment to SCR 60.03, "The test for appearance of impropriety is whether the conduct would create in reasonable minds a perception that

the judge's ability to carry out judicial responsibilities with integrity, impartiality and competence is impaired." See also ABA Model Code of Judicial Conduct Rule 2.4(B) ("A judge shall not permit family, social, political, financial, or other interests or relationships to influence the judge's judicial conduct or judgment").

31. Zephyr Teachout, *Corruption in America: From Benjamin Franklin's Snuff Box to Citizens United* (Cambridge, MA: Harvard University Press, 2014).

32. Indeed, among "prominent academics," she saw "a revival of interest in the centrality of corruption in the American political-legal tradition." Teachout, *Corruption in America*, 279.

33. Teachout, *Corruption in America*, 2, 4, 55.

34. Teachout, *Corruption in America*, 34; she identified "violence and corruption . . . force and fraud" as "the two primary tools for undoing democracy." *Corruption in America*, 272.

35. Teachout, *Corruption in America*, 35.

36. Teachout, *Corruption in America*, 35.

37. Teachout, *Corruption in America*, 295; see also Teachout, *Corruption in America*, 31, where she explained that the Constitution, Article I, Section 9 (the gifts and emoluments clause), "reflected a broad view of what constitutes corruption, a broad view of the importance of protecting against even the slightest temptation, and a commitment to using absolute, prophylactic rules to support a civic society in which people put public interests first in their public roles."

38. Teachout, *Corruption in America*, 290.

39. *Citizens United v. FEC*, 558 U.S. 310, 452 (2010) (Stevens, J., *concurring and dissenting*). See also Teachout, *Corruption in America*, 50 ("Though the word *corruption* was used hundreds of times in the [Constitutional] convention and the ratification debates, only a handful of uses referred to what we might now think of as quid pro quo bribes").

40. Teachout, *Corruption in America*, 9, 294.

41. Teachout, *Corruption in America*, 276 (emphasis added); see also *Corruption in America*, 38 ("By corruption, the early generations meant excessive private interests influencing the exercise of public power").

42. Teachout, *Corruption in America*, 284.

CHAPTER 4. THE TRIAL JUDGE: BIRTH, ABORTED

1. Monica Migliorino Miller, *Abandoned: The Untold Story of the Abortion Wars* (Charlotte, NC: Saint Benedict Press, 2012).

2. Miller, *Abandoned*, 198–99.

3. Ms. Miller's case gained heavy press coverage, and, on November 11, 1990, the day before jury selection, she was on the cover of *Insight*, the Sunday magazine of the *Milwaukee Journal*, followed by "Obedience and Disobedience," an article about her life and antiabortion advocacy. Rosalind Dawson, "Obedience and Disobedience," *Insight*, November 11, 1990.

The article detailed Miller's arrests and convictions—information that, typically, a jury would not learn. Even absent this Sunday feature, I was concerned about problems in picking a jury given that prospective jurors would be questioned regarding their beliefs about abortion. Thus, I had requested more than the usual number of prospective jurors from which we would draw twelve (or fourteen, with alternates). Now I worried we would need an even bigger pool of prospectives or be forced to postpone the trial until the article's impact had receded.

My worry was unwarranted. I asked sixty prospective jurors whether they had seen or read the article. Although the *Milwaukee Journal* was Wisconsin's biggest daily, and, although the *Journal* promoted its Sunday advertising with the claim that *Insight* was the magazine with the state's highest circulation, my question met what may have been a harbinger of the declining relevance of print media. Of the sixty prospective jurors, only four had seen the magazine the day before, and only one had read the article.

4. Nondisclosure also took an unexpected turn, but it was not mine. Miller wrote: "There was one important piece of information about me that Schudson did not know and that I deliberately withheld from him. At the time of the sentencing hearing, I was seven weeks pregnant. When [my attorney] filed the pre-sentencing report, which is supposed to inform the court of any personal circumstances which might influence a judge's sentence, he knew about my pregnancy; but I insisted that he not mention it. He agreed. I felt that if the judge was going to be lenient, I wanted his leniency for the sake of the unborn on whose behalf I had acted. I did not want him to make his sentencing decision based on sympathy or concern for my unborn baby but not for the others." Miller, *Abandoned*, 230.

5. In subsequent correspondence with me, Miller expressed regret about what she termed her "imprudent remark," and clarified that she had intended to convey that "even shooting a police officer who facilitated the deaths of the unborn was not intrinsically immoral" but that "she did not advocate such actions be taken."

6. See Leonard Sykes Jr., "Jail Sentence Ignites Debate over Protesting," *Milwaukee Journal*, February 24, 1991. See also Edmund Bond Miller, "Commentary: A Judge's Sentencing," *Fidelity* 11–15 (June 1991).

7. See *State v. Miller*, 173 Wis. 2d 908, 499 N.W.2d 301 (Ct. App. 1993).

8. Any such correlation, however, is uncertain and may vary according to myriad circumstances, some ironic. For example, consider "the connection between the decline in clinic blockades and the rise in restrictive abortion laws." Jennifer Szalai, "What We Don't Talk about When We Talk about Abortion," *New York Times*, February 15, 2008. See Katie Watson, *Scarlet A: The Ethics, Law & Politics of Ordinary Abortion* (New York: Oxford University Press, 2018).

9. See G. Kevin Jordan, Benjamin Read, Mary Zahn, and Doretha Moore, "Activists on Abortion Discuss Next Moves," *Milwaukee Sentinel*, July 1, 1992 ("Schudson said . . . he believes himself to be competent to hear the motion impartially, but 'appearances of fairness would be compromised.' Schudson's announcement came after . . . a special prosecutor . . . introduced a motion to stiffen bail requirements for Miller . . . in light of her two arrests at recent abortion demonstrations").

In 2018, strikingly similar circumstances involving the trial judge's spouse emerged in the sexual assault prosecution of Bill Cosby. In that case, however, the trial judge refused to recuse. See Maggie Astor, "Cosby Wants a New Judge," *New York Times*, March 22, 2018; Jon Hurdle, "Judge in Cosby's Trial Rejects Claim of Bias over His Wife's Work as a Therapist," *New York Times*, March 29, 2018. In almost all such challenges to refusals to recuse, appellate courts defer to trial judges' evaluations of their own biases and abilities to continue presiding over a case. Appellate courts consistently conclude that the trial judges are able to judge their own capacity for fairness. That may be so, but less tenable is the appellate deference to trial judges' evaluations of the *appearance* of fairness.

10. Nevertheless, seven years later, I received a death threat. According to information from the FBI, I had been included in "The Nuremberg Files," an anti-abortion list of targeted doctors, clinic owners and employees, and law enforcement officers and judges "working in the baby slaughter business."

11. See *McCullen v. Coakley*, 134 S. Ct. 2518 (2014). See also Adam Liptak and John Schwartz, "Court Rejects Zone to Buffer Abortion Clinic," *New York Times*, June 27, 2014.

12. While writing this book, I have exchanged several emails with Ms. Miller, shared chapters and excerpts with her and others featured in these case studies, and invited comments in an effort to ensure accuracy. To Miller, I wrote, in part: "In addition to drawing from the court record, I would like to include portions of our correspondence and, perhaps, excerpts from *Abandoned*. I hope to relate aspects of the agony I felt (and still feel)." Miller replied: "I would not expect to be asked to approve or review what you write about my case—and I do believe that you will be fair and honest. If you are inclined you can send to me the pages that concern that trial and your decision for my comments or opinion—and you'd not be obligated to change anything—but of course sending those pages to me is *entirely up to you*."

A year later, after reviewing a draft of this chapter, Miller responded, in part: "I have to say you are remarkably honest—really [it's] nearly staggering what you are able to admit in terms of how you may have allowed yourself to be influenced in my case. What you have done here is laudable and very fair."

CHAPTER 5. THE APPELLATE JUDGE: BIRTH, PREMATURE

1. See *Peterman v. Midwestern Nat'l Ins. Co.*, 177 Wis. 2d 682, 687–90, 503 N.W.2d 312 (Ct. App. 1993).

2. *Peterman v. Midwestern Nat'l Ins. Co.*, 177 Wis. 2d 698. "Estoppel" is the legal doctrine barring a party from taking legal advantage of his/her own wrongdoing.

3. *Peterman v. Midwestern Nat'l Ins. Co.*, 177 Wis. 2d 707–8 (Schudson, J., concurring) (quoting *DeShaney v. Winnebago Count Dep't of Social Servs.*, 489 U.S. 189, 212–13 (1989) (Blackmun, J., *dissenting*)).

4. Judge Smith's position was historically anchored. See, e.g., Sir Mathew Hale's seventeenth-century code of judicial conduct: "I be not biased with compassion to the poor, or favor to the rich." John Campbell, *The Lives of the Chief Justices of England* (Jersey City: F. D. Linn, 1881), 208. Sir Mathew's compassionless code is also cited in Charles Gardner Geyh, *Courting Peril: The Political Transformation of*

the American Judiciary (New York: Oxford University Press, 2016), 66, n.31. Geyh's impressive work is one of two to which I refer throughout this book, the other being *How Judges Think* by Richard A. Posner, for their discussions of the legalistic/ compassionate debate. Geyh described the "rule of law paradigm" and the "legal culture paradigm"; Posner, "legalism" and "realism." While compatible in many ways, their theories do not always coincide with each other or with mine. Still, both books have both informed and challenged me. I am grateful to Professor Geyh and Judge Posner for advancing my understanding of several themes I develop here.

5. Judge Smith's and my relationship, to that point, had been very good. We had enjoyed mutual admiration that had come from several felony cases I had prosecuted before him during his years on the trial bench. He was, in my opinion, a fine trial judge; I was, in his words, "the Olivier" of the courtroom. Indeed, it was Judge Smith who, following his election to the appeals court, encouraged me to run against his colleague, the presiding judge.

6. *Peterman v. Midwestern Nat'l Ins. Co.*, 177 Wis. 2d 682, 704, n.10, 503 N.W.2d 312 (Ct. App. 1993). The debate continues. Indeed, according to Geyh, "the influence of emotion on judicial decision making" has become a "subfield of law and psychology" that "gained sudden prominence in 2009, when President Obama identified 'empathy' as a relevant qualification for [Sonia Sotomayer's] service on the Supreme Court." Geyh, *Courting Peril*, 59. "The comment drew a sharp rebuke from critics who claimed that empathy . . . had no place on a Supreme Court that should decide cases with reference to applicable law alone" (78):

> [I]n a 2007 speech, [Senator Obama] said compassion, not just the letter of the law, should come into play. "We need somebody [on the Supreme Court] who's got the heart, the empathy, to recognize what it's like to be a young teenage mom," he said. "The empathy to understand what it's like to be poor or African-American or gay or disabled or old. And that's the criteria by which I'm going to be selecting my judges."
>
> But conservatives see his focus on empathy as code for steering cases on the basis of desired outcomes. "On matters that he really cares about, there's no meaningful difference between his political views and his constitutional views," said M. Edward Whelan III, president of the Ethics and Public Policy Center and a former Scalia clerk. In effect, "the empathy standard that he's used in nominating justices is just camouflage for judicial lawlessness."

Peter Baker, "Obama's Mission to Remake Court: A Struggle over Power, Law, and Legacy," *New York Times*, February 29, 2016, A1.

In this regard, President Obama would find what some might see as surprising support from Judge Posner, often a hero to conservatives. Posner wrote of "psychology" as "an understudied influence on judicial behavior" (Posner, *How Judges Think*, 377) and explained that, because of "legalism's inability in many cases to decide the outcome (or decide it tolerably . . .)" (11), judges necessarily rely not only on "political preferences" (10) but also on "personal characteristics and personal and professional experiences" (10), "personality traits, or temperament (and thus emotionality . . .)"

(12), "intuition, emotion, and preconception . . . as contrasted with explicit, logical, step-by-step reasoning" (98), personal "idiosyncrasies" (11), and even "nonlegalist influences . . . likely to operate subliminally" (65). Moreover, far from lamenting what others might think a liberal lapse into squishy soft sentimentality, Posner explained: "The character of an emotional reaction, at once gripping and inarticulable, does not make emotion always an illegitimate or even a bad ground for a judicial decision. . . . Emotion can be a form of thought, though compressed and inarticulate. It is triggered by, and more often than not produces rational responses to, information" (106).

Chapter 6. Standard of Review: Casting the Legal Drama

1. Charles Gardner Geyh, *Courting Peril: The Political Transformation of the American Judiciary* (New York: Oxford University Press, 2016), 90.

2. *Obergefell v. Hodges*, 135 S. Ct. 2584 (2015).

3. *Obergefell v. Hodges*, 135 S. Ct. 2584, 2611 (2015) (Roberts, C.J., *dissenting*).

4. *Obergefell v. Hodges*, 135 S. Ct. 2584, 2612 (2015) (Roberts, C.J., *dissenting*).

5. *Obergefell v. Hodges*, 135 S. Ct. 2584, 2611–12 (2015) (Roberts, C.J., *dissenting*).

6. Adapted from WIS JI-Criminal 50 Preliminary Instruction—Credibility (Rel. No. 48—5/20/10); 2010, Regents, Univ. of Wis. This is but one of many similar instructions; each state enacts its own.

7. Never? Well, almost. The exceptions are so exceptional that they would only distract from our discussion. My anecdotal data: in ten years, I presided over approximately 270 jury trials in criminal cases; I never overturned a verdict, including the two with which I disagreed.

8. Regarding the relative authority of judges and juries to decide between the death penalty and life imprisonment, law continues to evolve. Recently, the Supreme Court concluded, "The Sixth Amendment [right to a jury trial] requires a jury, not a judge, to find each fact necessary to impose a sentence of death." *Hurst v. Florida*, 136 S. Ct. 616, 619 (2016). See Adam Liptak, "Justices Halt Florida Way of Deciding Death Cases," *New York Times*, January 13, 2016. See also Alan Blinder, "Unanimity Is Required in Executions, Florida Rules," *New York Times*, October 15, 2016.

9. The exceptions are important. In many states, if a defendant chooses to testify, two questions are allowed: "Have you ever been convicted of a crime?" and, if so, "How many times?" The legal rationale is that every witness's credibility is for the jury to evaluate, and, depending on the number (and, sometimes, the nature) of criminal convictions, the defendant's record may fairly influence a jury's assessment of the defendant's credibility.

In rare cases, not only the criminal convictions but also a defendant's prior conduct—good or bad—may be allowed in evidence. Positive "character" evidence— testimony about a good reputation—sometimes may be introduced (and rebutted by other evidence) if a defendant's honesty or truthfulness is at issue. Negative conduct—testimony about prior "bad acts"—even if they did not lead to a criminal charge or conviction, also may be allowed. While unusual, that most often occurs in sexual assault trials if the evidence is of behavior so similar to the charged offense—same or similar style of assaults, for example—that such prior conduct is probative of the actual charge on trial. See Billie Wright Dziech and Charles B. Schudson, *On Trial: America's Courts and Their Treatment of Sexually Abused Children* (Boston: Beacon Press, 1991), 130.

Such evidentiary circumstances may require a trial judge to make difficult discretionary decisions, some of which may prove pivotal. Moreover, such decisions may turn less on law than on the trial judge's attitudes and understandings and, further, those attitudes and understandings may change with "shifting social mores." See Graham Bowley, "Cosby's Retrial Will Play Out in 'Different Era': The #MeToo Moment," *New York Times*, January 18, 2008. In the first trial of the sexual assault charges against Bill Cosby, the prosecution asked the judge to permit nineteen women, in addition to the victim of the alleged assault on trial, to testify about their similar encounters with Cosby. The judge, however, allowed only one of them to testify. That trial ended in a mistrial—a "hung jury" unable to reach a verdict. At the re-trial many months later, the same judge allowed five additional witnesses to testify about Cosby's comparable conduct against them. See Graham Bowley, "Judge in Cosby's Trial for Sexual Assault Will Allow Five More Accusers to Testify," *New York Times*, February 16, 2018.

On April 26, 2018, following his re-trial, Bill Cosby was found guilty of three counts of aggravated indecent assault. "Perhaps most damaging to Mr. Cosby was the testimony from five other women who told jurors they, too, were Cosby victims" who had been "drugged and sexually assaulted" in much the same way, thus allowing for the prosecution's argument that the victim's assault "was part of a signature pattern of predatory behavior." Graham Bowley and Jon Hurdle, "Jury Finds Cosby Guilty In a Sexual Assault Case Seen as a Turning Point," *New York Times*, April 26, 2018.

What made the difference for the same judge in making the two different rulings? What made the difference for two different juries—the first deadlocking, the second finding Cosby guilty? Was it the #MeToo movement's emergence between the two trials? It is impossible to know, and certainly, in evaluating the decision-making of one judge and two dozen jurors, many factors in both trials would need to be considered. The judge offered little if any explanation for his rulings (see Bowley, "Judge in Cosby's Trial for Sexual Assault Will Allow Five More Accusers to Testify"), but "[i]n a joint statement . . . the jurors who voted to convict" in the re-trial "said that they believed [Cosby's] accuser's account and were persuaded of his guilt by the facts, not the momentum of social change captured in the 'MeToo movement.'" Still, I think it reasonable to ask whether, fairly or otherwise, that movement may have influenced the trial judge's attitudes and understandings, and his rulings about the additional witnesses, and whether, in turn, those additional witnesses may have made the difference for any or all of the jurors at the second trial. See Graham Bowley and Matthew Haag, "Cosby Jury Says Accuser's Credibility Led to Guilty Verdict," *New York Times*, April 30, 2008.

10. *State v. Miller*, 1993 Wisc. App. LEXIS 96, 1, 12–14, 173 Wis. 2d 908, 499 N.W.2d 301 (Ct. App. 1993). (Within the quoted portion of this decision, I have

omitted eight citations—all case precedents reiterating the required criteria and standards of review.)

11. *State v. Miller*, 1993 Wisc. App. LEXIS 96, 1, 15, 173 Wis. 2d 908, 499 N.W.2d 301 (Ct. App. 1993).

12. *Peterman v. Midwestern Nati. Ins. Co.*, 177 Wis. 2d 682, 691 (Ct. Ap. 1993).

13. *Obergefell v. Hodges*, 135 S. Ct. 2584, 2612, 2624 (2015) (Roberts, C.J., *dissenting*).

14. Richard A. Posner, *How Judges Think* (Cambridge, MA: Harvard University Press, 2008), 47, 49.

15. In this chapter, I have failed to acknowledge the slight differences between and among the standards of review for the US Supreme Court and all other appellate courts. For a helpful discussion of these distinctions, see Posner, *How Judges Think*, 269–323 (Chapter 10, "The Supreme Court Is a Political Court"). Posner explains, in analytically astute detail, the traditional *political* and *policymaking* power of the US Supreme Court (and, I would note, of some state supreme courts as well).

Chapter 7. The Trial Judge: Life, and a Lost Teenager

1. Stephen Sondheim, "Children Will Listen," *Into the Woods*, Rifting Music Inc., 1988.

2. See Model Code of Judicial Conduct R. 2.4(A), "in place since the Canons of Judicial Ethics were promulgated in 1924," which provides that "a judge 'shall not be swayed by public clamor, or fear of criticism.'" See Charles Gardner Geyh, *Courting Peril: The Political Transformation of the American Judiciary* (New York: Oxford University Press, 2016), 12, 21.

3. See Billie Wright Dziech and Charles B. Schudson, *On Trial: America's Courts and Their Treatment of Sexually Abused Children* (Boston: Beacon Press, 1991), 25–26.

4. A. M. Platt, *The Child Savers: The Invention of Delinquency* (Chicago: University of Chicago Press, 1977), 10.

5. See Dziech and Schudson, *On Trial*, 25 (bracketed word and emphasis added).

6. See Ralph Adam Fine, *Escape of the Guilty* (New York: Dodd, Mead, 1986), 183–84.

7. *In the Interest of S. W., a child under eighteen years of age*, State of Wisconsin, Circuit Court Branch I, Milwaukee County, Case No. 03213184, Decision and Order (November 7, 1983). The case title may seem strange. Reflecting the Progressive Era's approach, many states still caption juvenile cases, even those involving criminal charges, with benevolent titles such as "*In the Interest of* _____," rather than the adversarial, "*State v.* _____." And all states still protect juvenile confidentiality, many by using initials rather than full names. Additional portions of the *S. W.* decision, not included here, relate the shameful, heartbreaking details of other cases in which bureaucratic abuse resulted in tragedy.

8. A press report helps answer some obvious questions:

When the 16-year-old girl ran away from the Newberry House group home, nobody told her parents.

The girl continued to call and visit her . . . parents, telling them she was there on free time. . . . She talked about Newberry House, describing to them how well she was following the rules.

"We had no reason to doubt it," said her mother in an interview.

It wasn't until seven weeks after she had run away that her parents found out. The mother said they were surprised with the news when they attended a routine court hearing for their daughter.

The final insult was that they had been billed $199 for their daughter's treatment for the month, even though the girl spent only three days in the group home. They eventually were reimbursed.

"Judge Is Incensed as a Girl Is 'Lost,'" *Milwaukee Journal*, October 30, 1983.

9. The inadequacy of resources was extreme. Studies, prepared by the Department as well as by independent consultants, established that Milwaukee County social workers and probation officers carried caseloads three times the national average. For years, juvenile courts and social services had been drastically underfunded and remained so, in part because of a long-standing dispute between the state and the county regarding financial responsibility for services. *Seventeen years earlier*, a front page editorial had cried out:

The staff of [the county's juvenile] probation workers is so small and the case load so large that supervision of delinquents is at best superficial. Loose supervision increases the likelihood that a child will commit additional delinquent acts. Repeated delinquency adds to the load on probation officers and the farcical cycle continues.

A boy who is sent to the court for his first offense is usually released on probation. His probation officer, who may have a work load of 75 cases, has little time to gain the boy's confidence, counsel him, guide him to better ways. The boy learns nothing from his first experience. Soon he is in trouble again, in and out of court again—perhaps several times. Finally he is committed to a state correctional institution.

"A Farce Is Right," *Milwaukee Journal*, December 2, 1966. By the time SW came to court, caseloads exceeded one hundred. I would revise the editorial in one respect— the boy did indeed learn something from his first experience . . . he learned about law and lack of authority, credibility and enforcement; he learned about a justice system's lack of care and caring. As Sondheim warned, "children will listen."

10. *In the Interest of S. W., a child under eighteen years of age*, State of Wisconsin, Circuit Court Branch I, Milwaukee County, Case No. 03213184, Decision and Order (November 7, 1983), 26–27.

11. *In the Interest of S. W., a child under eighteen years of age*, State of Wisconsin, Circuit Court Branch I, Milwaukee County, Case No. 03213184, Decision and Order (November 7, 1983), 36.

12. John Fauber, "Two Social Workers Found in Contempt," *Milwaukee Sentinel*, November 9, 1983.

13. Barbara A. Koppe, "Judge Raps Fines for Caseworkers," *Milwaukee Journal*, November 9, 1983.

14. Tom Ahern, "Union Set to Petition for Transfer of Judge Schudson," *Milwaukee Sentinel*, November 10, 1983.

15. My conduct, I think, crept close to the edge of an ethical standard: "A judge may not, while a proceeding is pending . . . make any public comment that may reasonably be expected to affect the outcome . . . of the proceeding." See Wisconsin Code of Judicial Conduct, Wis. § SCR 60.04(1)(j). "Judges have not always been so severely constrained," wrote Robert M. O'Neil in *Trial* magazine. "Chief Justice Marshall, albeit under a pseudonym, answered his critics through a series of letters to a newspaper editor, defending both the Court over which he presided and the merits of particular decisions." Robert O'Neil, "Assaults on the Judiciary," *Trial* 34, no. 9 (1998): 56.

16. "Schudson Should Stay Put," *Milwaukee Journal*, November 15, 1983.

17. *In the Interest of S.W.: Milwaukee County Department of Social Services,* et al. *v. Circuit Court,* et al., Case No. 83–2366 (Wis. Ct. App.), Order, February 16, 1984.

18. *In the Interest of S.W., a child under eighteen years of age,* State of Wisconsin, Milwaukee County Circuit Court Branch I, Case No. 03213184, Decision and Order II at 8, May 29, 1984. I was not the only judge to invoke contempt authority to direct an executive department to deliver protective services for children. Prompted by federal lawsuits brought by the American Civil Liberties Union in the 1980s, judges and judicially created supervisory panels took control of social services departments in several states. See, e.g., J. C. Barden, "Panel to Direct Child Welfare in Connecticut," *New York Times*, December 21, 1990. Still, the exercise of such authority remains rare and politically problematic. "Whether judges consciously moderate their interpretations of law to avoid confrontations with or resistance from legislators, governors, presidents, voters, or fellow judges matters less than that their interpretations of law are so moderated." Geyh, *Courting Peril*, 56. Such moderation is prevalent among elected state judges. Therefore, it is no surprise to find such civil rights suits pursued in federal courts, before appointed federal judges politically protected by lifetime tenure.

CHAPTER 8. THE APPELLATE JUDGE: LIFE, AND A SEX PREDATOR

1. The Latin motto of Dartmouth College, "Vox clamantis in deserto" translates to "the voice of one crying out in the wilderness." It first appears in the Bible in Isaiah 40:3 and subsequently in Matthew, Mark, Luke, and John. See Julia O'Sullivan, "The Origin of Vox Clamantis in Deserto," *The Dartmouth*, March 7, 2017.

2. See Meg Kissinger, "On Trial: Hot, Noisy Courtrooms Are Jeopardizing Justice," *Milwaukee Journal*, July 6, 1988 ("Schudson and Circuit Judge Michael J. Skwierawski [presiding judge of the Felony Division] say conditions are so deplorable in their courtrooms . . . that they refuse to conduct trials there. 'It's impossible. I will not hold a jury trial here,' Skwierawski said. 'The conditions are unbearable.'"). I bought an air conditioner and installed it in my chambers window so that we could

hold some hearings. But it could not cool the cavernous courtroom, and we wouldn't risk the health of jurors by requiring them to sit hours in overheated conditions.

3. "[B]y 1982, the public seemed to have discovered child sex abuse, both its trauma and its prevalence." Rachel Aviv, "The Science of Sex Abuse: Is It Right to Imprison People for Heinous Crimes They Have Not Yet Committed?" *New Yorker*, January 14, 2013, 36. That "discovery" was consistent with my experience. For five years, reviewing all published appellate decisions on child sexual abuse for the book I was writing, I concluded that more child sexual abuse prosecutions, convictions, and appeals had occurred between 1980 and 1990 than in the preceding two hundred years.

4. See "Locked Away," a three-part series in the *New York Times*. Monica Davey and Abby Goodnough, "Doubts Rise as States Hold Sex Offenders after Prison," *New York Times*, March 4, 2007; Abby Goodnough and Monica Davey, "A Record of Failure at a Center for Sex Offenders," *New York Times*, March 5, 2007; Abby Goodnough and Monica Davey, "For Sex Offenders, Dispute on Therapy's Benefits," *New York Times*, March 6, 2007. Chronologically, the years and states of the new laws are 1990—Washington; 1994—Kansas, Minnesota, and Wisconsin; 1995—Arizona and California; 1997—Illinois and North Dakota; 1998—Florida, Iowa, New Jersey, and South Carolina; 1999—Massachusetts, Missouri, Texas (outpatient treatment only; no commitment center), and Virginia; 2003—Pennsylvania; 2006—Nebraska and New Hampshire; 2007—New York. Davey and Goodnough, "Doubts Rise."

5. *Kansas v. Hendricks*, 521 U.S. 346 (1997). After losing his Supreme Court appeal, Leroy Hendricks was confined for many years. He remained "locked up at a cost to [Kansas] taxpayers of $185,000 a year—more than eight times the cost of keeping someone in prison there." At age seventy-two, he was spending "most days in a wheelchair or leaning on a cane, because of diabetes, circulation ailments and the effects of a stroke" and "may not live long enough to 'graduate' from treatment." Few ever do.

> Nearly 3,000 sex offenders have been committed since the first law passed in 1990. In 18 of the 19 states, about 50 have been released completely from commitment because clinicians or state-appointed evaluators deemed them ready. Some 115 other people have been sent home because of legal technicalities, court rulings, terminal illness or old age.
>
> In discharging offenders, Arizona, the remaining state, has been the exception. That state has fully discharged 81 people. . . .
>
> An additional 189 people have been released with supervision or conditions.

These laws "keep large numbers of rapists and pedophiles off the streets after their prison terms." See Davey and Goodnough, "Doubts Rise." They may be among the factors resulting in a substantial reduction in the number of actual *acts* of child sexual abuse. According to University of New Hampshire professor David Finkelhor, perhaps America's most respected researcher specializing in the study of child sexual

abuse, even after correcting for fluctuations in overall rates of crime, the number of
child sexual abuse incidents has fallen dramatically. (The specific impact of predator
commitments is difficult to measure. States without such laws have seen equivalent
reductions. Still, the commitment of a predator in one state may contribute to statistical reductions in others if that predator had been assaulting children across state
lines.) See David Finkelhor and Lisa Jones, "Have Sexual Abuse and Physical Abuse
Declined since the 1990's?" (Durham, NH: Crimes against Children Research Center, 2012) (CV267), http://www.unh.edu/ccrc/pdf/CV267_Have%20SA%20%20
PA%20Decline_FACT%20SHEET_11-7-12pdf; see also David Finkelhor, Kei Saito,
and Lisa Jones, "Updated Trends in Child Maltreatment, 2014" (Durham, NH:
Crimes against Children Research Center, 2016), http://www.unh.edu/ccrc/pdf/
Updated%20trends%202014.pdf.

6. For courts, the first factor was pretty standard stuff; for many years, judges and
juries have determined mental illness in various proceedings, including those involving pleas of insanity. The second factor was new; it required courts to forecast sexual
assault. In recent years, however, their predictions have involved a little less art and
a little more psychological "science." But such science, still in its infancy, is unset-
tled. "Actuarial formulas . . . play a central role in deciding who is dangerous enough
to be committed." Davey and Goodnough, "Doubts Rise." "Most actuarial tools
used to predict someone's risk of recidivism consider only unchanging factors, like
their number of past offenses and the sex of their victims. Some scientists say that
so-called dynamic factors—how much treatment an offender gets, for example, and
how old he has grown—should factor heavily into actuarial risk assessment, too."
Goodnough and Davey, "For Sex Offenders," 18.

In the first generation of predator commitment trials, the primary actuarial
instrument came to be the Static-99. According to Aviv, it was "developed through
studies of rapists and child molesters" and "places individuals in classes of risk based
on ten factors correlated with recidivism, including age, whether the defendant has
ever had a live-in relationship that lasted at least two years, and whether his victims
were strangers." Such actuarial instruments, she wrote, "predict sexual violence
about as well as the S.A.T. forecasts freshman grades," and, she contends, "[n]either
correlation is particularly strong." See Aviv, "The Science of Sex Abuse," 40.

7. See Wis. Stat. § 980.08.

8. "Even the look of commitment centers reflects the dichotomy at the core of
their stated reason for being—to lock away dangerous men (only three women have
been civilly committed) but also to treat them. Most of the centers tend to look and
feel like prisons, with clanking double doors, guard stations, fluorescent lighting,
cinder-block walls, overcrowded conditions and tall fences with razor wire around
the perimeters." Davey and Goodnough, "Doubts Rise," 18–19. For a sex predator
committed under the federal law, the transfer from prison to treatment center
demarcated a distinction without much difference: "He wore the same uniform as
other inmates and was subject to the same punishments, schedule, and rules." Aviv,
"The Science of Sex Abuse," 40.

9. See *State v. Schulpius (In re Schulpius)*, 2004 WI App 39, 270 Wis. 2d 427, 678 N.W.2d 369.

10. See *State v. Schulpius (In re Schulpius)*, 2004 WI App 39, 270 Wis. 2d 427, 678 N.W.2d 369, ¶¶ 44–59. My dissenting opinion then went on to discuss possible remedies.

> At oral argument, Schulpius' counsel maintained that outright release was the only proper remedy to protect Schulpius' rights and deter the government's violations of court orders. The Assistant Attorney General disagreed. He suggested other remedies—perhaps an award of monetary damages; perhaps financial penalties for officials or departments responsible for failing to follow the court orders; perhaps, if no supervised-release facility in Milwaukee County exists, court direction of expenditures to create one. Or at most, the Assistant Attorney General urged, if Schulpius must be released, he should be supervised.
>
> Interestingly enough, in the most fundamental way, the parties' positions are not far apart. Both Schulpius and the State seek compliance with court orders; both want enforcement of the law the legislature enacted, not a charade. But can any remedy give Schulpius his due, prevent such Kafkaesque confinement of others, and, at the same time, protect the community? I believe so; but to understand how, one must think through each of the several options.
>
> Damages? That's silly; Schulpius' new-found wealth would be of little benefit behind bars, and the status quo would continue. Financial penalties for government officials or departments? That's spittin' into the wind; the government could continue to violate court orders and, ultimately, the penalties would pass on to the taxpayers. Continued confinement with, again, the *false* promise of possible supervised release? What could more certainly *reduce* incentives for confined predators to cooperate in treatment?
>
> And where would such remedies lead? Just play them out—any one of them. *Any remedy short of supervised release actually endangers our community more than release itself.* The status quo would continue. The State, rather than creating a Milwaukee County facility to house, treat and supervise predators, would keep Schulpius and other predators confined even when courts ordered their supervised release. Wisconsin then would need to increase staff and eventually build institutions to make room for all the unlawfully confined predators who qualify for the supervised release that will never come.
>
> Then what would happen? What, in all likelihood, would Wisconsin really do? Now swallow hard; here's the last bite of Kake-Kafkaesque. Faced with tight budgets and overcrowded institutions, Wisconsin could solve this fiscal and constitutional riddle in only one way: by no longer seeking commitment of sex predators in Milwaukee County (and, eventually, in other counties claiming to be unable to provide suitable facilities). Thus, quite certainly, judicial acquiescence in this governmental misconduct leaves not only a constitutional stain, but a *more endangered community*. . . .

If we see Schulpius only as a sex predator, we warehouse him without regret. But if we recognize the constitutional rights Schulpius carries, we respond with the remedy as we must. And by completing the several possible remedy-scenarios, we see the results of judicial acquiescence in unconsciona-ble governmental conduct: in the short run, Milwaukee County remains safe from Schulpius, but in the long run, Milwaukee County, along with the rest of Wisconsin, becomes *more endangered by more sex predators* whom the State should but won't commit.

Therefore, I accept the Assistant Attorney General's last option as, truly, the only option. Only immediate *supervised* release can address the *more than four years* of violations of court orders and, at the same time, offer the best possible community protection. (*State v. Schulpius (In re Schulpius)*, 2004 WI App 39, 270 Wis. 2d 427, 678 N.W.2d 369, ¶¶ 60–64 (Schudson, J., *dissenting*))

11. *State v. Schulpius (In re Schulpius)*, 2004 WI App 39, 270 Wis. 2d 427, 678 N.W.2d 369, ¶¶ 68–71 (Schudson, J., *dissenting*).

12. *State v. Schulpius (In re Commitment of Schulpius)*, 2006 WI 1, 287 Wis. 2d 44, 707 N.W.2d 495.

13. *State v. Schulpius (In re Commitment of Schulpius)*, 2006 WI 1, 287 Wis. 2d 44, 707 N.W.2d 495, ¶¶ 37–39.

14. *State v. Schulpius (In re Commitment of Schulpius)*, 2006 WI 1, 287 Wis. 2d 44, 707 N.W.2d 495, ¶¶ 33–36. Quoting my colleagues' decision, the Supreme Court also reasoned, "'Any judicial decision that puts the community at risk because of what agents of government may have done or not done must balance the 'potential injury' to society's interests against the 'potential benefits' that would flow from any rule designed to deter future conduct by those agents, even where . . . those agents might have violated rules designed to protect constitutional rights'" (¶ 40).

15. *State v. Schulpius (In re Commitment of Schulpius)*, 2006 WI 1, 287 Wis. 2d 44, 707 N.W.2d 495, ¶ 42 (emphasis added) (quoting *State v. Sprosty*, 227 Wis. 2d 316, 331 (1999)). Nevertheless, by the time Schulpius's case climbed to the Wisconsin Supreme Court, after much more than his "four years" of lock-up in violation of Judge Franke's order had passed, all seven justices somehow were able to write, "[W]e are satisfied that the [Department] has made substantial attempts to establish a residential facility or dwelling that would enable individuals committed under Chapter 980, such as Schulpius, to be placed on supervised release in Milwaukee County. . . . [W]e find encouragement in the efforts undertaken by the [Depart-ment] to resolve this issue and, hopefully, prevent it from recurring." *State v. Schul-pius (In re Commitment of Schulpius)*, 2006 WI 1, 287 Wis. 2d 44, 707 N.W.2d 495, ¶ 44. Really . . . "satisfied" by years of unsuccessful attempts, and "encouraged" by such complete failure?

16. *State v. Schulpius (In re Commitment of Schulpius)*, 2006 WI 1, 287 Wis. 2d 44, 707 N.W.2d 495, ¶ 48.

17. See Wis. Stat. § 980.08(5m). Enacted May 22, 2006, just four months after the Supreme Court's decision in Schulpius's appeal, this statute prohibits placement

of a predator in any facility that did not exist prior to January 1, 2006, thus precluding construction of a facility that could house conditionally released sex predators.

18. Wis. Stat. § 980.08(4)(cg)3 & 5.

19. Taken together, these actions by the state supreme court and the state legislature, as unconscionably as any I witnessed in three decades of public service, ignored the words that came to be considered perhaps the most important warning ever written in the US Supreme Court: "Our Government is the potent, the omnipresent teacher. For good or for ill, it teaches the whole people by its example. Crime is contagious. If the Government becomes a lawbreaker, it breeds contempt for law." *Olmstead v. United States*, 277 U.S. 438, 485 (1928) (Brandeis, J., *dissenting*).

20. Monica Davey, "Minnesota's Detaining of Sex Offenders after Prison Is Ruled Unconstitutional," *New York Times*, June 18, 2015. See also Aviv, "The Science of Sex Abuse," 41 ("In Minnesota, which has one of the largest commitment programs, six hundred and seventy inmates work on correcting distorted thoughts about sex . . . , but in eighteen years only one man has been discharged from the program. (The man was released [in 2012], after concluding a course of treatment that began in 1994)"). Judge Frank was deciding a class action suit presented by fourteen sex predators committed under the *federal* sex predator commitment law— the Adam Walsh Child Protection and Safety Act—enacted in 2006. Named after Adam Walsh, a seven-year-old boy who was kidnapped and decapitated, the law allows the federal Bureau of Prisons to seek civil commitment of inmates, beyond their criminal conviction release dates, who would have "serious difficulty in refraining from sexually violent conduct or child molestation if released."

21. Joseph Goldstein, "Housing Rules Keep Sex Offenders in Prison beyond Release Dates," *New York Times*, August 22, 2014. The federal system also has devolved into comparable "consumer" fraud. Established in 2007, the federal sex predator commitment law was "designed as a five-phase treatment regime, but the final stage, which would help inmates reintegrate into the community, [as of 2013] has not yet been implemented." Aviv, "The Science of Sex Abuse," 45.

22. Aviv, "The Science of Sex Abuse," 38.

23. "Politics and emotion also factor heavily into who gets committed, with decisions made by elected judges . . . who may be more affected by the raw facts of someone's offense history or the public spectacle over their crimes than the dry science of risk prediction." Davey and Goodnough, "Doubts Rise," 18. Thus, will courtroom decks always seem stacked against sex predators? No doubt, but perhaps not only for the reasons raw statistics might imply: "By 2007, roughly forty-five hundred sex offenders had been civilly committed nationwide, and just over ten per cent had been released." Aviv, "The Science of Sex Abuse." What does that tell us? Maybe not much. After all, few predators are treatable. The growing body of evidence establishes their incorrigibility. Thus, while Kafkaesque violations of due process are no less deplorable, a conditional release rate of 10 percent is not necessarily unfair.

24. See Bruce Vielmetti, "Sex Offender Shawn Schulpius Granted Release from Secure Treatment," *Milwaukee Journal Sentinel*, February 28, 2013.

25. Anthony Lewis, *Gideon's Trumpet* (New York: Vintage Books, 1964), 227.

CHAPTER 9. THE TRIAL JUDGE:
DEATH, AND A CHERISHED CHILD

1. Isabel Allende, "The Judge's Wife," in *The Compact Bedford Introduction to Literature* (Boston: Bedford Books, 1997), 422–27.

2. On appellate courts, as we will see in chapter 10, *random* case assignment also can be consequential. But interestingly enough, in the US Supreme Court, it is the *nonrandom* method of case assignment that may make big differences. Adam Liptak explains:

> When the chief justice is in the majority, he gets to decide who will write the Supreme Court's opinion. [When the chief justice expects to dissent, the senior justice in the majority chooses.] This is, Justice Felix Frankfurter once wrote, "perhaps the most delicate judgment demanded of the chief justice."
>
> Chief Justice John G. Roberts Jr. has approached the task with characteristic rigor.
>
> In one sense, a new study concluded, he is scrupulously fair: Every justice gets very close to the same number of majority opinions. In another sense, he plays favorites, doling out major assignments and unappealing ones with keen attention to strategy.

Adam Liptak, "Doling Out Major Opinions and 'Dogs,' Roberts Pursues a Strategy," *New York Times*, November 9, 2015. The study, prepared by Harvard law professor Richard J. Lazarus, is interesting in a number of ways, the most meaningful of which may relate to Justice Kennedy's assignments, given his pivotal vote in many five-four decisions: "'The assignments to Justice Kennedy have a distinct purpose,' Lazarus wrote: 'to lock in his vote in close cases.'"

3. One last variable: where the jury finds the defendant sane, and *in those states that allow the death penalty*, a third phase—the "sentencing phase"—may come next.

4. Some state legislatures, responding to public concern that parole could reduce "life imprisonment" to much less than *life in prison*, enacted laws adding a new layer of decision-making discretion, requiring judges to order that "life means life" or, instead, to specify the date for parole eligibility.

5. One newspaper story ended:

> Schudson said the "loss of a child was the most excruciating loss" to a parent.
>
> "Yet your decision to take your child's life was an act that may have been perceived by you as an act of love and caring, but it was cruel beyond belief."
>
> . . .
>
> "Children are precious. They are real human beings and are not here to satisfy the needs and wants of adults, even their parents."

Mike Christopulos, "Father Who Killed Son in Custody Dispute Gets Life," *Milwaukee Sentinel*, March 2, 1989. Another account concluded:

> "To those of us in the courtroom, sitting before us was a man—Anthony McClain Sr.—of character and kindness," Schudson said, addressing McClain.

"Throughout the trial we watched you shedding tears of excruciating pain and absolute sincerity."

But the feeling of sympathy was inescapably linked to the fact that McClain brought the pain upon himself, Schudson said.

"You may have felt that your decision to take your own child's life was an act of love, but indeed it was . . . cruel . . . ," Schudson said. "You put an end to a life that was vibrant . . . ready to thrive—ready to thrive in part because of your own efforts."

Ferdinand de Leon, "Prosecutor Feels Sorry for Man Who Killed Son," *Milwaukee Journal*, March 5, 1989.

6. George Bradt, "Wanamaker Was Wrong—The Vast Majority of Advertising Is Wasted," Forbes, September 14, 2016. John Wanamaker, one of America's most prominent merchants, served as US postmaster general.

7. Veblen's memorable phrase first appeared in his 1914 book, *The Instinct of Workmanship and the Industrial Arts*. See Erin Wais, "Trained Incapacity: Thorstein Veblen and Kenneth Burke," *KB Journal* 2, no. 1 (2005).

8. See 18 U.S.C. § 3553(b)(1), directing that a court "shall impose a sentence of the kind, and within the range" established by the guidelines, subject to departures in specified cases where the judge finds "an aggravating or mitigating circumstance of a kind, or to a degree, not adequately taken into consideration by the Sentencing Commission in formulating the guidelines."

9. See Richard A. Posner, *How Judges Think* (Cambridge, MA: Harvard University Press, 2008), 178–79 ("The United States Sentencing Commission, which drafted the guidelines, drew on the knowledge of criminologists, federal probation officers, and other experts, though the sentencing guideline ranges established by the Commission mostly tracked what had been average judicial sentencing practice before the guidelines").

10. The appeals indirectly touched these judicial concerns. Both focused on whether a judge could order a sentence that exceeded the guideline maximum. In one, the defendant challenged a judge's decision to exceed the maximum on the basis of aggravating factors the jury had not considered in reaching its verdict; in the other, the prosecution challenged a judge's decision declining to do so. See *United States v. Booker*, 543 U.S. 220, 221–23 (2005).

11. Posner, *How Judges Think*, 72.

12. Posner commented: "Apart from brief orientation sessions and occasional continuing legal education seminars, judges in our system are not actually 'trained,' which is an interesting commentary on the methodological rigor, or rather the lack thereof, of judging. Judicial 'training' is learning by doing—a further clue to the largely tacit character of judicial reasoning." Posner, *How Judges Think*, 118. And, as I have explained:

Whether appointed or elected, most trial judges often deal with laws and issues they have never before encountered. It is not unusual for a civil lawyer with no trial experience to become a judge assigned to a criminal trial court. It is not unusual for a judge with no background in child development or family dynamics to be assigned to a juvenile or family court. Some judges study hard and learn fast. Most do not. . . . While many view judges as entrenched and resistant to change, that image may be more apparent than real. Every state has judges who bellow, 'This is my court, and I don't care what you say the law is'; but many judges are willing to listen and learn. In fact, judges may constitute a professional group unique in its readiness for change. They are not supposed to have personal allegiances to particular procedures or philosophies. Having followed a rule for years, a judge is expected to alter it immediately upon command from a higher court. In fact, that is exactly what judges frequently do with far less resistance than most outside the legal system would suspect.

Billie Wright Dziech and Charles B. Schudson, *On Trial: America's Courts and Their Treatment of Sexually Abused Children* (Boston: Beacon Press, 1991), 178–80.

13. See "Where He's Been," www.keynoteseminars.net. Most of my presentations were cosponsored by the National Council of Juvenile and Family Court Judges, which, along with the National Judicial College, is located at the University of Nevada–Reno. Both organizations offer courses for state trial judges and, occasionally, for American tribal judges and foreign judges as well. The College hosts almost all its programs at the Reno campus; the Council offers programs there, too, but also operates throughout the country conducting courses hosted by state judicial conferences and nonjudicial organizations, including the American Academy of Pediatrics, the American Probation and Parole Association, and the National District Attorneys Association. As their full names indicate, the College offers courses for judges in all assignments, while the Council concentrates on judges in juvenile and family courts. State appellate judges regularly attend state judicial education programs for trial judges, as well as separate seminars designed specifically for appellate practice. They may do so at their own state's conferences and at institutions including New York University, which offers excellent courses for state and federal appellate judges from throughout the country. Federal judges have their own educational programs.

14. By 2002 the percentage of federal cases going to trial had declined to 1.8 percent. "In state systems, trials have become scarcer still, with only 0.6 percent of 2002 cases filed culminating in trial. The 'trial judge' has thus become an oxymoron, who looks less like an archetypal umpire, than a case manager." Charles Gardner Geyh, *Courting Peril: The Political Transformation of the American Judiciary* (New York: Oxford University Press, 2016), 28. True, to a point, though trials, particularly jury trials, still consume the most substantial percentage of a trial judge's time.

15. Without knowing the legal term, most people learn, if only from TV and movies, that defendants have the right of "allocution"—to speak directly to the judge in open court before being sentenced. Thus, most people would assume that victims also have the right to address the judge. But in most states, they do not (though judges may permit them to do so). Some states have addressed this, enacting statutes to provide protections for victims and witnesses. Wisconsin was the first,

enacting a "bill of rights" declaring that victims should be "honored and protected by law enforcement agencies, prosecutors and judges . . . no less vigorous[ly] than . . . criminal defendants," Wis. Stat. § 950.01, and specifying that victims do indeed have the right to speak at sentencing. See Wis. Stat. § 950.04(iv)(m); Dziech and Schudson, *On Trial*, 33–34.

16. *North Carolina v. Alford*, 400 U.S. 25 (1970).

17. The proposition that preclusion of such pleas (at least in all noncapital cases) would bring the wheels of justice grinding to a halt is wrong. "Indiana, New Jersey and Pennsylvania prohibit *Alford* pleas." See *State v. Garcia*, 192 Wis. 2d 845, 860 n.4, 532 N.W.2d 111 (1995). All states should do so; their courtroom wheels would keep turning.

18. On the Wisconsin Court of Appeals, I authored opinions elaborating my objections to *Alford* pleas. See, e.g., *State v. Smith*, 196 Wis. 2d 646, 539 N.W.2d 336 (Ct. App. 1995) (Schudson, J, *dissenting*) (*rev'd* 202 Wis. 2d 21 (1996)).

19. While formulas vary from state to state, Wisconsin's were not unusual. During my trial court years, a prisoner would become eligible for parole after serving one-fourth the length of a judicially pronounced sentence and, with minor variations due to good time, would reach mandatory release after serving less than two-thirds. Thus, for example, an armed robber sentenced to twenty years would become eligible for parole after five years and reach mandatory release after no more than ten years, four months, and nine days. Sending my felony court colleagues the Corrections Department's charts detailing the dates, I wrote:

> I believe it essential to fair sentencing in every case to practice "truth in sentencing." That means that in analyzing what should be the appropriate sentence, and in explaining the sentence to the defendant, victims, lawyers and public, the judge should speak in terms that include understanding of the parole eligibility time, the mandatory release time, and sometimes even the average length of time served. . . .
>
> The sentencing result is not necessarily tougher or softer. However, it is consistently more informed and fair. In addition, it should help judges pierce the public's cynicism that would understandably include doubts about what sentences really mean. . . .
>
> This kind of analysis has led me to order sentences that are considerably longer than those recommended in some cases. However, in so doing, the analysis has allowed me to specifically address the very concerns raised by both parties, particularly when they seek long-term incarceration and treatment, but recommend a sentence length that actually undermines the potential for that.
>
> The same process has led me to order some sentences that are considerably shorter that those recommended.

20. See *Sentencing Seminar Syllabus*, National Judicial College (September 1988).

21. Thus, in 1987, the National Council of Juvenile and Family Court Judges published *Child Sexual Abuse—Issues and Actions: Manual and Administrator's Guide;*

A Training Curriculum to Improve Judicial Response, and provided crash courses at judicial conferences throughout the country.

22. Now having had the privilege of teaching more than one hundred courses for judges throughout America and abroad, I offer these added, concluding reflections on judicial education:

1. It is hard to imagine any professionals, other than judges, allowed to begin their duties with so little training. In many states, little if any orientation is required. In the ensuing years, however, judges complete annual continuing education, choosing from courses at state judicial conferences under the auspices of state supreme courts and administrative offices.

2. Judicial education courses, whether provided through the National Judicial College, the National Council of Juvenile and Family Court Judges, or state judicial conferences, are almost always excellent. Faculty—usually judges but sometimes specialists from fields including computer technology, economics, medicine, psychology, and literature—are carefully selected and additionally trained in adult education teaching techniques. Indeed, some of the finest courses I've ever taken anywhere came through judicial education—economics for judges at the University of Kansas; appellate skills at New York University; law and literature taught by Brandeis and University of Wisconsin faculty; teacher training led by the National Council of Juvenile and Family Court Judges; and courses on brain science and bias through the National Association of State Judicial Educators.

3. Such superb programs make a difference, challenging America's judges, improving their practices, and truly transforming some of their most important understandings.

CHAPTER 10. THE APPELLATE JUDGE: DEATH, AND THREE WIDOWS

1. Franklin P. Adams, *FPA Book of Quotations; a New Collection of Famous Sayings, Reflecting the Wisdom and the Wit of Times Past and Present and Including the Virtuous, Humorous, and Philosophic Commentary on Life by Men and Women of Every Age, Together with Riches from the Profound Wells of the Bible, Proverbs, and Anonymity* (New York: Funk and Wagnalls, 1952), 466.

2. Robert Habush, one of America's most famous litigators, served as president of the Association of Trial Lawyers of America (ATLA). (In 2006 the organization changed its name to the American Association for Justice [AAJ].)

3. Kurt Chandler, *Courtroom Avenger: The Challenges and Triumphs of Robert Habush* (Chicago: American Bar Association, 2014), 214–15.

4. Chandler, *Courtroom Avenger*, 223.

5. See Wis. Stat. § 895.85(3) ("The plaintiff may receive punitive damages if evidence is submitted showing that the defendant acted maliciously toward the plaintiff or in an intentional disregard of the rights of the plaintiff").

6. See Wis JI-Civil 1701.1. See also *Trinity Evangelical Lutheran Church v. Tower Ins. Co.,* 261 Wis. 2d 333, 352 n.5 (2003).

7. "[J]urors explained how they had reached the amount of the awards. The award for compensatory damages to each widow—$1.4 million—equaled $100,000 multiplied by the fourteen horrific seconds the workers experienced from the time of the loud banging of the crane to the time they came to rest on the infield ground. 'We were thinking about what these gentlemen went through in those fourteen seconds,' said a juror somberly.'" Chandler, *Courtroom Avenger*, 256. The punitive damages were double the amount of the $47 million contract held by Mitsubishi to build the retractable roof. These amounts were in addition to $27 million already secured through partial pre-trial settlements with some of the insurers of both Mitsubishi and the stadium's general contractor (see 222–23).

8. See *BMW of N. Am., Inc. v. Gore*, 517 U.S. 559, 570 (1996).

9. In issues relating to "tort reform," I know of no case better than *Guzman v. St. Francis Hosp.*, 2001 WI App 21, 240 Wis. 2d 559, 623 N.W.2d 776, to illustrate how reasonable judges may reach honest and reasonable differences of opinion, *and* to cause concern that political positions may have masqueraded as legal "reasoning."

In *Guzman*, Judge James Smith, Judge Mary Brown, and I considered a challenge to the state legislature's recently enacted $350,000 limit (often called a "cap") on "non-economic damages" in cases of medical malpractice. However misleading reputations may be, many court-watchers considered Judge Smith a scholarly but doctrinaire conservative, Judge Brown an obsessively political liberal, and me an unpredictable independent. Thus, they may have expected Judge Smith to approve the cap, Judge Brown to disapprove, and me to cast the swing vote. I concluded that the cap was unconstitutional; that, by imposing a *legislative policy* that limited these damages in *all* cases, the cap, automatically reducing what a jury otherwise might award in each case, violated the right to a jury trial. Judge Brown agreed with my analysis; Judge Smith did not. Thus, I authored the majority opinion. But, just before its issuance, Judge Brown changed her mind, though she never told me why. Consequently, Judge Smith then wrote the majority opinion allowing the legislative cap on damages, and Judge Brown wrote a concurring opinion "reluctantly" agreeing "that the statute barely passes constitutional muster" (588 (Brown, J., *concurring*)). I dissented (591–607 (Schudson, J., *dissenting*)).

The plaintiff then appealed to the Wisconsin Supreme Court, where one of the seven justices recused and the other six divided three-three. When such an even split occurs in the highest court, the next highest court's decision becomes law. Accordingly, Judge Smith's majority opinion prevailed, setting an important precedent. These votes—two-one and three-three—typify the closeness of calls on tort reform in America's appellate courts.

10. "Scholars have identified a number of early English statutes authorizing the award of multiple damages for particular wrongs. Some 65 different enactments during the period between 1275 and 1753 provided for double, treble, or quadruple damages." *BMW of N. Am., Inc. v. Gore*, 517 U.S. 559, 580–1 (1996). "Present-day federal law allows or mandates imposition of multiple damages for a wide assortment of offenses, including violations of the antitrust laws, and the Racketeer Influenced

and Corrupt Organizations Act, and certain breaches of the trademark laws, and the patent laws" (581, n.33).

11. See *BMW of N. Am., Inc. v. Gore*, 517 U.S. 559, 568 (1996) ("Punitive damages may properly be imposed to further a State's legitimate interests in punishing unlawful conduct and deterring its repetition"). See also *Trinity Evangelical Lutheran Church v. Tower Ins. Co.*, 2003 WI 46, 261 Wis. 2d 333, 661 N.W.2d 789 ("[T]he purpose of punitive damages is to punish the wrongdoer, and to deter the wrongdoer and others from similar conduct, rather than to compensate the plaintiff for any loss").

12. For a summary of the state-by-state status at the time of the Supreme Court's decision, see *BMW of N. Am., Inc. v. Gore*, 517 U.S. 559, 614–19 (1996) (appendix to dissenting opinion of Ginsburg, J.) (Ginsburg, J., *dissenting*) ("State legislatures have in the hopper or have enacted a variety of measures to curtail awards of punitive damages"). Sensitive to criticism of windfalls for plaintiffs and their lawyers and seeing an opportunity to strengthen publicly funded programs, some states have modified punitive damages in a politically appealing way—taking substantial percentages of punitive damage awards from victims and allocating them to state treasuries, university systems, schools for the disabled, health care and rehabilitation services, legal services, and trust funds for crime and tort victim compensation. See *BMW of N. Am., Inc. v. Gore*, 517 U.S. 559, 614–19 (1996) (Appendix list: "Allocation of Punitive Damages to State Agencies").

13. See *Pac. Mut. Life Ins. Co. v. Haslip*, 499 U.S. 1, 39 (1991) (Scalia, J., *concurring*) ("State legislatures and courts have the power to restrict or abolish the common-law practice of punitive damages, and in recent years have increasingly done so").

14. See *BMW of N. Am., Inc. v. Gore*, 517 U.S. 559, 585 (1996).

15. See *BMW of N. Am., Inc. v. Gore*, 517 U.S. 559, 600 (1996) (Scalia, J., *dissenting*).

16. Focusing not only on *BMW* but also on two other cases in which Justice Scalia authored separate opinions on punitive damages, Posner observed: "People have multiple desires, often conflicting, and they must weigh them against each other in coming to a decision. . . . Justice Scalia surely disapproves of extravagant awards of punitive damages to tort plaintiffs, but he disapproves more of the concept of substantive due process that his colleagues have used to impose a constitutional limit on those awards." Richard A. Posner, *How Judges Think* (Cambridge, MA: Harvard University Press, 2008), 284–85. See also *TXO Prod. Corp. v. All. Res. Corp.*, 509 U.S. 443, 470 (1993) (Scalia, J., *concurring*); *State Farm Mut. Auto. Ins. Co. v. Campbell*, 538 U.S. 408, 429 (2003) (Scalia, J., *dissenting*).

17. *BMW of N. Am., Inc. v. Gore*, 517 U.S. 559, 599 (1996) (Scalia, J., *dissenting*). Justice Scalia's readiness to discard precedent should not surprise careful Supreme Court observers. Throughout his career, he was among the leaders of judicial "restraint," conservative style, which meant *activism*. Indeed, that very quality was an important factor leading to his appointment by President Reagan. See Lincoln Caplan, "Judicial Restraint Means Activism on the Right," *Washington Post*, January 19, 1986 ("Like so much else in modern conservative thinking, the Reagan approach defines itself in reaction to perceived excesses of liberalism. In adopting its own legal notions, the [Reagan] administration has transformed a distinguished conservative

tradition. It has turned judicial restraint into a new form of activism"). See also David Savage, "The Sharp-tongued Conservative Who Transformed the Supreme Court," *The Week*, February 26, 2016 ("He broke with fellow Reagan appointees— Justices Sandra Day O'Connor and Anthony Kennedy—because they refused to overturn the court's precedents on abortion, school prayer, and other issues").

18. *BMW of N. Am., Inc. v. Gore*, 517 U.S. 559, 607–14 (1996) (Ginsburg, J., *dissenting*).

19. See Nina Totenberg, "Scalia v. Ginsburg: Supreme Court Sparring, Put to Music," NPR, *All Things Considered*, July 10, 2013 (updated July 11, 2013), www.npr .org/2013/07/10/200137481. I do not mean to make too much of this. Liberal-Conservative crossover is a relatively frequent occurrence on business issues before the Supreme Court. See Noam Scheiber, "As Americans Take Up Populism, Supreme Court Embraces Business," *New York Times*, March 12, 2016. See also Mark Tushnet, *In the Balance: Law and Politics on the Roberts Court* (New York: Norton, 2013); Jonathan H. Adler, *Business and the Roberts Court* (New York: Oxford University Press, 2016). Further, I do not mean to suggest that Justice Scalia was less doctrinaire than characterized by critics. Open-minded humility, they say, was not in his repertoire. Linda Greenhouse noted that "while earlier in his Supreme Court tenure, he prided himself on hiring one politically liberal law clerk among his four clerks every year, he abandoned that practice at least a decade ago." Linda Greenhouse, "Resetting the Post-Scalia Supreme Court," *New York Times*, February 18, 2016. Jeffrey Toobin described him as "[b]elligerent with his colleagues, dismissive of his critics, nostalgic for a world where outsiders knew their place and stayed there," adding: "Scalia described himself as an advocate of judicial restraint, who believed that the courts should defer to the democratically elected branches of government. In reality, he lunged at opportunities to overrule the work of Presidents and of legislators, especially Democrats." Jeffrey Toobin, "Antonin Scalia: Looking Backward," *New Yorker*, February 29, 2016. Even posthumously, his name courts controversy. See Nicholas Fandos, "University Critics Draw Line at Naming School for Scalia," *New York Times*, April 29, 2016 (regarding the proposal to rename the George Mason University Law School for Justice Scalia); Nicholas Fandos, "University in Virginia Firms Up Plan to Honor Scalia," *New York Times*, May 18, 2016. And who weighed in on the controversy in support of honoring him? Ruth Bader Ginsburg "described the school's renaming as 'altogether fitting.'" Steve Eder, "Rolling Back U.S. Regulations Will Test One Scholar's Finesse," *New York Times*, July 10, 2017.

Never having known or worked with Justice Scalia, I am not taking sides. What I would add, however, to enhance our understanding of appellate judges generally, are punctuation points to Greenhouse's observation about the importance of Justice Scalia's law clerk selection.

While appellate judges cannot pick their judicial colleagues, they do pick their clerks. And, because clerkships are coveted, judges are able to choose from among many fine lawyers and graduating law students. For me, clerk selection was fun and frustrating—fun, because I enjoyed meeting so many excellent applicants; frustrating, because I often found more than one I wanted. In fact, on two occasions, unable to decide, I picked two women to share the position—an ideal situation for them, as they balanced childbearing and careers, and for me, as I benefited from twice the talents. Still, I *always* knew what I wanted: clerks *not* like me. Silently applying criteria that might not have been lawful in a job listing, I sought clerks whose experiences differed from mine, even according to gender, race, religion, and politics. I wanted clerks who would challenge my thinking and cause me to question and learn. I *never* was disappointed and will always be grateful for the dedicated efforts of my outstanding clerks.

This is more than a perfunctory "thank you." I am not alone in emphasizing law clerks' irreplaceable contributions. Consider the comments of Indiana University School of Law professor Frank Sullivan Jr., writing of his many years as an Indiana Supreme Court justice: "Hardly anything . . . approaches the satisfaction of the keen friendships that I have developed with the twenty-eight lawyers who served as my law clerks. . . . [H]ow much they taught me—to be sure, some of it merely generational: as each year went by, the clerks were that much younger than me!—as women, African-Americans, Hispanics, and Asian-Americans, they brought background and experience to the issues confronting our court that I simply did not have." Frank Sullivan Jr., "What I've Learned about Judging," *Valparaiso University Law Review* 48 (2013): 195–216. The veiled influence of law clerks may be significant, as a noteworthy case reveals. In 1971, an unnamed law clerk was largely responsible for turning the US Supreme Court's five-three rejection of Muhammad Ali's challenge to his conviction for draft evasion into an eight-zero vindication of his conscientious objector claim. See Bob Woodward and Scott Armstrong, *The Brethren: Inside the Supreme Court* (New York: Simon and Schuster, 1979). See also Dave Anderson, "How a Clerk Spared Ali from Prison," *New York Times*, December 17, 1979 (reprinted, June 11, 2016).

20. Wis. Stat. § 895.85(3).

21. Looking back at my file, I found eleven pages of notes I had prepared, not for oral argument itself but just for our meeting to organize the issues. I was reminded that the case consisted of three consolidated appeals and cross-appeals involving six plaintiffs, two defendant corporations, three insurance companies, and all their attorneys, necessitating an intricate flow chart identifying the players, their teams, and their arguments. In twelve years, only one other appeal—the so-called Seinfeld case of national renown—came close to presenting such complications. (In that case, I authored our fifty-five-page decision, needing approximately half my working hours for six months to do so.) See *Mackenzie v. Miller Brewing Co.*, 234 Wis. 2d 1 (Ct. App. 2000).

Such appeals and their time-consuming authorship are rare. Most judges greet them reluctantly, knowing that such a case can consume one's efforts for months. For that reason among others, most appellate courts, to fairly allocate the burden, assign authorships on a "rotating" basis. Then, individual practices vary. Able and conscientious judges accept personal responsibility for actual authorship, relying on their clerks for important but limited assistance. Others, less industrious, delegate almost all research and writing to them.

Authorship assignment takes us to one of the least known and most blatantly corrupting influences on appellate decision-making. Hidden and utterly indefensible, it operates this way. Because the judges know the rotating order of authorships, each judge, every month, knows what's coming. But what if a judge wants to dodge a time-consuming case? No problem—as long as that judge is willing to violate ethical standards and abandon merit-based decision-making. That judge need only declare an intention to *dissent*. Then authorship moves to the next judge (and the unethical judge can sit back, wait for the majority opinion, and write a brief concurring or dissenting opinion, or perhaps even "reconsider" and come on board with the majority). Does this actually happen? Yes, but not often. Honesty and peer pressure are almost always strong enough to prevent such perfidy. Still, such unprincipled pettiness plays a part, particularly in close and time-consuming cases where judges may look at the rotation and lean one way or the other in order to avoid or obtain authorship.

22. Posner, *How Judges Think*, 5.

23. Wis. Stat. § 757.81(4)(c).

24. See Wis. SCR §§ 60.04(3)(a), 60.01(1). See also Wis. SCR § 60.02 ("A judge should participate in establishing, maintaining and enforcing high standards of conduct and shall personally observe those standards so that the integrity and independence of the judiciary will be preserved"); Wis. SCR § 60.03 ("A judge shall avoid impropriety and the appearance of impropriety in all of the judge's activities"); Wis. SCR § 60.03 (comment) ("The test for appearance of impropriety is whether the conduct would create in reasonable minds a perception that the judge's ability to carry out judicial responsibilities with integrity, impartiality and competence is impaired").

25. Wis. Stat. § 757.93(1)(a) ("All proceedings [of the Wisconsin Judicial Commission] relating to misconduct . . . are confidential"); Wis. Stat. § 757.94(1) ("A complaint or communication alleging judicial misconduct . . . with the [judicial] commission . . . is privileged").

26. *Wischer v. Mitsubishi Heavy Indus. Am., Inc.*, 2003 WI App 202, ¶¶ 58–83, 267 Wis. 2d 638, 673 N.W.2d 303 (Schudson, J., *dissenting*).

27. Chandler, *Courtroom Avenger*, 259.

28. Sir Tom Stoppard (1937–), whose words from his play *The Real Thing* are the ones I quoted to open the preface and now repeat here. Stoppard is a Czech-born British playwright, knighted in 1997. See also Posner, *How Judges Think*, 149 ("Important judicial activities go on below the radar . . . such activities of appellate judges as carefully reading and commenting on the circulated draft of another judge on the panel").

29. Posner, *How Judges Think*, 218.

30. See Augustus Y. Napier and Carl Whitaker, *The Family Crucible* (New York: HarperCollins, 1978).

CHAPTER 11. THE TRIAL JUDGE: RELIGION, AND WHITE SUPREMACISTS

1. Proceedings and Debates of the Virginia State Convention of 1829–30, 616 (1830) (quoted in *Williams-Yulee v. Fla. Bar*, 135 S. Ct. 1656 (2015)).

2. See publications of the Southern Poverty Law Center and its periodic state-by-state surveys of hate groups throughout America: www.splcenter.org.

3. See Mark Ward, "Shooting Not Justified, Prosecutor in Skinheads Case Says," *Milwaukee Journal*, April 4, 1989; "Teen in Car Testifies on Skinhead Shooting," *Milwaukee Journal*, April 5, 1989.

4. O'Malley also testified that he fired only after seeing one of the occupants stick a handgun out the car window. See "Lawyer Grills Teens Shot at by Skinheads," *Milwaukee Journal*, April 6, 1989. See also Eldon Knoche, "'Skinhead' Gunman Says He Was Afraid," *Milwaukee Sentinel*, April 8, 1989 ("I was in fear of one of my friends or myself being killed"); Mark Ward, "Witness Tells of Shots from House," *Milwaukee Journal*, April 8, 1989 (O'Malley testified that "he fired one shot from a rifle upstairs, another man upstairs fired two shots from a rifle and a third man downstairs fired one shot from a sawed-off shotgun"). The existence of a handgun in the car and whether one of the car's occupants ever pointed it out the window remained in dispute due, in part, to inadequate police investigation. See Eldon Knoche, "'Skinheads' Sentenced to Very Different Terms," *Milwaukee Sentinel*, July 6, 1989; Matt Devine, "Judge Scolds Police, Media during 'Skinhead' Sentencing," *Milwaukee Journal*, July 6, 1989.

5. See Ward, "Witness Tells of Shots." During the trial, the jurors visited the crime scene. The article reports: "Jurors could see holes made by shotgun pellets riddling the side of the house where Lange had been fired on during a fight a week before the shooting incident. O'Malley said that incident, which he said began as a fight between Lange and several Hispanics, combined with warnings received from police, convinced residents of the house that they were in danger."

6. Moreover, Gahn knew this evidence was legally secure. Insulated by "Miranda" warnings from the police who questioned him, O'Malley's statements were admissible.

7. See Mark Ward, "Skinhead Found Guilty on All Counts," *Milwaukee Journal*, April 13, 1989.

8. See "Why Courts Must Sock It to the Skinheads," *Milwaukee Journal*, April 14, 1989.

9. A press report summarized the evidentiary distinctions I identified, leading to the different sentences:

- O'Malley fired a more powerful M-1 rifle; Lange fired a .22-caliber rifle. O'Malley's shot caused the more serious injuries.
- O'Malley shot first from the upstairs window; Lange, standing nearby, fired in reaction.
- O'Malley had not been shot earlier; Lange, having been shot in the face six days earlier, had more fear of an attack.
- O'Malley showed no remorse; Lange acknowledged he overreacted to the threat of a car slowly driving by the house and appeared to accept responsibility.
- O'Malley was the leader; Lange, a follower.

See Knoche, "'Skinheads' Sentenced." See also Devine, "Judge Scolds Police."

10. Journalist Dennis McCann captured important moments and moods of O'Malley's trial. But while he mentioned the defense theory, he dismissed it, failing to report the confirmation of the defendant's account:

It is for a jury of his peers—actually, a jury of his grandparents' peers because you probably couldn't find a dozen just like him—to rule on skinhead hero Patrick O'Malley's guilt or innocence in a South Side shooting last summer.

That is as it should be.

But guilt or innocence aside, other verdicts are fair game for those who watched O'Malley's trial from the cheap seats, and here are the obvious ones: dumb, depressing, comical, disturbing, silly, sad.

And I'm unanimous about that.

O'Malley, 18, is the neo-Nazi, white-power missionary who became one of the leaders of Milwaukee's skinhead movement last summer. It was a bully-kid movement that thrived on hatred and bigotry, on tough talk and race-baiting that finally hauled in trouble. It all peaked the night O'Malley and another teen were arrested after shots fired from their house struck a car carrying five North Side youths. They wounded one and scared the bejeezus out of the rest.

O'Malley's trial was, on one level, a basic lesson in American justice because it gave even a teenage neo-Nazi his eight days in court. On another level it was good theater, occasionally tedious, sometimes amusing, often disturbing.

O'Malley played the lead. Some of his friends attended in the uniform of the street—T-shirts and flight jackets, shorn heads and black boots—but O'Malley dressed up for the jury. He wore sports coats and sweaters, even a tie the day he testified, and was so keen on spiffing up that he grew hair. He was a natty neo-Nazi and an occasionally charming one, flashing a bright Irish smile and glad-handing with friends. He even talked with the black legal assistant brought in by defense lawyer James C. Wood, who no doubt hoped the jury would notice and think, hey, this kid isn't so bad.

But you can put a pig in a dress and take her to a dance and you still won't have a pretty date. Even Wood was obliged to liken his client's philosophy to that of the Ku Klux Klan, and there was no mistaking the swastika that bulged on the bicep of one of O'Malley's skinhead buddies. If O'Malley and his pals so impressed an 11-year-old neighbor that he asked his mother if he, too, could shave his head, they did not inspire a bailiff who watched them swagger and said, "These guys, there's so much hate in these people."

Which is just what begat all this trouble in the first place.

The skinheads had so alienated blacks and Hispanics and others with their divisive and hate-filled talk of white power last summer that they began to fear for their own safety. The defense contended that one gang had threatened to firebomb the skinhead house or attack it with Gatling guns, rockets and other weapons stolen from an armory in Chicago.

Right. But, skinheads being kids, they decided to fortify their own little house. They sent two guys with enough hair to pass as normal to buy rifles and ammunition at Woolworth's and cheap walkie-talkies from Toys R Us.

Really. Toys R Us. They posted guards, moved the furniture into the kitchen to save it from firebombs, filled cans with water and waited.

The poor chumps who showed up weren't the much-feared gang, though. They were five North Side high school kids, four of them black, out on a hot summer night getting their kicks by driving by the house of the notorious skinheads. They weren't babes in the woods, maybe, but they swore to a boy that the baseball bat and sharp stick they brought along weren't to start a fight, but to end one. They bought some juice and, in man's uncanny way of getting the right brainstorm at the wrong time, decided to throw the bottles at the heavily armed skinhead house.

"It was," as one youth later testified in one of those rare moments when sworn testimony was also revealing truth, "a dumb thing to do." It was also a classic mismatch. Throw-tinkle-BLAM-BLAM-BLAM-BLAM and done.

The skinheads have split up now, O'Malley's contingent rejected by those who share his hair style but not his ugly creed. He continues to follow the twisted path of separatism, achieving such status that his band, Hammerhead, reportedly was invited to play at last month's Aryan Woodstock in California. That planned white supremacist mega-concert died for lack of permits.

He has grown his hair out, but he refused to grow up.

That is a dumb thing to do.

Dennis McCann, "Hate on Trial with Skinhead," *Milwaukee Journal*, April 12, 1989. The following week, Lange's trial also received substantial press coverage. See Mark Ward, "Lawyer in 2nd Skinhead Trial Says Defendant Saw Danger," *Milwaukee Journal*, April 18, 1989; Eldon Knoche, "2nd 'Skinhead' Tells of Fears," *Milwaukee Journal*, April 19, 1989; Anne Waukau, "2nd 'Skinhead' Found Guilty in South Side Shooting Case," *Milwaukee Sentinel*, April 22, 1989; Jim Stingl, "Lawyer in Skinhead Case Drew Flak from Other Attorneys," *Milwaukee Journal*, April 22, 1989 (describing criticism attorney Eduardo Borda, a Chilean American, received for defending a neo-Nazi).

11. This is particularly true under extreme stress or during an "emotional hijacking." The brain's amygdala supplies fight-or-flight protection by releasing cortisol and adrenaline, powerful chemicals that fuel the bloodstream for strength and speed. But as they fortify fight or flight, they also weaken logical problem-solving. Thus, physiologically, as strength and the potential for sudden response rise, judgment and self-control drop; as the need for decisiveness arrives, the capacity for calm and correct conclusiveness departs. See, e.g., Daniel Goleman, *Emotional Intelligence: Why It Can Matter More Than IQ* (New York: Bantam Books, 1994); Daniel Goleman, *Primal Leadership: Realizing the Power of Emotional Intelligence* (Boston: Harvard Business School Press, 2002). See also Daniel H. Pink, *A Whole New Mind: Why Right-Brainers Will Rule the Future* (New York: Riverhead Books, 2005).

12. See Mark Ward, "Skinheads Sought Different judge: Bid to Replace Jewish Judge Denied; Fair Trial Is Promised," *Milwaukee Journal*, September 2, 1988.

13. See Alan Blinder, "Top Alabama Judge Orders Halt to Same-Sex Marriage Licenses," *New York Times*, January 6, 2016; Campbell Robertson, "Chief Justice in Alabama Is Suspended a Second Time," *New York Times*, October 1, 2016.

14. See Eben Pindyck, "One Step at a Time: 50 Years Ago, a Group of Primarily Black Marchers Attempted to Change the City," *Milwaukee Magazine*, August 2017, 13–14.

15. Ruth F. Brin, "An Assumption of Faith," *Harvest: Collected Poems and Prayers* (Duluth, MN: Holy Cow! Press, 1999), writing of Caleb and Joshua, who filed a "minority report" countering the conclusion of ten fellow spies and urging "[t]hat a band of nomad slaves could conquer a settled land, [t]hat a people decimated by illness and warfare could overcome fortified cities."

16. See, e.g., Laurie Goodstein, "Links to Religious Group Raise Issues for Nominee," *New York Times*, September 29, 2017, reporting that the nomination of Professor Amy Coney Barrett, of Notre Dame Law School, for a seat on the US Seventh Circuit Court of Appeals raised questions as the Senate Judiciary Committee considered—or avoided consideration of—whether her Catholicism and "membership in a small, tightly knit Christian group called People of Praise" might compromise her independence. "'The dogma lives loudly within you,' declared Senator Dianne Feinstein, Democrat of California, in what has become an infamous phrase. Senator Orrin Hatch, Republican of Utah, accused his colleagues of employing an unconstitutional 'religious test' for office." By a vote of fifty-five to forty-three, the Senate confirmed Barrett. See Kevin Freking, "Senate Confirms Notre Dame Professor for Federal Court amid Religious Fight," *South Bend Tribune*, November 1, 2017.

CHAPTER 12. THE APPELLATE JUDGE: POLITICS, "OUT ON THE POINT"

1. See Shawn E. Tuma, "Law in Texas Literature: Texas Justice—Roy Bean Style," *Review of Litigation* 21, no. 3 (2002): 551–92. See also Timothy Egan, *Lasso the Wind: Away to the New West* (New York: Knopf, 1998), 157–65.

2. See, e.g., the sentences of Cook County judges in the Greylord cases: Hon. John J. Devine (fifteen years); Hon. Daniel P. Glecier (six years); Hon. Martin F. Hogan (ten years); Hon. Reginald J. Holzer (thirteen years); Hon. Richard LeFevour (twelve years); Hon. John H. McCollum (eleven years); Hon. John J. McDonnell (six years); Hon. Michael E. McNulty (three years); Hon. John M. Murphy (ten years); Hon. Wayne W. Olson (twelve years); Hon. John F. Reynolds (ten years); Hon. Roger Seaman (five years); Hon. Raymond Sodini (eight years). Several of these sentences added fines, probations, and orders for community service.

3. Frank Mastropolo, Lauren Pearle, and Glenn Ruppel, "Pa. Supreme Court Throws Out Thousands of Juvenile Delinquency Cases," ABC News, October 29, 2009, http://abcnews.go.com/2020/pa-supreme-court-throws-thousands-juvenile-delinquency-cases/story?id=8952028.

4. ABC News explained:

Ciavarella and Conahan had allegedly devised a plot to use their positions as judges to pad their pockets. They shut down the old county-run juvenile detention center by first refusing to send kids there and, then, by cutting off funds, choking it out of existence.

They then replaced the facility with a cash cow—a privately owned lockup built by the judges' cronies—and forged a deal for the county to pay $58 million for a 10-year period for its use. At the time, Conahan was serving as president judge of the Luzerne County Common Pleas Court, a position that allowed him to control the county-court budget. Ciavarella was the Luzerne County juvenile court judge.

Mastropolo, Pearle, and Ruppel, "Pa. Supreme Court Throws Out Thousands of Juvenile Delinquency Cases." Extensive news coverage exposed outrageous sentences. See Stephanie Chen, "Pennsylvania Rocked by 'Jailing Kids for Cash' Scandal," CNN, February 24, 2009, http://www.cnn.com/2009/CRIME/02/23/pennsylvania .corrupt.judges/ ("At a friend's sleepover . . . , 14-year-old Phillip . . . pocketed change from unlocked vehicles in the neighborhood to buy chips and soft drinks. The cops caught him. There was no need for an attorney, said Phillip's mother . . . who thought at most, the judge would slap her son with a fine or community service. But she was shocked to find her eighth-grader handcuffed and shackled in the courtroom and sentenced to a youth detention center . . . [t]hen . . . to a boarding school for troubled teens for nine months"); Ian Urbina and Sean D. Hamill, "Judges Plead Guilty in Scheme to Jail Youths for Profit," New York Times, February 13, 2009 ("At worst, Hillary . . . thought she might get a stern lecture when she appeared before a judge for building a spoof MySpace page mocking the assistant principal at her high school. . . . She was a stellar student who had never been in trouble, and the page stated clearly at the bottom that it was just a joke. Instead, the judge sentenced her to three months at a juvenile detention center on a charge of harassment. She was handcuffed and taken away as her stunned parents stood by").

5. See Eyder Peralta, "Pa. Judge Sentenced to 28 Years in Massive Juvenile Justice Bribery Scandal," NPR, August 11, 2011, http://www.npr.org/sections/thetwo-way/ 2011/08/11/139536686/pa-judge-sentenced-to-28-years-in-massive-juvenile-justice-brib ery-scandal. The unfairness of such kickbacks is obvious. Less understood, however, is the constitutional basis—the Fourteenth Amendment—for the reversal of the criminal convictions.

The Fourteenth Amendment to the US Constitution provides, in part: "nor shall any State deprive any person of life, liberty, or property, without due process of law." Such "due process"—words often repeated, without pause to ponder their meaning— signifies the steps that, at a minimum, must be taken to ensure fairness in any legal proceeding that could lead to a person's loss of property, freedom, or life. Under our Constitution, such is the "process" that is "due." In words that seem aimed at the heart of scandals like Pennsylvania's, Justice Ruth Bader Ginsburg explained: "The impartiality guaranteed to litigants through the Due Process Clause adheres to a core principle: 'No man is permitted to try cases where he has an interest in the outcome.'

Our cases have 'jealously guarded' that basic concept, for it 'ensures that no person will be deprived of his interests in the absence of a proceeding in which he may present his case with assurance that the arbiter is not predisposed to find against him.'" *Republican Party v. White*, 536 U.S. 765, 814 (2002) (Ginsburg, J., *dissenting*). See also *In re Murchinson*, 349 U.S. 133, 136 (1955) ("A fair trial in a fair tribunal is a basic requirement of due process"). Thus, as Geyh noted, in *Tumey v. Ohio*, 273 U.S. 510 (1927), the Supreme Court "used the due process clause to invalidate a state court scheme in which judges were paid from fines they assessed against defendants—a conflict of interest that would tempt less than forthright judges to impose unwarranted fines to line their pocketbooks." Charles Gardner Geyh, *Courting Peril: The Political Transformation of the American Judiciary* (New York: Oxford University Press, 2016), 104. The "significance of affording parties due process in judicial proceedings is entrenched in western culture dating back at least as far as the Magna Carta [1215]" (138).

6. And no reason to dismiss Cook County's Greylords with "Well, that's Chicago." Bribery, whatever a court system's traditions, still is a function of *individual* character. Recall the effort to extradite the nursing home owners (chapter 2). Against high-priced attorneys hired by financially powerful defendants, I litigated that issue in Chicago before Cook County Chief Judge Richard J. Fitzgerald. His conduct and rulings led me to trust in his integrity. Years later, reading 2010 news clippings of his death, I learned that Fitzgerald "was the only member of the Cook County circuit judiciary entrusted by the federal government with details of . . . Operation Greylord." Trevor Jensen, "Services Set for Retired Judge Richard Fitzgerald, Hero of FBI Probe," *Chicago Tribune*, April 19, 2010. According to Illinois Supreme Court Justice Thomas R. Fitzgerald (no relation), quoted in Jensen's article: "In that whole sordid business he was the one shining light."

7. See *State v. Gesch*, 167 Wis. 2d 660, 482 N.W.2d 99 (1992).

8. The procedure is different in federal courts, where the trial judges, with relatively little input from the attorneys, do almost all the questioning of prospective jurors.

9. In L. C. Clay's case, the statute provided, in part: "The court shall examine on oath each person wh~   'ed as a juror to discover whether the juror is related by blood. ~   o any party or to any attorney appearing in the case,
                              e case, or has expressed or formed any opinion, or
                              n the case. If a juror is not indifferent in the case,
t   tat. § 805.08(1).
                              ula may be modified to account for the number
of   other factors, including the number of defen-
dar   e selected, and whether the charge is punishable
by   .g., Wis. Stat. § 972.03.
1   imprudent. The prospective's answers offered
ampl   us, the prosecutor's ethical obligation should
have   e motion. Further, other prospectives were
availab   n would have caused no problem but would

have preempted an appealable issue. The proof was in the appellate pudding—the issue was so clear that the assistant attorney general, representing the prosecution before our court, conceded the prosecutor's and judge's error.

12. The state supreme court clarified why, even when an objectionable prospective never becomes a juror on the case, fresh jury selection and a new trial are required. Otherwise, a defendant would be left "in an unavoidable and extremely unfair 'catch 22'" accepting the selection of the objectionable juror in order to preserve all four peremptory strikes (and preserve an appealable issue), or removing the objectionable juror by using one of the four peremptory strikes that should have remained available to remove another prospective. The supreme court concluded: "We will not force a defendant into such a 'lose-lose' position. The peremptory challenge is one of the most important of the rights secured to the accused." *State v. Gesch*, 167 Wis. 2d 660, 671, 482 N.W.2d 99 (1992).

13. Amanda Frost and Stephani Lindquist, "Countering the Majoritarian Difficulty," *Virginia Law Review* 96, no. 4 (2010): 719–97. In fact, as Geyh added in *Courting Peril*: "[S]everal studies have shown that criminal sentences spike in the months leading up to an election." Geyh, *Courting Peril*, 55.

14. See chapter 10, n.25. Again this is awkward. Still, I must clarify that while, for both legal accuracy and educational completeness, I must include Judicial Commission referral among my options, I am neither stating nor implying anything about whether, in fact, I ever made any such referral and, if so, whether the Commission took any action.

15. In contrast to the misleadingly limited quotations in the majority opinion, I quoted the questioning of the prospective juror in its entirety and concluded:

> [A]lthough the trial court attempted to salvage [the prospective juror] by tugging him toward an impartial harbor with leading questions, and although [the prospective juror] intermittently acquiesced to the obvious directions that those questions implied, the full record establishes [his] partiality as a matter of law. . . .
>
> On appeal, the *State* confronts this extraordinary record and does *not* reach the majority's remarkable conclusion that the trial court did not err. Rather, the State argues only "harmless error" because [the prospective juror] was removed from the jury by a peremptory challenge. Under [the Wisconsin Supreme Court's decision in Gesch], however, such harmless error analysis is inapplicable.
>
> . . . [The statute] is clear: "*If a juror is not indifferent in the case, the juror shall be excused.*" [statute cited] [emphasis added]. This record is astounding. [The prospective juror] was "not indifferent." He knew it and, on appeal, the State does not argue otherwise. The majority, however, joins the trial court in attempting a salvage operation that the law does not permit.

State v. Clay, No. 94-1193-CR, 1995 Wisc. App. LEXIS 899, 49–52 (Ct. App. July 25, 1995) (Schudson, J., *dissenting*).

16. See *State v. Ramos*, Case No. 94-3036-CR, unpublished slip op., 558 N.W.2d 704, 1996 WL 515652 (Wis.Ct.App. Sept. 12, 1996); this time around, Judge Jones dissented, but only to assert that it was "more appropriate for our supreme court to resolve Ramos's claim." See his dissent in this case. The Wisconsin Supreme Court, in a five-two decision, affirmed our decision. See *State v. Ramos*, 211 Wis. 2d 12, 564 N.W.2d 328 (1997). How fitting that "Clay" was the source of such controversy, for, like formations from a potter's wheel that seem complete only to change before firing, Clay's legal legacy continued to be reshaped. Appeals involving variations of the same issue kept coming, and, within a few years, the Wisconsin Supreme Court backed off a bit, circumscribing the "automatic reversal" rulings of *Gesch* and *Ramos* and, applying "harmless error" analysis, affirming some convictions. See, e.g., *State v. Mendoza*, 227 Wis. 2d 838, 596 N.W.2d 736 (1999); *State v. Kiernan*, 227 Wis. 2d 736, 596 N.W.2d 760 (1999). See also Sarvenaz J. Raissi, "Analyzing Juror Bias Exhibited during Voir Dire in Wisconsin: How to Lessen the Confusion," *Marquette Law Review* 84 (2000): 517–40.

CHAPTER 13. INDIGESTION: FOOD, MOOD, AND MORE

1. Richard A. Posner, *How Judges Think* (Cambridge, MA: Harvard University Press, 2008), 110.

2. Ed Yong, "Justice Is Served, but More So after Lunch: How Food-Breaks Sway the Decisions of Judges," *Discover Magazine*, April 11, 2011.

3. See Yong, "Justice Is Served." See also Leva Danziger and Avnaim-Pesso, "Extraneous Factors in Judicial Decisions," PNAS, February 25, 2011, http://dx.doi.org/10.1073/pnas.1018033108. See also Associated Press, "Study: Judges' Lenience Depends on Time of Day," April 17, 2011: "We find that the likelihood of a favorable ruling is greater at the very beginning of the work day or after a food break than later in the sequence of cases," the researchers report. . . . When people are making a lot of decisions in a row, they look for ways to simplify the process when they get mentally tired, [said Jonathan Levav of Columbia University], and the easiest thing is to maintain the status quo—that is, leave the prisoner in jail." See also Daniel Pink, *When: The Scientific Secrets of Perfect Timing* (New York: Riverhead Books, 2018).

4. Alex Kozinski, "What I Ate for Breakfast and Other Mysteries of Judicial Decision Making," *Loyola of Los Angeles Law Review* 26 (1993): 993; on Kozinski, see chapter 1, n. 5. See also David M. O'Brien, *Judges on Judging: Views from the Bench* (Chatham, NJ: Chatham House, 1997); Gregory C. Sisk, Michael Heise, and Andrew P. Morriss, "Charting the Influences on the Judicial Mind: An Empirical Study of Judicial Reasoning," *New York University Law Review* 73, no. 5 (1998): 1377–500.

5. See, e.g., the work of Dan Ariely, a professor of psychology and behavioral economics at Duke University: www.danariely.com.

6. Course catalog, Dartmouth Experimental College, Winter 1968.

7. See, e.g., Charles B. Schudson, "Brains and Biases: Bringing Emotional Intelligence to America's Courts," 2011 Joint Annual Conference of the National Association for Court Management and the National Association of State Judicial Educators, Las Vegas, Nevada, July 11, 2011. See also *NASJE Curriculum Design: The Journey*

toward Diversity, Fairness, and Access through Education, National Association of State Judicial Educators (2015).

8. An "implicit bias" or "implicit association test" (IAT) measures the speed with which one makes word associations. Computer generated, it shows photos of black and white faces and asks the test-taker to correlate them with positive or negative words, the premise being that faster connections reflect more automatic neurological processes. See Raina Kelley, "The Roots of Racism: What We Don't Know Can Hurt Us," *Newsweek*, July 13, 2009. Shawn C. Marsh, social psychologist and director of the National Council of Juvenile and Family Court Judges, Juvenile and Family Law Department, explains:

> Although some researchers use physiological methods to get at implicit bias (e.g., functional magnetic resonance imaging), the most popular method involves latent response or reaction time measures. This approach is based on the idea that two pieces of information that are tightly associated in our minds should be easier to sort together. For example, for many European Americans, it is easier, based on response time, to pair a white face with a "good" word (e.g., honest) than it is for them to pair a black face to a "good" word. Further, for many European Americans, it is easier, based again on response time, to pair a black face with a "bad" word (e.g., violent) than it is for them to pair a white face with a "bad" word. Latent response time measures assess the speed with which you make these pairings. . . . Regardless of method, the body of research on implicit bias suggests it operates not just as a function of race but also gender, age, and other categories—although not consistently or in the same manner or degree for all participants.

Shawn C. Marsh, "The Lens of Implicit Bias," *Juvenile and Family Justice Today* (Summer 2009): 16–19. See self-tests available at several sources, including https://implicit.harvard.edu/implicit/demo/takeatest.html. Project Implicit was founded in 1998 by three scientists—Tony Greenwald (University of Washington), Mahzarin Banaji (Harvard University), and Brian Nosek (University of Virginia). Project Implicit Mental Health launched in 2011, led by Bethany Teachman (University of Virginia) and Matt Nock (Harvard University). For more information, see www.projectimplicit.net/about.html. For an excellent explanation of the Implicit Association Test, see Leonard Mlodinow, *Subliminal: How Your Unconscious Mind Rules Your Behavior* (New York: Pantheon Books, 2012), 154–57. Mlodinow explores many facets of subliminal and nonverbal communication that have significant implications for the ways in which judges receive information and reach decisions. *Subliminal* is particularly helpful in detailing recent developments in brain science, physiological factors that affect decision-making, and neutral or unavoidable elements that sometimes account for biases. For example:

> Though your evaluation of another person may feel rational and deliberate, it is heavily informed by automatic, unconscious processes—the kind of emotion-regulating processes carried out within the ventromedial prefrontal

cortex. . . . [W]e can't avoid mentally absorbing the categories defined by the society in which we live. They permeate the news, television programming, films, all aspects of our culture. And because our brains naturally categorize, we are vulnerable to acting on the attitudes those categories represent. But before you recommend incorporating [ventromedial prefrontal cortex] obliteration into your company's management training course, remember that the propensity to categorize, even to categorize people, is for the most part a blessing. It allows us to understand the difference between a bus driver and a bus passenger, a store clerk and a customer, a receptionist and a physician, a maître d' and a waiter, and all the other strangers we interact with, without our having to pause and consciously puzzle out everyone's role anew during each encounter. *The challenge is not how to stop categorizing but how to become aware of when we do it in ways that prevent us from being able to see individual people for who they really are.* (156–57; emphasis added)

9. Charles Blow, "A Nation of Cowards?," *New York Times*, February 21, 2009. Mr. Blow explains:

Project Implicit, a virtual laboratory . . . , has administered hundreds of thousands of online tests designed to detect hidden racial biases. In tests taken from 2000 to 2006, they found that three-quarters of whites have an implicit pro-white/anti-black bias. (Blacks showed racial biases, too, but unlike whites, they split about evenly between pro-black and pro-white. And, blacks were the most likely of all races to exhibit no bias at all.) In addition, a 2006 study by Harvard researchers published in the journal Psychological Science used these tests to show how this implicit bias is present in white children as young as 6 years old, and how it stays constant into adulthood. . . .

So why do so many people have this anti-black bias?

I called Brian Nosek, an associate professor in psychology at the University of Virginia and the director of Project Implicit, to find out. According to him, our brains automatically make associations based on our experiences and the information we receive, whether we consciously agree with those associations or not. He said that many egalitarian test-takers were shown to have an implicit anti-black bias, much to their chagrin. Professor Nosek took the test himself, and even he showed a pro-white/anti-black bias.

Similar self-tests are available to measure implicit bias based on gender, sexual orientation, and other classifications. Derrick Johnson, president of the NAACP, maintains that, for public officials, testing for implicit bias should be mandatory. Derrick Johnson, "Everyone Should Be Tested for Implicit Bias," *New York Times*, May 11, 2018.

10. Nicholas Kristof, "Our Biased Brains," *New York Times*, May 7, 2015 (quoting Harvard University professor and Project Implicit cofounder Mahzarin Banaji). But see also Emily Badger, "We Are All a Little Biased," *New York Times*, October 7, 2016. Implicit bias training programs for police officers may lead participants to

"falsely believe they've rooted out their biases and so don't need to worry about them any more. 'Just wanting to eliminate implicit bias is not sufficient. . . . You can't unlearn implicit biases.'"

11. Consider examples offered by Shawn C. Marsh:

> Wikipedia alone lists over 300 types of cognitive biases and fallacies. One example is the *just-world hypothesis*, which is the tendency for people to want to believe that the world is fundamentally just, causing them to rationalize an otherwise inexplicable injustice as deserved by the victim. Another . . . is *implicit egotism*. An example . . . is that we tend to like our first and last initials better than other letters in the alphabet (a bias documented in at least 14 countries and called the *name letter effect*). . . . In the 2000 presidential campaign, for instance, people whose last names began with *B* and *G* were more likely to contribute to the election funds of *Bush* and *Gore*, respectively. Our names also seem to influence our decision where to live (e.g., statistically disproportionate number of residents named Mildred live in Milwaukee) and what we do for a living (e.g., statistically disproportionate number of lawyers are named Larry).

Shawn C. Marsh, "Psychology and the Courts: Exploring the Sometimes Wacky World of Decision-Making," National Council of Juvenile and Family Court Judges, April 12, 2012, https://www.ncjfcj.org/psychology-and-courts-exploring-sometimes -wacky-world-decision-making.

12. Michelle Alexander, *The New Jim Crow: Mass Incarceration in the Age of Colorblindness* (New York: New Press, 2010), 106 (emphasis added). See also Anthony Amsterdam and Jerome Bruner, *Minding the Law* (Cambridge, MA: Harvard University Press, 2000).

13. Kristof, "Our Biased Brains."

14. See Dahlia Lithwick, "Women: Truly the Fairer Sex," *Newsweek*, April 20, 2009 (citing Christina L. Boyd, Lee Epstein, and Andrew D. Martin, "Untangling the Causal Effects of Sex on Judging," *American Journal of Political Science* 54 [2010]: 389–411). Consider also the recent research on gender imbalance in the frequency of interruptions in US Supreme Court oral arguments: "'Conservatives interrupt liberals at significantly higher rates than liberals interrupt conservatives,'" and "male justices . . . interrupt female justices far more often than the other way around. 'Even though female justices speak less often and use fewer words than male justices, . . . they are nonetheless interrupted during oral argument at a significantly higher rate.'" Tonja Jacobi and Dylan Schweers, "Justice, Interrupted: The Effect of Gender, Ideology and Seniority at Supreme Court Oral Arguments," Northwestern Law and Econ Research Paper No. 17-03, *Virginia Law Review* 103 (2017): 1422, 1383, https://ssrn.com/abstract=2933016. See also Adam Liptak, "Let Me Finish, Please: Conservative Men Dominate the Debate," *New York Times*, April 18, 2017.

Even more recent research also is revealing. In a study of 619 trial court judges, in comparison to 504 laypersons, University of Illinois psychology professor Andrea Miller found that judges discriminated, based on their gender attitudes, as much or

more than laypersons—to the detriment of both men and women—in child custody cases and employment decisions determining family caregiving duties. "'My
first takeaway is that judges are human,'" Miller commented. "But she was surprised
that judges' expertise in family law did not reduce their tendency to be influenced
by their personal ideas about gender. 'The legal system is set up to believe that
judges are superhuman logical thinkers and fair decision-makers,' Miller said. 'And
this research shows that even people who are extremely motivated to be fair and make
correct decisions are not immune to the same mistakes that everyone else experiences.'" Diana Yates, "Study: Judges as Susceptible to Gender Bias as Laypeople—
and Sometimes More So," *Illinois News Bureau*, April 19, 2018, http://news.illinois
.ed/view/6367/640610.

    15. See Lithwick, "Women: Truly the Fairer Sex" (quoting Carol Gilligan, *In a
Different Voice: Psychological Theory and Women's Development* [Cambridge, MA:
Harvard University Press, 1982]).

    16. Posner, *How Judges Think*, 107. He added: "Because the unconscious mind
has greater capacity than the conscious mind, the knowledge accessible to intuition
is likely to be vast. . . . Thus, the more experienced the judge, the more confidence
he is apt to repose in his intuitive reactions" (108). Moreover, "[t]he broader the
range of experiences found in an appellate panel, the less likely it is that relevant
considerations will be overlooked" (116). On the basis of his nineteen years as a justice of the Indiana Supreme Court, Frank Sullivan agreed: "[T]he more relevant real-
life experience that can be brought to bear in judging, the better the judging. . . .
Men and women from different backgrounds and experiences . . . often produce
new perspectives on issues—and entirely new ways of looking at, examining, and
solving problems. *This is why diversity . . . on multi-member appellate courts is so desirable.*" Frank Sullivan Jr., "What I've Learned about Judging," *Valparaiso University
Law Review* 48 (2013): 199–200 (emphasis added). See also Geyh, *Courting Peril*:
"the right of parties to an impartial hearing . . . is not compromised but arguably
furthered by the diversity of perspective that comes from judges with varying backgrounds" (133); "a judge's race and gender contribute to his or her life experience that
can inform judicial discretion in salutary ways, by enabling judges to better understand the circumstances of parties with common experience and convey that understanding to fellow judges" (142). Such salutary benefits are far less likely in trial
courts where a judge's biases are neither mixed with nor buffered by the biases of
others. Still, for trial judges, "when it comes to implicit bias, forewarned is, to no
small extent, forearmed" (142). But the complications keep coming; such confident,
intuitive judging may mislead: "[I]t is even more important to doubt your own leanings, to be skeptical of your instincts. It is frequently very difficult to tell the difference between how you think a case should be decided and how you hope it will
come out. It is very easy to take sides in a case and subtly shade the decision-making
process in favor of the party you favor." Kozinski, "What I Ate for Breakfast," 997.
See also Daniel Kahneman, *Thinking Fast and Slow* (New York: Farrar, Straus and
Giroux, 2013); Thomas Gilovich, Dale Friffin, and Daniel Kahneman, *Heuristics and*

Biases: The Psychology of Intuitive Judgment (New York: Cambridge University Press, 2002); Roger Johnson, "And We Thought We Were Thinking Rationally: Recognizing the Biases That Shape Human Experience," Lawrence University, Björklunden Seminars, 2017; Roger Johnson, "How We Decide," Lawrence University, Björklunden Seminars, 2018 (see http://lawrence.edu/s/bjorklunden/bjorkseminars for more information about the seminars).

17. Geyh, *Courting Peril*, 58. See also Posner, *How Judges Think*, 104 ("even a villain, according to advice given actors who play villains, is not a villain in his own eyes").

18. Posner, *How Judges Think*, 72. Judicial bias, unrecognized or unacknowledged, also may come from educational and professional backgrounds. Professor Glenn Harlan Reynolds, University of Tennessee College of Law, has written that "the judicial branch has been the domain of people who are not merely highly educated, but educated in the particular way that law schools educate." He noted that, over time, the Supreme Court had "become more elite," with every Justice . . . a graduate of an Ivy League law school but, unlike many previous Justices, none coming from the "heartland" and none having experience as a war veteran, an elected official, a presidential cabinet officer, or many other roles related to myriad issues that come before the Supreme Court. Glenn Harlan Reynolds, "'Front Row Kids' Dominate U.S. Courts/Judges May Not Even Realize They're Biased," *USA Today*, October 30, 2017.

Such educational or professional limitations may significantly skew decision-making, particularly when the understanding of legal issues depends on the understanding of research data and policy questions. Professor John Pfaff, Fordham University Law School, explained:

> In 2013, for example, *Shelby County v. Holder* invalidated a critical portion of the Voting Rights Act of 1965, making it arguably one of the most consequential cases in recent years. [Chief] Justice John G. Roberts Jr., arguing that the South had taken great strides that made the protections of the act unnecessary, based his decision in part on a Senate Judiciary Committee analysis that misinterpreted how the Census Bureau reports race and ethnicity data and wrongly suggested that registration gaps between minorities and whites had shrunk significantly, an error that neither he nor his clerks caught.
>
> . . . None of the justices has any serious training in statistics, and the clerks who assist them are almost all recent law school graduates, who rarely have any formal statistical background. Empirical facts are central to what the court does, but its members lack expertise.
>
> . . . When presented with potentially critical empirical evidence in a major gerrymandering case . . . , Chief Justice Roberts joked that "it may be simply my educational background" before describing the material as "sociological gobbledygook." (John Pfaff, "The Justices Need Fact-Checkers," *New York Times*, October 19, 2017)

See also Adam Liptak, "To Test if a Voting Map Is Partisan, Do the Math," *New York Times*, January 16, 2018.

19. Adam Liptak, "Another Factor Said to Sway Judges to Rule for Women's Rights: A Daughter," *New York Times*, June 17, 2014. See also *Nev. Dep't. of Human Res. v. Hibbs*, 538 U.S. 721 (2003). Having a daughter is not the only seemingly simple circumstance that can contribute to the evolution of judicial views. Consider, for example, the impact of cell phones and modern technology on the Supreme Court's search-and-seizure opinions. See Linda Greenhouse, "The Justices Have Cellphones, Too," *New York Times*, June 26, 2014. See also *Riley v. California*, 134 S. Ct. 2473 (2014).

20. David Brooks, "The Choice Explosion," *New York Times*, May 3, 2016.

21. Named for Katharine Cook Briggs and her daughter, Isabel Briggs Myers, who, almost one hundred years ago, developed the self-test based on theories of Carl Jung, "Myers-Briggs" is a forty-question inventory of psychological preferences yielding sixteen personality profiles. Each profile—neither "good" nor "bad" but distinctive—presents communication styles and value preferences that help clarify how individuals most comfortably receive information and communicate. Used in many professional circles, it is neither diagnostic nor judgmental but, most agree, provocative and remarkably accurate. See Peter B. Myers and Katharine D. Myers, *Myers-Briggs Type Indicator Profile* (Palo Alto, CA: Consulting Psychologists Press, 1998). See also, e.g., Joan Bishop and Ileen D. Gerstenberger, "Who Are You? The Myers-Briggs Type Indicator and Your Leadership Style—Making It Work for You," 2011 Annual Conference of the National Association for Court Management and the National Association of State Judicial Educators, Las Vegas, July 11–12, 2011.

For studies in court contexts, see Thomas N. Langhorne, "Court Teams' Decision-Making: The Role Personalities, Logic, Personal Values, and Life Experiences Play," 2011 Annual Conference of the National Association for Court Management and the National Association of State Judicial Educators, Las Vegas, July 11–12, 2011. Langhorne aggregates data of judges who have taken the Myers-Briggs test. No surprise—the judicial personality is not typical. Compared to the general population, judges "tend to be much more introverted, intuitive, thinking [as distinguished from feeling] and judging [as distinguished from perceiving]." Langhorne, "Court Teams' Decision-Making."

22. See Don Richard Riso and Russ Hudson, *The Wisdom of the Enneagram: The Complete Guide to Psychological and Spiritual Growth for the Nine Personality Types* (New York: Bantam Books, 1999).

23. Geyh, *Courting Peril*, 91.

24. Geyh, *Courting Peril*, 4. See also at 91 ("the indeterminate nature of law may give law itself a degree of elasticity that incorporates extralegal influences. . . . the 'rule of law' often allows for a range of proper answers").

25. At the time, this code provision was Wisconsin SCR § 60.01(10). Subsequent revisions and renumberings yield some confusion. For the balance of this discussion, I cite the current words and code numbers. The COMMENT to Wis. SCR § 60.04 specifies, "The proscription against communications concerning a proceeding includes

communications from . . . law teachers, and other persons who are not participants in the proceeding."

26. Wis. SCR § 60.04(1)(g)3.

27. Wis. SCR § 60.04(1)(g)2.

28. See *In re Tesmer*, 219 Wis. 2d 708, 580 N.W.2d 307 (1998).

29. *In re Tesmer*, 219 Wis. 2d 708, 580 N.W.2d 307 (1998), ¶¶ 59–68 (Bablitch, J., *dissenting*).

30. See Benjamin Weiser, "Stumped, Your Honor? Call a Judge," *New York Times*, May 20, 2015.

31. "Compassion fatigue" (also known as "vicarious victimization" or "secondary trauma"), the condition that most often affects judges, particularly those serving in juvenile, criminal, and family courts, has been defined as "the cumulative physical, emotional and psychological effects of being continually exposed to traumatic stories or events when working in a helping capacity." Linda Albert, Deborah Smith, and Gregory Van Rybroek, "Keeping Legal Minds Intact: Mitigating Compassion Fatigue among Judges," Wisconsin Supreme Court 2009 Juvenile Law Seminar, Waukesha, Wisconsin, September 23–25, 2009. See Charles R. Figley, *Compassion Fatigue: Coping with Secondary Traumatic Stress Disorder in Those Who Treat the Traumatized* (New York: Brunner/Mazel, 1995). See also National Judicial College, *Judicial Wellness: A Stress Management Guide for and by Judges* (Salem, MA: Administrative Office of the District Court, 1996); Peter G. Jaffe, Claire V. Crooks, Billie Lee Dunford-Jackson, and Judge Michael Town, "Vicarious Trauma in Judges: The Personal Challenge of Dispensing Justice," *Juvenile and Family Court Journal* 54, no. 4 (2003): 1–9; Jared Chamberlain and Monica K. Miller, "Evidence of Secondary Traumatic Stress, Safety Concerns, and Burnout among a Homogeneous Group of Judges in a Single Jurisdiction," *Journal of the American Academy of Psychiatry and the Law Online* 37, no. 2 (2009): 214–24.

Such secondary trauma touches not only judges but court staff as well. In recent years, several organizations, including the National Center for State Courts and the National Association of State Judicial Educators, have become increasingly active in addressing the needs of clerks, stenographers, bailiffs, and others. See, e.g., Tina M. Mattison, "Vicarious Trauma: The Silent Stressor," National Center for State Courts, ICM Fellows Program, 2012, http://www. ncsc. org/-/media/Files/PDF/Education% 20and% 20Careers/CEDP% 20Papers/2012/Vicarious% 20Trauma. ashx; Tiffany Zelski Hammill, "Capstone Experience: Addressing the Effects of Vicarious Trauma Experienced by Court Employees," National Association of State Judicial Educators "Call-inar," May 11, 2017.

32. Julia Preston, "Immigration Judges Found under Strain," *New York Times*, July 11, 2009 (emphasis added). See also Julia Preston, "Immigration Courts Buckling under Huge Backlog of Cases," *New York Times*, December 2, 2016.

33. Caitlin Dickerson, "Immigration Judges Face Up to Their Prejudices," *New York Times*, October 5, 2016 (emphasis added) (exploring the compounding problems of implicit bias and unmanageable caseloads).

34. Posner, *How Judges Think*, 251.

CHAPTER 14. JUDICIAL CAMPAIGNS:
DECLARATIONS AND CONTRIBUTIONS

1. Wis. SCR § 60.06(3).

2. Judicial campaigning at political party meetings is addressed differently or not at all by codes of judicial ethics. In some states, where judicial elections are partisan, the allowance is clear. In others, including Wisconsin, where "[n]o judge or candidate for judicial office or judge-elect may . . . [b]e a member of any political party" or "[p]articipate in the affairs . . . of a political party," SCR § 60.06(2)(b)(1) & (2), the code carves out an exception: "Nothing in this subsection shall be deemed to prohibit a judge, judge-elect, or candidate for judicial office, whether standing for election or seeking an appointment, from appearing at partisan political gatherings to promote his or her own candidacy." SCR § 60.06(2)(e).

3. Wis. SCR § 60.06(3). Federalism accounts for America's patchwork quilt of ethical code provisions on judicial election/selection, regulation of which comes from the relatively short history of judicial conduct codes. "When the 1960s began, no state had an enforceable code of conduct or a formal disciplinary process. By 1981, all fifty states had disciplinary processes in place, and by 2008, all fifty states had adopted codes of judicial conduct." Charles Gardner Geyh, *Courting Peril: The Political Transformation of the American Judiciary* (New York: Oxford University Press, 2016), 38. Restrictions on campaign comments were "relatively new to judicial elections" and "not universally adopted." See *Republican Party v. White*, 536 U.S. 765, 786 (2002). Some state standards were modeled on the ABA's Canons of Judicial Conduct, adopted in 1924, "but these rules did not achieve widespread adoption until after the Second World War." *Williams-Yulee v. Fla. Bar*, 135 S. Ct. 1656, 1676 (2015) (Scalia, J., *dissenting*). Over time, more and more judicial conduct codes came to curtail campaign rhetoric. Still, such codes, some just now entering adolescence, are continuing to feel growing pains, suffer peer pressures, and try to find their fits. (Interestingly enough, the US Supreme Court remains "the only court in the land that is not subject to a code of conduct." Geyh, *Courting Peril*, 150.)

4. While they understood the value of judicial "silence" on the campaign trail, countless voters were puzzled by the fact of an elective judiciary. Campaigning, I encountered many who asked why they were electing judges at all; they confessed their ignorance of the candidates and issues in judicial elections. Many said that, as a result, they simply did not vote in judicial elections (and, in fact, in April 1996, the statewide voter turnout in the supreme court election in which I ran was 7 percent). Thus, I cannot fully embrace Geyh's contention that "voters tend to regard [judicial] elections as legitimacy enhancing." Geyh, *Courting Peril*, 117.

5. Diane S. Sykes, "Ethics and Rhetoric in Wisconsin Judicial Elections," *Wisconsin Interest* (2000): 34. (When she wrote this, Sykes was serving on the Wisconsin Supreme Court. In 2003, President George W. Bush nominated her to the Seventh Circuit Federal Court of Appeals; she was confirmed in 2004.)

6. *Republican Party v. White*, 536 U.S. 765, 816 (2002) (Ginsburg, J., *dissenting*).

7. *Williams-Yulee v. Fla. Bar*, 135 S. Ct. 1656, 1685 (2015) (Kennedy, J., *dissenting*). And teach not only the voters, but the candidates as well. Writing of the "visceral

experience of politics—like the visceral experiences of art, theater, and love," Teachout describes valuable lessons learned on the campaign trail: "The experience of politics is profoundly invigorating, and while people who have lived a political life will undoubtedly admit there are dingy deals and terrible pressures, they may be more likely to believe in the human capacity for civic attention and love. Those involved in politics will bring a more subtle understanding of the psychological ways in which gifts and money change politics." Zephyr Teachout, *Corruption in America: From Benjamin Franklin's Snuff Box to Citizens United* (Cambridge, MA: Harvard University Press, 2014), 273–74.

    8. *Buckley v. Ill. Judicial Inquiry Bd.*, 997 F.2d 224, 227 (7th Cir. 1993).

    9. See *Stretton v. Disciplinary Bd. Of Supreme Court*, 944 F.2d 137 (3d Cir. 1991); *Buckley v. Ill. Judicial Inquiry Bd.*, 997 F.2d 224 (7th Cir. 1993). In *Buckley*, the US Court of Appeals was addressing consolidated cases, one of which presented a challenge to disciplinary action by the Illinois Judicial Inquiry Board against a judge who, in the course of his campaign for state supreme court, had circulated literature stating that he had "never written an opinion reversing a rape conviction." *Buckley v. Ill. Judicial Inquiry Bd.*, 997 F.2d 224, 226 (7th Cir. 1993). This, the disciplinary board maintained, violated an Illinois ethical rule stating that "a candidate, including an incumbent judge, for a judicial office . . . should not make pledges or promises of conduct in office other than the faithful and impartial performance of the duties of the office; announce his views on disputed legal or political issues; . . . provided, however, that he may announce his views on measures to improve the law, the legal system, or the administration of justice, if, in doing so, he does not cast doubt on his capacity to decide impartially any issue that may come before him" (225).

    10. At issue was the challenge of an attorney who, during his two campaigns for the Minnesota Supreme Court, had distributed literature criticizing the state supreme court's decisions on abortion, crime, and welfare, and sought an injunction to stop the Minnesota Lawyers Professional Responsibility Board from disciplining him for violating an ethical standard prohibiting a judicial candidate from "announc[ing] his or her views on disputed legal or political issues." *Republican Party v. White*, 536 U.S. 765, 768 (2002). The Minnesota Republican Party joined in the case, arguing that, because the code precluded candidates from announcing their positions, voters were unable to learn information essential to informed voting (770).

    11. The majority's decision spawned extensive commentary and many warnings, including one cautioning that the field of judicial candidates would narrow from "good lawyer[s] of established repute" to ones "politically acceptable to a broader range of public sentiment." Geoffrey C. Hazard Jr., "The Role of the Bar in Politicized Judicial Elections," *Willamette Law Review* 39, no. 4 (2003): 1351.

    12. Thus I question the import of statistical studies minimizing the impact of *Republican Party v. White*, 536 U.S. 765 (2002). See Geyh, *Courting Peril*, 135 n.20, 155 n.87. While the "self-censorship" of judges and judicial candidates has prevailed "[f]or generations, if not centuries," and while some judges still may "continue to decline overtures to announce their views in judicial campaigns," the more powerful points are that (1) judicial candidates now may announce their positions; (2) many

do so; and (3) almost all others are chilled by "the political transformation" of recent years that "renders the persistence of such [silence] perilous" (155, 134).

13. Sykes, "Ethics and Rhetoric," 34. Sykes continued: "Any litmus test approach to judicial selection misunderstands the nature and role of the judiciary, and any capitulation to this sort of political pressure weakens the institution's credibility and integrity." Two years before the Supreme Court decided *Republican Party v. White*, 536 U.S. 765 (2002) (and four years before she was confirmed to the federal bench), Judge Sykes reflected on her state supreme court campaign and the media's role in compounding the conflicts inherent in judicial campaigning:

> [W]hat we have seen is an increased willingness to campaign on a specific legal/policy agenda. . . . This phenomenon is fed by the media and special interest players in the political arena who are so influential to the success or failure of any candidacy. There is now an expectation among many reporters, editorial writers, and political action committees that Supreme Court candidates will weigh in on important legislative initiatives and declare how they would have voted on high-profile court cases. Refusing to do so . . . carries a potential political price: bad press and loss of endorsements, both editorial and organizational. And so the candidates are drawn in. What all this threatens to do is turn judicial elections into legislative ones, which in turn threatens to populate the judiciary with men and women of legislative rather than judicial mindset. . . . The media, it seems, wants to have it both ways: it decries the politicization of the judiciary and then demands that judges behave like politicians. ("Ethics and Rhetoric," 36)

14. See Jed Handelsman Shugerman, *The People's Courts: Pursuing Judicial Independence in America* (Cambridge, MA: Harvard University Press, 2012).

15. See Michael Bennett and Cruz Reynoso, "California Rural Legal Assistance (CRLA): Survival of Poverty Law Practice," *Chicana/o Latina/o Law Review* 1 (1972): 1–79. See also Jose R. Padilla, "California Rural Legal Assistance: The Struggles and Continued Survival of a Poverty Law Practice," *Chicano Latino Law Review* 30 (2011): 163–76. The coincidence of California's prominence in such litigation and Ronald Reagan's political career proved consequential. "California agribusinesses expended considerable energy and money to elect Ronald Reagan Governor in November 1966," and Reagan, in turn, both as governor and president, fostered efforts to cut funding for legal services. Bennett and Reynoso, "California Rural Legal Assistance," 10.

16. In both federal and state systems, in both appointive and elective processes, "conservatives . . . worked hard and effectively to ensure representation of their views on the courts." Adam Liptak, "Why Judges Tilt to the Right," *New York Times*, January 31, 2015. Citing a study by the political scientists Adam Bonica of Stanford and Maya Sen of the Kennedy School of Government at Harvard, Liptak wrote, "They have cultivated candidates for the bench, notably through the Federalist Society, the conservative legal group active on law school campuses." See also Adam Bonica and Maya Sen, "The Politics of Selecting the Bench from the Bar: The Legal

Profession and Partisan Incentives to Politicize the Judiciary," *IDEAS Working Paper Series from RePEc*, 2015, http://j.mp/11g7YJZ.

17. Thomas R. Phillips, "Comment," *Law and Contemporary Problems* 61 (1998): 127–249 (commenting on Paul D. Carrington, "Judicial Independence and Democratic Accountability in Highest State Courts"). Phillips served as the chief justice of the Texas Supreme Court from 1988 to 2004.

18. Shugerman, *The People's Courts*, 12. Also, one might look again at chapter 10's consideration of legislative enactments and judicial decisions limiting punitive damages.

19. Shugerman, *The People's Courts*, 241–46.

20. See Shugerman, *The People's Courts*, 254–55. Also in 1996, Justice David Lanphier became Nebraska's first supreme court justice to lose a retention election. "Opposition to Lanphier coalesced around two supreme court decisions in which Lanphier was involved. One was a unanimous decision authored by Lanphier striking down a term limits amendment that had been approved by the voters. The other was a series of court rulings that reinserted malice as an element of second-degree murder, resulting in the overturning of a number of murder convictions." Nebraskans had approved a term limits amendment, with 70 percent voting in favor. They denied Justice Lanphier's retention by about the same margin. See "Judicial Selection in the States: Nebraska," National Center for State Courts, http://www.judicialselection.com/judicial_selection/index.cfm?state=NE.

21. Shugerman, *The People's Courts*, 241. Business interests began "capitalizing on socially conservative issues and pouring money into key races. Trial lawyers and other interests that had already been invested in judicial elections responded by spending more and doubling down. . . . The increasing power of political advertising made it easier for local and national groups to challenge incumbents, and the expense of this advertising required incumbents and challengers to raise more money."

22. A. G. Sulzberger, "Ouster of Iowa Judges Sends Signal to Bench," *New York Times*, November 3, 2010. The signals continue, sounding in more and more states. See Erik Eckholm, "Outraged by Court in Kansas, G.O.P. Sets Out to Reshape It," *New York Times*, April 2, 2016 ("Look at [Arkansas, Kansas, Oklahoma, Pennsylvania, Washington, and Wisconsin] where political attacks on judicial decisions are common and well-financed attack ads are starting to jar the once-sleepy elections for State Supreme Court seats"); Michael Wines, "Judges Say, Throw Map Out; Lawmakers Say, Judges First," *New York Times*, February 14, 2018 ("Rather than simply fighting judicial rulings [in gerrymandering cases]," and with greater use of impeachment to intimidate judges, "elected officials in some states across the country—largely Republicans, but Democrats as well—are increasingly seeking to punish or rein in judges who hand down unfavorable decisions"). In challenges to judicial rulings on gerrymandering, impeachment may be emerging as the most recent blatant political attack on judicial independence. See Adam Liptak, "Justices Won't Block Pennsylvania Redistricting," *New York Times*, March 20, 2018; see also National Center for State Courts, "Gavel to Gavel: Pennsylvania: After U.S. Supreme Court Declines to Overturn PA Supreme Court's Redistricting Decisions, 12 PA House

Members Move Forward with Impeachment of PA Supreme Court Justices," *NCSC Connected Community*, March 27, 2018; *League of Women Voters, et al. v. Commonwealth of Pennsylvania*, et al., no. 159 MM 2017, Supreme Court of Pennsylvania, February 19, 2018.

23. Judicial retention elections originated in Missouri in 1940. Why? The national momentum for merit selection of judges had stalled, making minimal progress for many years. But in the 1930s, Missouri's judicial scandals, involving Kansas City's "Boss" Tom Pendergast, recharged the movement. (Among the Missouri judges boosted by the Pendergast machine was Harry Truman, first elected in 1922 and still in judicial office until his elevation to higher positions starting in 1934.) See Shugerman, *The People's Courts*, 198–203.

The "Missouri Plan," the most lasting legislative effort to combine the best of both worlds, appointive and elective, was designed by the American Judicature Society and the American Bar Association. With slight variations from state to state, it relies heavily on merit-selection commissions. Ironically, however, California is the outlier. See Shugerman, *The People's Courts*, 197–207. Shugerman explained:

> Rose Bird [the state secretary of agriculture who, despite having no judicial experience, was appointed as chief justice by Governor Jerry Brown in 1977,] was famously defeated in a retention election. But that retention election proves the rule. In every other merit plan state, the professional commission nominates a list of candidates, and the governor is limited to that list. However, in California, the governor nominates one specific candidate, and the professional commission simply approves or disapproves that candidate. . . . Fifty-two years later, that . . . made a big difference in the political calculus of Rose Bird's opponents. (244, 254)

California and Tennessee were among the few states whose retention elections rejected incumbents. "*All* of the million-dollar [judicial] races between 2000 and 2009 were the [contested, nonretention] partisan or nonpartisan kind. None of the retention elections came close to that level of spending." Shugerman, *The People's Courts*, 253. But soon enough, judicial retention elections, like their contested cousins, devolved from polite affairs to heated, high-cost conflicts. According to the NYU Law School Brennan Center for Justice, in 2010, the year Iowa voters rejected the three supreme court justices, more was spent on judicial retention elections nationwide than in the previous decade. See Sulzberger, "Ouster of Iowa Judges."

24. Shugerman, *The People's Courts*, 243.

25. See Liptak, "Why Judges Tilt to the Right."

26. Those were the days—$20,000 was enough to produce and air a TV ad; print campaign calendars, buttons, and bumper stickers; and leave a small balance (donated after the election to the Milwaukee Task Force on Battered Women and the Milwaukee Boys and Girls Club). My opponent spent a little more, almost all from his own resources.

27. Some codes actually delineate the ethically permissible "thank you" manners. See, e.g., *Williams-Yulee v. Fla. Bar*, 135 S. Ct. 1656, 1663 (2015) ("[Florida's Canon 7]

allow[s] judicial candidate[s] to . . . 'learn the identity of campaign contributors, and send thank you notes to donors'") (citing Florida Judicial Ethics Advisory Committee interpretation, "An Aid to Understanding Canon 7," 51–58 (2014)). See also, e.g., "COMMENT" to Wis. SCR § 60.06(4) ("Acknowledgement by a judge or candidate for judicial office of a contribution in a courtesy thank you letter is not prohibited"). Other standards support "blind" systems that shield judges from knowledge of their donors. See Commentary to Canon 7B(2), Model Code of Judicial Conduct ("Unless a candidate is required by law to file a list of his campaign contributors, their names should not be revealed to the candidate"). Now, however, almost all states require such filings; thus the judges know the names of their contributors and the amounts contributed.

28. On this point as well, the codes are far from unanimous, some even reaching opposite conclusions. Florida, for example, specifies that judicial candidates, "including an incumbent judge . . . shall not . . . solicit attorneys for publicly stated support," though their campaign committees may do so. See Canon 7C(1), Florida Code of Judicial Conduct (1973). But Wisconsin says: "A judge or candidate for judicial office may solicit or accept endorsements supporting his or her election or appointment personally or through his or her committee . . . [and is] not prohibited from soliciting and accepting endorsements from lawyers and others." Wis. SCR § 60.06(5). The COMMENT to that subsection provides four important points, not necessarily found in codes of other states: (1) "In light of the restrictions on campaign rhetoric . . . , the receiving of endorsements is an important method of informing the electorate of broad-based and presumably informed support for a particular candidacy"; (2) "[S]olicitation and acceptance of endorsements from current litigants are prohibited"; (3) Judicial candidates "may solicit and accept endorsements from entities . . . such as newspapers and trade organizations"; and, anticipating the impossibility of full and accurate implementation and the impracticality of continuous monitoring, (4) "Neither culling nor cross-checking of names on mailing lists or dockets is required."

29. The code's exact words leave no doubt: "A judge [or] candidate for judicial office . . . should *avoid direct involvement with the committee's fundraising efforts*." Wis. Stat. SCR § 60.06(4) (emphasis added). From conversations with colleagues, I know "involvement" was common. How direct? Behind the scenes of my campaigns, I strategized, designed literature, and drafted the letters soliciting contributions. That, I believe, balanced on the ledge of "direct involvement." "Dialing for dollars" would have fallen off the cliff. Still, sometimes, locating the edge of the ledge may be difficult. Justice Scalia asked: "Does the First Amendment permit restricting a candidate's appearing at an event where somebody *else* asks for campaign funds on his behalf? Does it permit prohibiting the candidate's *family* from making personal solicitations? Does it allow prohibiting the candidate from participating in the creation of a Web site that solicits funds, even if the candidate's name does not appear next to the request?" *Williams-Yulee v. Fla. Bar*, 135 S. Ct. 1656, 1680 (2015) (Scalia, J., *dissenting*).

30. The collective yawn was deafening. Thus, regretfully, I found no media support for the premise presented by Wisconsin Supreme Court Chief Justice Shirley S. Abrahamson: "Good judging *is* good politics. . . . But judges have to talk about judicial independence and make it a campaign issue." Shirley S. Abrahamson, "Making Judicial Independence a Campaign Issue," *Wisconsin Lawyer* 78, no. 2 (2005): 16.

31. Wis. SCR § 60.03; the COMMENT to SCR 60.03 elaborates, "The test for appearance of impropriety is whether the conduct would create in reasonable minds a perception that the judge's ability to carry out judicial responsibilities with integrity, impartiality and competence is impaired." Similar provisions appear in almost all judicial conduct codes. See also *Caperton v. A. T. Massey Coal Co.*, 556 U.S. 868 (2009), where, in a case involving judicial campaign contributions, the Supreme Court chronicled state judicial ethics codes and commented on their "reforms . . . to eliminate even the appearance of partiality" (888).

32. *Republican Party v. White*, 536 U.S. 765, 790 (2002) (O'Connor, J., *concurring*). Appearances also were important in *Williams-Yulee*, where the Supreme Court declared: "A State may decide that the threat to public confidence created by personal solicitation exists apart from the amount of money that a judge or judicial candidate seeks. Even if Florida decreased its contribution limit, the appearance that judges who personally solicit funds might improperly favor their campaign donors would remain." *Williams-Yulee v. Fla. Bar*, 135 S. Ct. 1656, 1672 (2015). See also *Williams-Yulee v. Fla. Bar*, 135 S. Ct. 1656, 1675 (2015) (Ginsburg, J., *concurring*) ("How does the electorate perceive outsized spending on judicial elections? Multiple surveys . . . indicate that voters overwhelmingly believe direct contributions to judges' campaigns have at least 'some influence' on judicial decision making").

33. Chief Justice Thomas R. Phillips of the Texas Supreme Court agreed, and more:

Most active trial lawyers want judges to move cases efficiently with few reversible errors, not to be a "friend" on the bench. Even in appellate court races, many lawyers and lay people contribute primarily out of a perceived professional or civic obligation to support able public servants, not out of a hope to buy a philosophical predilection.

. . . "Could Texas Supreme Court justices be schizophrenic enough to rake in $1 million in campaign contributions with one hand while impartially swinging the gavel with the other?"

The answer, of course, is Yes. If judges are so weak as to be influenced by a contribution that goes only to their campaign coffers to pay election expenses, how could they possibly resist the pressures common to all judges of personal friendships and professional associations among those who appear before them? They can and do resist because judges make their rulings within the numerous formal and informal constraints that surround the process of the rule of law.

Phillips, "Comment," 136–37. See also *Republican Party v. White*, 536 U.S. 765, 796 (2002) (Kennedy, J., *concurring*) ("By condemning judicial elections across the board, we implicitly condemn countless elected state judges and without warrant.

Many of them, despite the difficulties imposed by the election system, have discovered in the law the enlightenment, instruction, and inspiration that make them independent-minded and faithful jurists of real integrity"). Nevertheless, Phillips conceded the public "appearance" of unfairness, noting that "public opinion polls across the nation have shown nearly universal public skepticism about whether judges are in fact impartial in cases involving contributors." Phillips, "Comment," 137.

Chief Justice Phillips came to be a much-admired judicial educator and a teacher I valued. Still, it would be unfair to ignore an interesting footnote to his distinguished career. Shugerman wrote:

> In 1987, the Texas Supreme Court had nine Democrats and no Republicans, with a solid pro-plaintiff majority. As luck would have it, six seats on the Texas Supreme Court would be on the ballot. Clements, the Republican governor, had recently appointed Tom Phillips to be the youngest chief justice (thirty-nine years old) in Texas history. As an interim appointment, Phillips was on the ballot that November, and he hired another young gun to run his race: the thirty-eight-year-old Karl Rove.
>
> Rove moved to Texas to work for a Republican state legislator, and at that time, Democrats held almost every statewide office and a nine-to-one advantage in the legislature. In 1978, Rove worked on George W. Bush's unsuccessful congressional campaign and on Clements's successful campaign for governor. Then Rove took the lead for Phillips in coordinating the Republican challengers in a unified "Clean Slate '88" campaign. Their well-financed campaign focused on tort reform and populist themes. In a memo to Phillips, Rove wrote, "No Republican has won by running as an establishment candidate. Our party's candidates have won by appearing as champions of the little man and not the big boys." Rove targeted trial lawyers for jeopardizing jobs for average Texans, and he promised corporate donors that a Republican court would limit compensation for injured employees and consumers and would put caps on damage awards.
>
> Of the six seats on the ballot, "Clean Slate" Republicans won three, and conservative pro-defendant Democrats won two more seats by echoing Rove's attacks on trial lawyers and tort reform themes. The 1988 campaign was the end of the pro-plaintiff Texas Supreme Court, and it was the beginning of the Republican takeover of the court. Ten years later, the court had nine Republicans and no Democrats. . . . Rove pulled off a similar flip in Alabama in the 1990s. (Shugerman, *The People's Courts*, 249–50)

34. Nina Totenberg, "Morning Edition," National Public Radio, April 30, 2015.
35. *Williams-Yulee v. Fla. Bar*, 135 S. Ct. 1656, 1662 (2015).
36. Florida Code of Judicial Conduct, Canon 7C(1)(g) (1973); see n.27, above, and *Williams-Yulee v. Fla. Bar*, 135 S. Ct. 1656, 1663 (2015). Such standards are relatively recent additions to judicial conduct codes. "The [American Bar Association] first proposed a canon advising against [personal solicitation of campaign contributions] in 1972, and a canon prohibiting it only in 1990. Even now, 9 of the 39 States that

elect judges allow judicial candidates to ask for campaign contributions." *Williams-Yulee v. Fla. Bar*, 135 S. Ct. 1656, 1676 (2015) (Scalia, J., *dissenting*).

Justice Scalia went on to assert, "Many States allow judicial candidates to ask for contributions even today, but nobody suggests that public confidence in judges fares worse in these jurisdictions than elsewhere." *Williams-Yulee v. Fla. Bar*, 135 S. Ct. 1656, 1676 (2015) (Scalia, J., *dissenting*). Not so; that is exactly what many do indeed suggest. *Personal* solicitation is important to judicial appearances. As Chief Justice Roberts emphasized: "[W]e are mindful that most States with elected judges have determined that drawing a line between personal solicitation by candidates and solicitation by committees is necessary to preserve public confidence in the integrity of the judiciary. These considered judgments deserve our respect, especially because they reflect sensitive choices by States in an area central to their governance—how to select those who 'sit as their judges'" (1671).

37. See *Williams-Yulee v. Fla. Bar*, 135 S. Ct. 1656, 1663 (2015).

38. *Williams-Yulee v. Fla. Bar*, 135 S. Ct. 1656, 1672 (2015).

39. *Williams-Yulee v. Fla. Bar*, 135 S. Ct. 1656, 1662 (2015).

40. *Williams-Yulee v. Fla. Bar*, 135 S. Ct. 1656, 1673 (2015) (Ginsburg, J., *concurring*); see also *Republican Party v. White*, 536 U.S. 765, 798 (2002) (Stevens, J., *dissenting*) ("There is a critical difference between the work of the judge and the work of other public officials. In a democracy, issues of policy are properly decided by majority vote; it is the business of legislators and executives to be popular. But in litigation, issues of law or fact should not be determined by popular vote; it is the business of judges to be indifferent to unpopularity").

41. See, e.g., Rabbi Ari Kahn, "Justice, Justice," Aish.com, http://www.aish.com/tp/i/moha/48930397.html.

42. *Caperton v. A. T. Massey Coal Co.*, 556 U.S. 868 (2009).

43. Shugerman, *The People's Courts*, 1–2 (first bracketed portion added; second bracketed portion in original). "Selecting" a judge to hear one's own appeal is within the historic tradition of America's judicial corruption. For example, more than a century ago, Colonel Edward Butler, "the longtime boss of St. Louis," and city officials had their convictions for bribes and kickbacks overturned. The journalist Lincoln Steffens "discovered that over the years Butler had directed the nominations . . . of justices on the very bench that heard the graft cases on appeal." Doris Kearns Goodwin, *The Bully Pulpit: Theodore Roosevelt, William Howard Taft, and the Golden Age of Journalism* (New York: Simon and Schuster, 2013), 373.

44. The Supreme Court explained:

Justice Benjamin was careful to address the recusal motions and explain his reasons why, on his view of the controlling standard, disqualification was not in order. In four separate opinions issued during the course of the appeal, he explained why no actual bias had been established. He found no basis for recusal because Caperton failed to provide "objective evidence" or "objective information," but merely "subjective belief" of bias. Nor could anyone "point to any actual conduct or activity on [his] part which could be termed 'improper.'" In other words, based on the facts presented by Caperton, Justice Benjamin conducted a probing search into his actual motives and inclinations; and he found none to be improper. We do not question his subjective findings of impartiality and propriety. Nor do we determine whether there was actual bias. (*Caperton v. A. T. Massey Coal Co.*, 556 U.S. 868, 882 (2009))

45. See *Caperton v. A. T. Massey Coal Co.*, 556 U.S. 868, 887 (2009).
46. See *Caperton v. A. T. Massey Coal Co.*, 556 U.S. 868, 884 (2009).
47. *Caperton v. A. T. Massey Coal Co.*, 556 U.S. 868, 870 (2009).
48. See *Caperton v. A. T. Massey Coal Co.*, 556 U.S. 868, 872–76 (2009).
49. *Caperton v. A. T. Massey Coal Co.*, 556 U.S. 868, 873 (2009).
50. *Caperton v. A. T. Massey Coal Co.*, 556 U.S. 868, 884 (2009) (emphasis added).
51. *Caperton v. A. T. Massey Coal Co.*, 556 U.S. 868, 886 (2009).
52. *Caperton v. A. T. Massey Coal Co.*, 556 U.S. 868, 893 (2009) (Roberts, C.J., *dissenting*).
53. *Caperton v. A. T. Massey Coal Co.*, 556 U.S. 868, 887 (2009). The dissent acknowledged, "To its credit, the [majority] seems to recognize that the inherently boundless nature of its new rule poses a problem" (899) (Roberts, C.J., *dissenting*). The unclear lines and "boundless nature" of the *Caperton* "new rule," in combination with the rapidly increasing influence of financial contributions to judicial campaigns, may be expected to generate efforts to convince state legislatures to enact statutes, or persuade state supreme courts to enact rules—some setting specific limits on the amounts of contributions to judicial campaigns; others requiring recusal when contributions from a party that becomes a litigant has a case before a judge who was the recipient of the contribution. For example, in 2017, fifty retired Wisconsin jurists proposed that the Wisconsin Supreme Court "draw a 'bright line' on conflicts of interest" by establishing such a recusal rule. See Patrick Marley and Bill Glauber, "Former Wisconsin Judges Seek Rules on Campaign Donations," *Milwaukee Journal Sentinel,* January 11, 2017; see also "Recusal Proposal Makes Sense," *Milwaukee Journal Sentinel,* January 15, 2017.

The *Caperton* saga continues. A few years ago, Blankenship's legal trail turned into federal criminal court and back onto the front pages.

Donald L. Blankenship, whose leadership of the Massey Energy Company catapulted him from a working-class West Virginia childhood into a life as one of the wealthiest and most influential men in Appalachia, was sentenced . . . to a year in prison for conspiring to violate federal mine safety standards.

The prison term, the maximum allowed by law, came in Federal District Court here six years and one day after an explosion ripped through Massey's Upper Big Branch mine, killing 29 men. Although Mr. Blankenship was not accused of direct responsibility for the accident, the deadliest in American coal mining in about 40 years, the disaster prompted the inquiry that ultimately led to his conviction. Federal officials have said that last autumn's guilty verdict was the first time such a high-ranking executive had been convicted of a workplace safety violation.

Alan Blinder, "Mine Chief Is Sentenced in Conspiracy over Safety," *New York Times*, April 7, 2016. See also Rena Steinzor, "Judgment Day for Reckless Executives," *New York Times*, April 8, 2016 ("The sentence is noteworthy . . . not because of the law, but in spite of it. The Mine Safety and Health Act . . . treats the worst criminal violations as mere misdemeanors. The leniency of the available sentence is a failure of the law"). Rena Steinzor is a professor at the University of Maryland School of Law and the author of *Why Not Jail? Industrial Catastrophes, Corporate Malfeasance, and Government Inaction* (New York: Cambridge University Press, 2015).

On January 19, 2017, the US Fourth Circuit Court of Appeals affirmed Blankenship's conviction. See Michael Virtanen, "Appeals Court Affirms Conviction of Coal CEO in Deadly Blast," *AP Financial* (New York), January 19, 2017. But the Blankenship story continued. After serving his sentence, Blankenship became a candidate for the US Senate. See Trip Gabriel, "Mine Blast Sent Him to Prison; Miners May Send Him to Senate," *New York Times*, February 26, 2018. He was "soundly defeated." See Trip Gabriel, "Don Blankenship Loses West Virginia Republican Primary for Senate," *New York Times*, May 8, 2018.

54. See Frank Sullivan Jr., "What I've Learned about Judging," *Valparaiso University Law Review* 48 (2013): 195–216.

55. Sullivan, "What I've Learned about Judging," 213–14.

56. *Citizens United v. FEC*, 558 U.S. 310 (2010). For an exceptionally valuable analysis of *Citizens United* and a thoughtful appraisal of its pivotal position in the evolution of "corruption" in American law, see Teachout, *Corruption in America*, 227–45.

57. *Citizens United v. FEC*, 558 U.S. 310, 319–200 (2010).

58. *Citizens United v. FEC*, 558 U.S. 310, 337 (2010).

59. Teachout, *Corruption in America*, 230.

60. See *Citizens United v. FEC*, 558 U.S. 310, 371 (2010).

61. *Citizens United v. FEC*, 558 U.S. 310, 312 (2010).

62. See *Williams-Yulee v. Fla. Bar*, 135 S. Ct. 1656, 1674 (2015) (emphasis added) (Ginsburg, J., *concurring*).

63. *Citizens United v. FEC*, 558 U.S. 310, 360 (2010).

64. *Citizens United v. FEC*, 558 U.S. 310, 460 (2010) (emphasis added) (Stevens, J., *concurring and dissenting*).

65. Shugerman, *The People's Courts*, 263 (emphasis added).

66. And any such limits may no longer be constitutional if yet another recent, five-four Supreme Court decision comes to be applicable to judicial campaigns. See *McCutcheon v. FEC*, 134 S. Ct. 1434 (2014).

67. Notwithstanding his concerted efforts to calm the "crisis rhetoric" of Justice O'Connor and others, Geyh, and his thought-provoking arguments for a shift to a new "Legal Culture Paradigm" that seems to normalize what, in my view, is abnormal and new, acknowledges that "a series of developments more than half a century in the making has changed the landscape of judicial politics in new and different ways and compounded the political pressures under which courts operate." Geyh, *Courting Peril*, 1, 6.

68. Geyh noted that, in *Caperton*, the Supreme Court "all but invited the states to . . . formulate[] rules more rigorous than due process requires that disqualify judges from hearing cases in which they have received campaign support from lawyers or litigants . . . in amounts sufficient to call their impartiality into question." Geyh, *Courting Peril*, 151. Nevertheless, "in the aftermath of *Caperton*, American Bar Association resolutions to address disqualifications when campaign supporters appear before the judge have been proposed, diluted, and withdrawn." Geyh, *Courting Peril*, 123.

Chapter 15. Begging the Question: Elective or Appointive?

1. Alexis de Tocqueville, *Democracy in America*, ed. J. P. Mayer, trans. George Lawrence (New York: Harper and Row, 1966).

2. Zephyr Teachout, *Corruption in America: From Benjamin Franklin's Snuff Box to Citizens United* (Cambridge, MA; London, 2014), 273–74.

3. See "Quality Judges Initiative" and "Securing Judicial Independence: The O'Connor Judicial Selection Plan," University of Denver Institute for the Advancement of the American Legal System, www.IAALS.du.edu. See also John Schwartz, "Effort Begun to Abolish the Election of Judges," *New York Times*, December 24, 2009 ("Justice O'Connor said that no other nation elected its judges. 'Nobody,' she said emphatically").

4. *Republican Party v. White*, 536 U.S. 765, 788–89 (2002) (O'Connor, J., concurring).

5. *Republican Party v. White*, 536 U.S. 765, 789 (2002) (O'Connor, J., concurring).

6. *Republican Party v. White*, 536 U.S. 765, 789 (2002) (O'Connor, J., concurring). See Stephen B. Bright and Patrick J. Keenan, "Judges and the Politics of Death: Deciding between the Bill of Rights and the Next Election in Capital Cases," *Boston University Law Review* 75 (1995): 793–94.

7. Richard A. Posner, *How Judges Think* (Cambridge, MA: Harvard University Press, 2008), 135, n.11.

8. Adam Liptak, "Judges Who Are Elected Like Politicians Tend to Act Like Them," *New York Times*, October 4, 2016.

9. *Republican Party v. White*, 536 U.S. 765, 789 (2002) (O'Connor, J., concurring) (quoting former California Supreme Court justice Otto Kaus); see Julian N. Eule, "Crocodiles in the Bathtub: State Courts, Voter Initiatives and the Threat of Electoral Reprisal," *University of Colorado Law Review* 65, no. 4 (1994): 733–40. See also Gerald F. Uelmen, "Judges Hear the Crocodiles Snapping; Nationwide, the Trend Is to Stifle Correct but Politically Unpopular Rulings," *Los Angeles Times*, February 19, 1997.

10. Jed Handelsman Shugerman, *The People's Courts: Pursuing Judicial Independence in America* (Cambridge, MA: Harvard University Press, 2012), 5.

11. See U.S. Const. art. III, § 1.

12. Shugerman, *The People's Courts*, 7–8. Shugerman explained:

The idea of judicial independence is so capacious and flexible that it has been manipulated to serve various political and economic interests over time. While reformers throughout American history have talked about separating law and politics, they often were seeking specific legal and political outcomes in particular kinds of cases, sometimes using "rule of law" rhetoric to thwart popular movements. These elites may have sincerely believed in judicial independence and the rule of law, they may have been cynically using this rhetoric only to persuade an audience, or somewhere in between, or they may have been trying to convince themselves of the moral correctness of their own positions. It is difficult to know. . . . Nevertheless, advocates of judicial elections . . . repeatedly emphasized judicial independence.

Shugerman, *The People's Courts*. See also Carl A. Pierce, Judy M. Cornett, Alex B. Long, Paula Schaefer, and Cassandra Burke Robertson, *Professional Responsibility in the Life of the Lawyer*, 2nd ed., American Casebook Series (St. Paul, MN: West Academic Publishing, 2015):

> Beginning . . . in 1832 . . . a strong trend toward popular election quickly developed. Historians have debated the causes of this trend, with many focusing on the rise of Jacksonian democracy and the attendant fear that the selection of judges was the product of backroom swaps among political elites. Regardless of the causes popular election soon became common. Between 1846 and 1860, nineteen of the twenty-one constitutional conventions held among the states approved constitutions that allowed citizens to elect their judges. Every state that entered the Union between 1846 and 1912 provided for judicial elections.
>
> Gradually, more states began to experiment with a third form of judicial selection: merit selection. Merit selection combines elements of appointive and elective systems while (proponents argue) reducing some of the harmful effects of both. . . . Thus, in theory, judges and judicial candidates are spared some of the problems associated with running in a contested election while still being subject to the will of the voters. (618–19)

Given the appointive-elective pendulum swings of America's judicial history, it is all the more noteworthy that, as Chief Justice Thomas R. Phillips of Texas pointed out, "no state has ever abandoned retention elections once they have been instituted." Thomas R. Phillips, "Comment," *Law and Contemporary Problems* 61 (1998): 129.

13. Shugerman, *The People's Courts*, 9. See also Pierce et al., *Professional Responsibility*, 619 (proponents of judicial appointment with life (or at least long) tenure argue that merit appointment is "essential to preserving a judge's decisional independence" while "[p]roponents of popular election counter that voter accountability is actually desirable in light of the fact that judicial decisions often have dramatic policy ramifications").

14. Shugerman, *The People's Courts*, 11–12.

15. The National Center for State Courts has tracked the continuing developments in selection methods and the recently intensifying state legislative activity:

INTEREST IN CHANGING OR ALTERING THE SELECTION OF JUDGES IN
THE STATES HAS WAXED AND WANED FROM YEAR TO YEAR FOR DECADES.
What makes the last five years remarkable, however, is the extent to which
mere interest and curiosity in this area has moved into legislative activity
and enactments across such a large number of states. Also notable: There is
no particular direction or wave of change. Different state legislatures are
both adopting and repealing the exact same selection methods or financing
systems—in some instances within days of each other.

"Trends in Judicial Selection Methods/ *States seeing lots of legislative activity, but proposals to change selection methods vary widely*," NSSC Digest, BRIEFS, The National
Center for State Courts 100, no. 1 (2017). Indeed, in identifying legislative activity
in this area between 2012 and 2017, the National Center distinguishes no fewer than
eleven categories: (1) change to nonpartisan races, (2) change to partisan races, (3)
change of composition of judicial nominating commissions, (4) increase in number
of names commissions submit for legislature's or governor's approval, (5) designation
of legislatures to confirm commission members or judicial nominees, (6) increase in
percentage of popular vote required for retention, (7) elimination of merit-selection
commissions, (8) adoption of merit-selection commissions, (9) repeal of public
financing, (10) adoption of public financing, and (11) judicial recusal based on financial contributions. See also Trip Gabriel, "They Couldn't Beat the Courts, So They
Voted to Change Them," *New York Times*, October 19, 2017.

16. Concluding that merit selection best addresses "both the problems of money
and job security," Shugerman further explained:

> It is inevitable that big spending and partisanship will invade the merit system
> from time to time, but it would be a mistake to overlook the contrast between
> merit systems and competitive election systems. The advocates of merit re-
> forms campaigned in favor of more job security and less political competition,
> and their reforms generally delivered as advertised. Only 1 percent or 2 percent
> of judges running in retention elections have been defeated, far lower than the
> other election modes. This pattern is not accidental. It reflects the stated
> intentions of the merit reformers in the 1930s and in the 1950s–1970s. Reten-
> tion elections create a safety valve for popular participation and a mechanism
> for preserving judicial accountability, but without threatening judges as acutely
> as competitive elections. (Shugerman, *The People's Courts*, 257–58)

Even before the most recent Supreme Court decisions, "merit selection of judges
[was] a preferable manner in which to select the judiciary." ABA Model Code of
Judicial Conduct Canon 5(C)(2), Comment (2000). "The American Bar Association
strongly endorses the merit selection of judges, as opposed to their election. . . . Five
times between August 1972 and August 1984 the House of Delegates has approved
recommendations stating the preference for merit selection and encouraging bar
associations . . . to work for the adoption of merit selection and retention." "An
Independent Judiciary: Report of the ABA Commission on Separation of Powers

and Judicial Independence 96" (1997). And, as Texas Chief Justice Phillips pointed out, "the plain fact is that judges are far more likely to lose for far more inscrutable reasons in contested elections rather than retention elections." Phillips, "Comment," 128.

17. Shugerman also saw big money and growing political pressure on Missouri Plan judges: "The 2010 defeat of the three Iowa judges who had ruled in favor of gay marriage may be a harbinger of money spilling over into merit. In a high-profile fight over explosive social issues, some groups will be sufficiently motivated by punishing the incumbents, expressing their outrage and deterring other judges in other states." Shugerman, *The People's Courts*, 258.

18. See Shugerman, *The People's Courts*, 3 ("Almost 90 percent of state judges face some kind of popular election"). For estimates of 87 percent, see also Roy A. Schotland, "Financing Judicial Elections, 2000: Change and Challenge," *Law Review of Michigan State University-Detroit College of Law* 3 (2001): 849–99.

19. Shugerman, *The People's Courts*, 256.

20. Paul Reidinger, "The Politics of Judging," *American Bar Association Journal* 73 (1987): 52–54 (quoted in Shugerman, *The People's Courts*, 262). See also J. Clifford Wallace, former chief judge for the US Ninth Circuit Court of Appeals, "An Essay on Independence of the Judiciary: Independence from What and Why," *New York University Annual Survey of American Law* 58, no. 2 (2001): 241–58 ("The existence of any unchecked political pressure, however infrequently used, casts a long shadow over the independence of the courts, causing them to be aware of political considerations extraneous to the cases at hand. This interference with the process of justice is insidious, and only the strongest of judges will be able to act unconcerned about its possible use").

21. Shugerman, *The People's Courts*, 12.

22. Teachout, *Corruption in America*, 47.

23. Teachout, *Corruption in America*, 304–5.

24. Phillips, "Comment" (quoting *Oxford Dictionary of Humorous Quotations* [New York: Oxford University Press, 1995]).

AFTERWORD

1. Oliver Wendell Holmes Jr., letter to Lewis Einstein, July 23, 1906; Richard Posner, *The Essential Holmes: Selections from the Letters, Speeches, Judicial Opinions, and Other Writings of Oliver Wendell Holmes, Jr.* (Chicago: University of Chicago Press, 1992).

2. Michael Forsythe, "China's Chief Justice Rejects an Independent Judiciary, and Reformers Wince," *New York Times*, January 20, 2017. But see Michael Forsythe, "Chinese Judge Blasts Trump over Judiciary," *New York Times*, February 8, 2017:

> Judge He Fan of the Supreme People's Court of China published a scathing blog post about Mr. Trump's reaction to [a recent federal court] ruling blocking key parts of his executive order that barred visitors from seven predominantly Muslim countries. Judge He said that Mr. Trump had breached the

principle of an independent judiciary, and that people who attacked judges were "public enemies of the law." . . .

[T]he harsh public face presented last month by the chief justice, Zhou Qiang, obscures what is happening on his watch. [Chinese] judges . . . admire the American legal system and study it to improve China's rules. . . .

Judge He . . . may be using Mr. Trump's assault on the independence of America's judiciary to safely and indirectly level some criticism against China's own system.

3. See Rick Lyman, "Polish Parliament Acts to Upend Nation's Courts," *New York Times*, July 22, 2017; Rick Lyman, "Rift in Poland as Leader Kills Curbs on Courts," *New York Times*, July 25, 2017; Rick Lyman, "Polish President Offers Plan to End Court Crisis, but the Response Is Tepid," *New York Times*, September 26, 2017; Patrick Kingsley, "Judges Exit Suddenly in Hungary, Deepening Fears of Premier's Grip," *New York Times*, May 2, 2018; Benjamin Novak and Patrick Kingsley, "Hungary's Judges Warn of Threats to Autonomy," *New York Times*, May 3, 2018.

4. See Peter Irons, *Justice at War: The Story of the Japanese American Internment Cases* (New York: Oxford University Press, 1983).

5. See Spencer Averick and Ava DuVernay, *13th* (Netflix, 2016).

ACKNOWLEDGMENTS

1. March 23, 1908, letter to Miller Outcault; see Doris Kearns Goodwin, *The Bully Pulpit: Theodore Roosevelt, William Howard Taft, and the Golden Age of Journalism* (New York: Simon and Schuster, 2013). William Howard Taft served as president of the United States from 1909 to 1913 and as Chief Justice of the United States Supreme Court from 1921 to 1930.

2. "It is not enough to cure the plague, one must know how to weep for it. Yes, one must know how to weep!" Miguel de Unamuno, *Del Sentimiento Trágico de la Vida* [*Tragic Sense of Life*], 11th ed. (1912; repr., Madrid: Espasa-Calpe, S.A., Colección Austral, 1967). Miguel de Unamuno (1864–1936), philosopher, poet, playwright, essayist, novelist, and professor of Greek and classics, served as rector of the University of Salamanca. He was removed from his university positions, exiled, and imprisoned in response to his courageous opposition to Spanish dictatorship.

CHARLES BENJAMIN SCHUDSON was born in Milwaukee. A graduate of Dartmouth College and the University of Wisconsin Law School, he is a Wisconsin reserve judge emeritus and president of KeynoteSeminars, LLC (www.keynoteseminars.net).

Charlie served as a state and federal prosecutor, a trial and appellate judge, and an adjunct professor of law at Marquette University and the University of Wisconsin. He was the Law and Literature Scholar in Residence at Lawrence University and, for many years, a member of the faculties of the National Council of Juvenile and Family Court Judges, and the National Judicial College. He continues to teach at law schools and professional conferences throughout America and beyond, and at Lawrence University's Bjorklunden Seminars. In recent years, as a Fulbright fellow, he served as the scholar in residence at law schools abroad.

Charlie has been a featured guest on NPR's *All Things Considered*, PBS's *MacNeil/Lehrer Report*, and on *Oprah*. He has authored hundreds of published appellate decisions as well as other published works, including *On Trial: America's Courts and Their Treatment of Sexually-Abused Children* (Beacon Press). He is a member of the National Association of State Judicial Educators.

Charlie lives in Sedona, Arizona, and Ellison Bay, Wisconsin, where he hikes, bikes, swims, searches and rescues, and writes.

Index

conservative activists, 159, 245n16
Constitution: 1st Amendment, 66,
157–58, 170–71, 248n29; 6th
Amendment, 62, 208n8; 14th
Amendment, 232–33n5; appointive
federal judiciary established by, 6,
187–88n6; vs. Articles of Confederation, 187n4, 193n6; on corruption,
42, 204n37, 204n39; Preamble,
202n13; as rule of law, impetus for,
5; on state autonomy, 193n6
contempt law, 26–27, 80, 212n18
Cook, Carol, 27–28
Cook County Jail, 86
Cornett, Judy M., 255n12
coroners, investigations/
recommendations by, 29, 198n13
corporate misconduct. See *BMW of
North America, Inc. v. Gore*; punitive
damages; *Wischer v. Mitsubishi
Heavy Industries*
corporations as "persons," 33, 198n14
corruption: *Alford* pleas, 108–10; in the
American tradition, 42, 133, 204n32;
bribery, 42, 133–34, 179, 204n39,
231–33nn4–6; in case assignments,
100; Constitution on, 42, 204n37,
204n39; definitions of, 41–43,
203n26, 204n41; democracy undermined by, 42, 179, 204n34; electoral
(*see* judicial campaigning); for
electoral gain, 134, 138–39 (see also
State v. Clay); external and internal
sources of, 37; forms of, 8, 41–42;
political, judicial independence
threatened by, 7; selecting a judge to
hear one's own appeal, 251n43; selling judicial decisions, 41, 203n22;
Stevens on, 8; Teachout on, 8, 42–
43, 176, 204n32, 204n34, 204n37,
204n39, 204n41. *See also* impropriety
and the appearance of impropriety
Cosby, Bill, 205–6n9, 209n9
Crossroads Academy, 26–29

Dahmer, Jeffrey, 98–100
Danziger, Shai, 141
Davey, Monica, 214n6, 214n8, 217n23
Dean, Alice, 26
death penalty cases, 63, 174, 208n8,
218n3
deceit/lying, 28–29
decision-making: by appellate judges,
11–14, 189–90nn15–16; arrogance in,
40; bias in, 141–44, 236–38nn8–11,
238–39n14, 240n18 (see also *Caperton v. A. T. Massey Coal Co., Inc.*);
circumstance's role in, 144, 241n19;
compassion/emotion in, 56–57,
68–69, 179–80, 206–7n4, 207–8n6;
conferring about pending cases,
146–48, 241–42n25; food's role in,
140–41, 235n3; gender bias in, 142–
43, 238–39n14; humility in, 39–41,
203n20; impartial, 36, 114, 201n1,
201n4, 202nn7–8; inquiry's role in,
37, 39; intuition in, 143, 239n16; by
judges, generally, 11–14, 19, 189–
90nn15–16, 190–91nn20–22, 194n10;
judges on, 13, 191n23; logic and
intellectually honest reasoning
in, 38–39, 57–58, 69; mood's role
in, 140, 235n3; personality's role in,
144–46, 241n21; Posner on, 13–14,
191n23, 194n10; racial bias in, 142–
43; religion's influence on, 129–32,
231n16; result-oriented, 58–59,
207n6; in sex-discrimination cases,
142; by trial judges, 11–14. *See also*
standard of review
Declaration of Independence, 39,
202n16
defense theory, 125–26
DeGrave, William. See *Wischer v. Mitsubishi Heavy Industries*
de Leon, Ferdinand, 218–19n5
democracy: corruption as undermining, 42, 179, 204n34; and responsiveness to citizens, 5–6; secrecy in,

Jones, Michael (*pseudonym*), 119–24, 134, 137–39, 235n16
Jordan, G. Kevin, 205n9
judges: authority of, 34; on decision-making, 13, 191n23 (*see also* decision-making); differences that matter, 20; disqualification (recusal) of, 17–18, 51, 192–93n4, 205–6n9 (see also *Caperton v. A. T. Massey Coal Co., Inc.*); education of, 111–13, 220n13, 221–22nn21–22 (*see also* National Judicial College); ethical standards for/misconduct by, 121–22, 227nn24–25; former lawyers as, 22, 195n1, 201n22; former prosecutors as, 22–23, 34–35, 195n2; innovative, 194n9; instructions to juries, 39, 61, 129, 202–3n17; as investigators, 27; limits on expression by, 13, 190–91n21, 192n29 (*see also* confidentiality); merit selection of, 169, 176–77, 247n23, 255nn12–13, 256–57n16; as not being politicians, 164–65, 170–73, 251n40; public comments while proceedings are pending, 81, 212n15; public criticism's influence on, 70–71, 210n2; relationship to law, 17; secondary trauma experienced by, 149–51, 242n31; substitution of, 17–20, 192n2, 193n5, 194n7. *See also* appellate judges; trial judges
judicial campaigning, 155–72; advertising, 159–60, 162, 166–67, 246nn21–22; attorneys' investments in judicial elections, 160–61, 163, 165, 249n33; contributions, 159–73, 246n21, 247–48nn27–29, 249–50nn32–33, 250–51n36, 253n66 (see also *Caperton v. A. T. Massey Coal Co., Inc.*; *Williams-Yulee v. The Florida Bar*); death penalty appeals' role in, 159–60; declarations vs. silence, 6–7, 155–58, 172–75, 243n3, 244–45nn9–12; educational role of, 157,

173, 244n7; ethical code provisions on, 243nn2–3; judges vs. politicians, 164–65, 170–73, 251n40; media's effects on, 245n13; Missouri Plan, 160, 247n23, 257n17; at political party meetings, 243n2; in retention elections, 160, 175, 246n20, 247n23; same-sex marriage's role in, 160; and voter ignorance about judicial elections, 243n4
judicial independence: America as a model of, 4–5; appointive vs. elective judiciaries, 6–7, 173–77, 188n8, 255n12, 255–56n15, 257n20; and campaigning by judges (*see* judicial campaigning); in China, 178, 257–58n2; cynicism vs. optimism about, 175–76; and the Declaration of Independence, 39, 202n16; *de facto* and *de jure* systems to protect, 37; definitions of, 36–37; federal appointments, political battles over, 7, 188n8; federal vs. state judiciaries, 6–7, 96 (*see also* state judges); in a free society, 38–39, 202n13; in Germany, 179; impartiality as protected by, 37, 202nn7–8; judiciary vs. legislative and executive branches, 5; measuring, 37, 201–2n5; via merit selection, 169, 176–77, 247n23, 255nn12–13, 256–57n16; research on, 36–37; and "rule of law" rhetoric, 254–55n12; as a shield, 3–4, 187n1; Shugerman on, 254–55nn12–13; Supreme Court decisions undermining, 6–7 (see also *Caperton v. A. T. Massey Coal Co., Inc.*; *Citizens United v. Federal Election Comm'n*; *Republican Party of Minn. v. White*; *Williams-Yulee v. The Florida Bar*); systemic and individual, 37; tenure of judges, 6, 187n2. *See also* corruption; decision-making
Jung, Carl, 241n21